More Praise for
THE ART OF TOUGH

"In more than forty years in government, Barbara Boxer has truly mastered the 'Art of Tough.' Her life and work are an inspiration to politicians everywhere, both real and completely fake."

—Julia Louis-Dreyfus, actress and star of the HBO series *Veep*

"For decades I have worked with Barbara Boxer on issues that have touched our hearts and our lives. She is a woman of her word and she is one of the most generous leaders I have ever met in politics."

—Nancy Pelosi, 52nd Speaker of the U.S. House of Representatives (D-California)

"This book offers invaluable lessons about politics and life from one of the strongest progressive voices of the U.S. Senate. Barbara Boxer's life lessons are tried and true. They are pearls of wisdom her readers can live by."

—Rep. John Lewis (D-Georgia)

"From being told in the early 1960s that 'women aren't stockbrokers' to five terms in the House and four terms in the Senate, Senator Barbara Boxer tells the story of a woman who found her calling. My favorite quote is: 'So I ran.' Even if you differ with Senator Boxer politically, THE ART OF TOUGH educates and entertains. It's a must-read."

—Carole King, singer-songwriter and bestselling author

"When you read Barbara's words, you realize how important it is to be strong in the face of overwhelming powers. Her book will inspire all of us to be fearless in our pursuits, our convictions, and our lives."

—Lily Tomlin, comedian and actress

"Anyone who thinks that Washington can't be understood, has no great hearts, and is not crucial to our daily lives will be turned around on all counts by Barbara Boxer's irresistible story of her more than four decades there. Read this as a bridge into the coming political year, and you won't just vote, you'll fight to vote."

—Gloria Steinem, feminist, activist, and author

"Drawing on her decades of effective, principled advocacy of liberal ideals, Barbara Boxer provides a valuable description of how the legislative process works at its best. She weaves the political, official, and personal aspects of the job into a readable, instructive narrative of how democracy can be practiced."

—Former Congressman Barney Frank (D-Massachusetts)

"It takes a true warrior to fight against the biggest polluters who would degrade our environment. That warrior is Barbara Boxer, who has been my partner for years in protecting our oceans so that their beauty remains for future generations."

—Ted Danson, actor and environmentalist

THE ART OF TOUGH

TOUGH

*Fearlessly Facing
Politics and Life*

BARBARA BOXER

hachette
BOOKS

NEW YORK   BOSTON

Hachette Books
Hachette Book Group
1290 Avenue of the Americas, New York, NY 10104
hachettebooks.com
twitter.com/hachettebooks

Originally published in hardcover and as an ebook in 2016 by Hachette Books, Inc.
First trade paperback edition: June 2017

Hachette Books is a division of Hachette Book Group, Inc. The Hachette Books name and logo are trademarks of Hachette Book Group, Inc.

The publisher is not responsible for websites (or their content) that are not owned by the publisher.

Photo insert credits: (page 1) photo courtesy the author; © Kenneth Lee; House photo; (page 2) © Paul Hosefros/The New York Times/Redux; © Jo Fielder; (page 3) photo courtesy the author; House photo; (page 4) Courtesy of Presidential Materials Division, National Archives and Records Administration; photo courtesy the author; (page 5) photos © Getty Images; (page 6) House photo; other photos courtesy the author; (page 7) photos © REX photos, 1998; (page 8) Courtesy of William J. Clinton Presidential Library; Courtesy of William J. Clinton Presidential Library; photo courtesy the author; © Absolutely Loved Photography by Stefanie Riedel

The Hachette Speakers Bureau provides a wide range of authors for speaking events. To find out more, go to www.hachettespeakersbureau.com or call (866) 376-6591.

ISBN: 978-0-316-31147-2 (pbk.)

Printed in the United States of America

LSC-C

10 9 8 7 6 5 4 3 2 1

I dedicate this memoir to my loving family—my husband, Stewart; our children, Doug and Nicole; their loving spouses, Amy and Kevin; and four extraordinary grandchildren, Zach, Zain, Sawyer, and Reyna.

Without all of my family I would be nowhere.

And

In loving memory of my parents, Sophie and Ira Levy, whose wisdom was imparted in ways that lie deep within me.

And

In loving memory of Paula Kozlen, my dear friend who brought light to the darkest situation and reminded me to live every second of every minute of every day.

Contents

Foreword

Amid tall bookshelves, pungent cheese, and beautiful mid-century art, I first met Barbara Boxer in the Upper West Side home of two of the most important Democratic activists in the country. A few dozen friends had gathered to support her re-election campaign. Everyone in the room was abuzz with excitement to hear her speak—they knew her and her record well and wanted to hear all that she was working on. I was a newcomer, curious about this famous senator who was a leader in women's rights, LGBT rights, and environmental protection, and who was known to be a tough fighter. I was thinking about running for Congress someday and my eyes were glued on her. I watched how she spoke so casually, with such self-assurance, with passion and determination. I knew she was a powerful national leader, but I didn't know what an important person she would be in my own Senate career a decade later. I just watched in awe of her command of the facts, her strong, direct speaking style when making a point, and her no-nonsense approach to her job. I thought, "I want to be able to do that someday..."

Fast-forward ten years. Barbara and I are in the trenches fighting against the Department of Defense (DOD) and too many colleagues about reforming how the military addresses sexual assault in the armed forces. We had been down the road of intense negotiations, belligerent defiance by DOD commanders, and multiple hearings. We had spent time with survivors, hearing their stories and feeling the heartbreaking disappointment of not being able to deliver the reform so vitally needed. One afternoon, after everyone had filed out of a meeting with Majority Leader Harry Reid to make our plea for a vote before the end of the year, I sat for an extra moment on Harry's couch and looked over to Barbara. Her eyes were still set, her face resolute, and her frame leaning forward.

I said, "Barbara, I just don't know. I'm not sure this is ever going to move forward."

Without even a breath, she said, "Kirsten, this is the moment you can't give up. This is the time you dig deeper. You have to keep at it. It will make all the difference."

Words of steel, just at the right time. Just when I needed them. That particular battle against the DOD leadership raged on for months longer, and we ultimately lost that vote, but by the end we had fifty-five senators, from both sides of the aisle, standing with us. I learned from Barbara that day the first rule of the Art of Tough: Never give up. Especially when the chips are down and there seems to be no light at the end of the tunnel. I'm still fighting on behalf of survivors of sexual assault, and I will never doubt the importance of the fight. I will sorely miss Barbara by my side in the Senate but I'm certain her next chapter will be even bolder than the last.

Kirsten Gillibrand

Preface

Since the *The Art of Tough* hit the bookstores last year, some important things have changed. Among them: I completed my last term as a United States senator and the 2016 presidential election occurred. Those are two significant developments, both for me personally and for the country at large, causing me to reflect on the meaning and value of the art of tough. My conclusion? The message of the book is more important than ever.

The unexpected presidential election result in which the "loser" received almost three million more votes than the winner is unsettling to many, not to mention the fact that the election exposed a divide in America that was in many ways deeper and more personal than anticipated by all sides. Before the election, I had scheduled an appearance on Chelsea Handler's show to celebrate the election of the first female president of our nation. That's what we all thought was going to happen.

Well, I will be honest with you. The day after the election, I didn't think I could summon the strength to appear on Chelsea's show. But I did. I had to. That's what the *The Art of Tough* means. You look the defeat in the eye, you pick yourself up and continue fighting for what you believe in. Chelsea wrote me a note saying that appearance was very important to her, her crew, and her audience. I am grateful for that, and it underscored for me why I want— no, need!—to stay involved, keep my voice out there. The same voice that is right here in this book, from deep inside me.

But recovering from an election result is just the beginning of being tough. To stand up, to question, to defend your beliefs, that all requires toughness, regardless of the bullying we might face. The attacks I endured, which you'll read about, are attacks many of us face—mine were just more public. Humiliating insults must never succeed, because that is what the attacker wants, all in an effort to break your spirit and shut you down. But it takes courage and determination, and learning the rules of tough to make sure you wind up the winner. One thing we know for sure: We will all be challenged many times; sometimes fairly, sometimes unfairly—as students, workers, community members, parents, grandparents, and as elected leaders. It is at those times that reaching for *The Art of Tough* can help you get through it all. I hope you find it inspiring, entertaining, and informative, especially with all of the historical context.

I was thinking about those who expressed toughness best. Take President Abraham Lincoln. If Lincoln, perhaps our greatest president, didn't have it, where would we be?

Consider what he had to overcome:

Losing his mother when he was just nine years old

Having to help support his family as a child

Losing a race for the state legislature (he won two years later)

Being rejected from law school

Losing his fiancée to illness, leaving him with a broken heart

Being defeated for speaker of the state legislature

Losing the first time he ran for Congress (he eventually won)

Losing two races for the United States Senate.

He could have quit life after facing such overwhelming challenges, all of those losses. But he didn't. In 1860 he won the presidency. Then there is my personal hero, Anita Hill, who, despite being vilified in front of the whole country, testified that a nominee for Supreme Court justice had harassed her. She stood her ground, held her head up, and as a result, today workers are protected from sexual harassment in the workplace, and because of her, as you will see in the book, women found the toughness and the grit to run for some of the highest offices in the land. And take Rosa Parks. If she hadn't refused to go to the back of the bus in 1955, which was required in the south, who knows how much longer it would have taken to end that outrageous symbol of racial bigotry.

What if people abandoned toughness? America would be a dramatically different country. African American men would never have won the right to vote. They fought so hard, despite the bigotry, violence, and incredible odds against them. African-American women did not get that right until all women did, and women would never have gotten the right to vote if they had given up after being arrested and force-fed as they protested for equality in the early twentieth century.

In the early 1900s there were few safety standards for factories. After the Triangle Shirtwaist Factory fire in New York City in 1911 that killed 146 workers, mostly immigrants, dedicated New Yorkers refused to accept the fact that a business could lock all the doors to keep workers inside, and they worked to pass safety reforms including a focus on child labor, which America eventually outlawed in 1938.

None of these battles were easy.

So whenever you find yourself in circumstances where you have to reach for the strength, the courage and just the right touch of tough, I hope you will find how to do it in the words that follow.

Introduction

I wrote *The Art of Tough* to tell the everyday, behind-the-scene struggles that move our nation toward "a more perfect union." After ten years as a member of the House of Representatives and almost twenty-four years as a senator, my experience has proven that even though the days of duels and fistfights on the Senate floor are over, we still engage in a different form of hand-to-hand combat.

I never planned a life in elected office. It wasn't even possible for women when I was a girl. But as I came of age as a worker, wife, and mother, my increasing sense of indignation and sometimes outrage about the issues I saw around me—racial prejudice, war, women's inequality, the neglect of our children and our environment—compelled me to jump full tilt into the battle.

So here's my book: a no-punches-pulled personal memoir about the personalities and shenanigans of my colleagues on both sides of the aisle. I want to show you that what these folks do (or don't!) has a direct, powerful impact on your lives. It breaks my heart when I hear people say, "Why should I vote...all politicians are the same...it won't make a difference...nothing changes." Oh, my God, how wrong, how mistaken that is. The men and women whom you elect to office make a critical difference in whether or not that dream of "a more perfect union," so eloquently written in the Preamble to our Constitution, is achieved.

How can we become a nation "of, by and for the people" if we don't vote? This book connects the dots and it does it in a way that I think is different—through the eyes of an ordinary person who grew up in the middle class with a fierce sense of right and wrong from parents who had that compass. And it shows how important it is to have a sense of humor to get through the heartbreak that comes to all of us in our lives.

I hope to inspire you to engage in your own life with a spirit of determination to fight for change. It's what I call the "art of tough" and I've had to do it myself all my life.

"The art of tough" is a way of approaching all the challenges of life with techniques that can apply to everyone. Whether you're in politics like me, or hustling to get an education, running a small business, raising a kid while holding down a job, bootstrapping a career under difficult circumstances— the values, beliefs, and sense of purpose are the same.

Each of us has to take charge of his or her own battles and even get more involved politically, particularly after seeing what happens in the political back rooms and how it matters to each of us. One person inside those rooms—or someone purposely left out of those rooms—*can* make a difference.

Chapter One

The First Lessons of Tough

———————

I'm no martial artist or big-time, high-stakes moneymaker. I barely measure five feet, maybe five-three in my high heels, and nobody has ever accused me of having a menacing presence. No, but I have lived with an emotional intensity—a sense of indignation, determination, and sometimes outrage—that has often inspired opposing reactions among my political colleagues, voters, and right-wing "pundits" who have said these and other quotable things about me:

"[Barbara Boxer is] quite possibly the biggest doofus ever to enter the Senate chambers, including janitorial staff, pizza delivery kids, and carpenter ants."   —Doug Powers on July 11, 2005, on WorldNetDaily

"Barbara Boxer is a great candidate for the Democratic Party: female and learning disabled."   —Ann Coulter, from a speech on February 18, 2005

"Barbara Boxer continues to prove that she is unfit for any office higher than turd inspector."

—Comment on April 7, 2005, from blog reader Arthur
Schlep in response to the EPA/American Chemical
Company study of children and pesticides

"You're a detestable femi-Naz."..."A stupid nut."..."A dried-up prune."..."In my day you'd be running a brassiere store on the turnpike."..."You can suck my machine gun."   —Various detractors

Yes, you read it right. And here's one of the strangest of all, from the inestimable radio host Michael Savage.

"In the future, Barbara Boxer may be remembered as the Frau Doctor Mengele of the U.S. Senate. Dr. Joseph Mengele, the Nazi war criminal who directed merciless human experiments, may have decided to come back, as a woman."

> —Michael Savage on October 27, 1999, from Newsmax.com: "Is There a Mrs. Dr. Mengele in the Senate?"

But on the other side I have gotten these messages:

"God bless you."..."You're an eloquent shining star."..."As a veteran I hold you in high esteem for all the fights you have taken on our behalf."..."Thank you for being a fearless trailblazer."..."An inspiration to my daughter..."

Then there is this: "Your work and integrity inspire me." But just to keep me humble: "Apparently the people are not your concern, ever."

My all-time favorite is, "You rock, Senator."

You get the point, I'm sure. I don't elicit neutral responses, and it's always been that way. I don't know how to be neutral. I take things to heart, run them through my brain, and the distance from there to my mouth isn't big enough to have much of a filter.

It's all about the art of tough, which has been informed by the principles that I have lived by, learned mostly from my dad, Ira Levy, the only one of nine siblings born in the United States, and my mom, Sophie, one of six, who came to her beloved America as a baby in 1911, wrapped in the arms and dreams of her parents. They both taught me to face problems and challenges with values, beliefs, and a sense of purpose, providing me with a foundation of moral ideals that has always been with me. As the children of families who chose America to escape the prejudices in Europe, they saw what hate and fear and silence in the face of injustice could do.

As lovers of music, they often cited the lyrics from *South Pacific* that said: "You've got to be taught before it's too late, before you are six or seven or eight, to hate all the people your relatives hate, you've got to be carefully taught." My parents taught me not to hate, but to be strong. Without knowing it, they taught me "the art of tough" and here are the guidelines:

1. *Never compromise about doing the right thing.*

    We lived on the fifth floor of a six-story apartment building in the Crown Heights section of Brooklyn. One of my friends, Sheila, lived directly above us. Sheila's parents were a lot more lenient than mine, so quite often I would whine that "Sheila's mom lets her do this" and "Sheila's mom lets her do that."

    My mother thought Sheila was spoiled silly. She said what every parent everywhere has said over the generations: "If Sheila's mother let her jump off the roof, would you want to do that too?" In my eleven-year-old mind, it was a point well taken.

    One day Sheila and I were walking home from school and stopped in at the candy store. In a completely shocking moment, Sheila put a two-cent taffy lollipop in her pocket, grabbed my hand, and dragged me out of the store. My parents had taught me that taking *anything* that didn't belong to me was a sin, but Sheila was so persuasive and so popular, I let her pull me down the street without saying anything. But it weighed on my mind and, as usual, I took this dilemma to my mother.

    Mom was dismayed that I hadn't told Sheila off.

    "Don't you understand what it would mean to that candy store owner if everyone did what Sheila did? Yes, it was only two cents, but that can add up."

Since I hadn't participated in "the act," I should have been done with it. So I told my mother in what was probably a righteous voice, "But I didn't do anything!"

Mom's reply was quick and intense. "That's the problem. You stood by and said nothing, and you need to tell Sheila how you feel."

"But..."

"No buts—go! She's just one floor up."

It was no fun. I tried to be very nice but clear about what I thought of her behavior, and I'm sure Sheila told our other friends what a Goody Two-shoes I was. But I knew my mother was right. I had failed to do the right thing, and that is not the way to act when a misdeed takes place right in front of your eyes. And in the long run, Sheila respected me for telling her, and we remained best friends.

This event taught me something else that's stuck with me ever since. When admonishing me to confront Sheila, my mother gave me another piece of invaluable advice I have used often: "You can tell someone to go to hell," she said, "but if you do it with sensitivity, they'll thank you for it."

2. *Don't be afraid to step up.*

In 1950, when I was ten, my mother had a "mystery" illness. She had horrible rashes and a terrible cough. Nothing seemed to help; she was sent to the hospital for tests and rest. She was away from me for days. Even having her gone for hours was too much for me. My dad was home after school; his sister, my aunt Rose, who lived nearby, filled in. But for me, there was no substitute for Mom.

Adding to my heartache was the hospital rule that barred visits from children under twelve—something about spreading germs in one direction or another. I begged my dad to break the rules, and although he had snuck me into the theater for a Jimmy Cagney gangster movie or two, he wouldn't budge.

"Why not write a letter to the doctor, Babs? I will make sure he gets it."

"Will he be mad?"

"Don't worry about that—he needs to know how these hospital rules hurt kids who want to see their parents."

Thankfully, my mother came home soon after I wrote my letter. But it wasn't until 1978, after my father's death, that I found my letter, clearly never delivered, along with his other mementos in a large accordion-style manila folder in his desk.

Dear Doc:

I am Mrs. Levy's daughter and would love to see my mother very much. I didn't see my mother when she left, only a little while, about five minutes before I went to school. I have no sickness, only a little belly ache now and then. I won't make a lot of noise. I miss my mother very much so can't I see her? Thanks for reading this letter.

> Sincerely yours,
> Barbara Levy

As a backup, I also wrote to my mother.

Dear Mom:

How mean can a person be? If they don't let me in they really are mean. I will be so happy if I see you. In school I am in the Mexican group [a study group on Mexican culture and arts]. In fact I am the chairman.

> Love and many
> kisses to you,
> Babs

Delivered or not, I guess that letter to the "Doc" was my first "truth to power" correspondence, of which I have written many more in my lifetime.

3. *Beware of anger.*

Being tough doesn't give you license to dive into an angry rage. That can lead to uncontrollable violence. I know. I did an awful thing in anger when I was in sixth grade. There was one kid—his name was Albert—who was harassing me and driving me nuts: pulling my hair, chasing me around, and shouting nasty things. Every day!

Honestly, I don't know why he was doing it, but boys in those days engaged in this behavior around girls to get their attention. I was little—still am—and so was Albert, so I was an easy target for him.

The antics were mostly harmless, but to me it was adding up. I didn't want this attention from him, and I had just gone through the same sort of problem with another boy named Jay, who chased me down a dirt hill filled with broken glass and debris, which was my path home from school on a regular basis.

One day, the predictable happened on my usual "run away from Jay" activity. I tripped, flying through the air and landing, my knees and elbows scraped, thoroughly embarrassed. When I got home, Mom told me she was going to the principal's office to put an end to it.

Mom's visit to the school turned into a "she said versus she said" between my mother and Jay's mother, and the whole thing was a humiliation. So when it came to Albert, I decided to take matters into my own hands and put an end to Albert's harassment in a big way. Big mistake.

Toward the end of the school day, when the halls were emptying out and nobody was watching, Albert insulted me—something about my height and my clothes. He got up in my face and punched me in the shoulder. I lost it. I took my number-two sharp lead pencil out of my pencil case and stabbed him in the upper arm. Fortunately, no one saw this happen, but oh, my God, it was awful. Albert started crying and so did I, but neither of us made this public. Me, because I had lost it and I knew it; Albert because he deserved it and I'm certain he knew it. It became our nasty secret.

I was immediately stunned at my own loss of control. What I'd done was contrary to everything taught by my parents. I was so ashamed. I told no one about it, but my punishment was coming, the self-inflicted punishment of anguish.

The day after the stabbing, Albert didn't show up for school. My heart sank. He was also gone the day after that. On my way home on the third day, I saw a black crepe cloth over the front door of his house. Now I knew the truth. I had killed him.

I ran home and cried to my mother. After listening quietly, she expressed her total shock that I would do such a thing.

"I'm surprised at you, Barbara Sue," she said, using the name my parents used when they were serious. "You know what a terrible thing you've done. But I doubt that you've killed Albert, and will call the principal to make sure."

It turned out that Albert's grandfather had died and the household was in mourning. I felt really bad for the family, but I felt such joy to see my nemesis when he returned to school. I even hugged him. Me hugging Albert. He wasn't amused or particularly happy to see me, but after that, he left me alone.

I learned that using my fists or a sharp pencil was not the way to go. I had agonized, felt guilt and remorse, and it probably would have been better to tell Mom to make another trip to the principal's office, even though it would have been "babyish."

I felt so lucky that it had all turned out okay.

Over the years, and I admit this with some difficulty, I learned to channel my anger, control it, analyze it, talk it over with those I trust, and map out a strategy to confront the issue in a smart way. Taking a pause is good for me because sometimes I can overreact or misconstrue a situation. There are other ways to win an argument. I wasn't going to repeat that fiasco.

In my work over forty years, I've had to be much tougher than I thought. Guys like Albert were a piece of cake compared to what I was confronted with day after day. Of course there were good things too, which kept me going. The more I have been attacked for my views and actions, the more I've stood up to it, and the more support I have received.

That support has been the wind at my back, pushing me forward, and I'm truly grateful for it. That support has made me a much better person, secure and unafraid of the venom, able to get past it and do my work without anger.

4. *Forgive.*

I forgave Albert and he eventually forgave me. It was to our mutual advantage. You can't go on living or working with someone if you hold a grudge or let any kind of lingering resentment fester in your heart.

I saw my parents get mad at friends and relatives but never for long. They always let it go, forgave whatever perceived grievance there had been, kept their eyes on the big picture, and put it behind them.

My parents were the youngest of their siblings and called themselves "change-of-life babies," a common term used back then to describe children born to moms in their forties; "unexpected blessings" was another description.

Everyone came to our very modest home, a two-bedroom apartment on Lefferts Avenue that may have been a thousand square feet. Even so, the door to that apartment was open to all relatives. My dad's brother, Uncle Murray, was a charming guy, about fifteen years older than Dad, who would arrive unannounced, give us all giant hugs, and sleep on my mother's favorite piece of furniture: her beautiful gray velvet couch in the living room. His dapper shoes would be neatly laid out, peeking out from under the couch with the fancy fringes hanging down onto his shoe tops. Murray would stay for days on end. He never said when he would come; he never said when he would go.

He was filled with stories of his sales career in which he would sell whatever was "popular"—even religious statues to nuns and priests, he would recount. When embarking on the sales tour to these Catholic institutions to sell his wares, he would tell them his name was Murray Kelley, not Murray Levy.

Murray was a bantamweight boxer as a young man and had the cauliflower ears to prove it. He was, in brief, "exotic," and the total opposite of my intellectual dad.

He was also a guy who took advantage of my parents' generosity. He took and took and took. He never cleaned up our small apartment. He never offered to pay for a meal out or even in, and although he was funny and engaging, he clearly was unappreciative.

My parents were hurt by Uncle Murray year after year, but they forgave him. I would listen to their heartfelt discussions every time he left, and how they knew he had a hard life, no permanent home, and no lasting marriage.

"He keeps everything inside under that happy exterior," said my mother. "He needs us," said my dad.

So Murray continued to show up at the door filled with his stories and his charm, the clothes on his back, the shoes under the couch, and big hugs, for years and years and years, fully forgiven for his trespasses.

Great lesson, especially for the daily give-and-take of national politics where someone can steal your idea one day, but the next day is your biggest advocate. But it is true for everyone, in any situation in which conflict can be expected on a regular basis, whether it's at home or at work, you must be ready to forgive. Not that you should ever forget the really bad stuff. If it recurs, put that person in the part of your heart that can't be touched by them anymore.

5. *Fight against racism.*

Ebbets Field, home of the Brooklyn Dodgers, was six blocks from our apartment house, so during night games, I could hear the cheers, the boos, and the hoopla. I wanted to go to the games like crazy and Dad was very pleased to accommodate me.

Dad was the only one in his family to graduate from college, let alone law school. He viewed baseball the way many European immigrants did. A mastery of the subtle intricacies of the game made them more worthy, they felt, of the adopted land that they loved so much for saving them from oppression.

So off we went, and right away I fell in love with number forty-two, Jackie Robinson. Me and a few million others! My dad told me about

Jackie—what a trailblazer he was, what a great athlete; what incredible character he had to stand up to the bigotry, hatred, and spitting and derision from many fans and players on other major league teams. There was even some racial tension in the Dodger clubhouse itself at first. My father told me that some players insinuated they would sit out rather than play alongside Robinson, but the mutiny ended when Dodgers management took a stand for Robinson. Manager Leo Durocher informed the team, "I don't care if the guy is yellow or black, or if he has stripes like a fuckin' zebra. I'm the manager of this team, and I say he plays. What's more, I say he can make us all rich. And if any of you cannot use the money, I'll see that you're traded."

Robinson did it all by maintaining his dignity, controlling his anger, and playing baseball like nobody else in the world. He set off excitement just by walking to the plate. I remember seeing his pigeon-toed stance as if it were yesterday. Jackie's presence on the bases in the fifties was electric. The way he moved away from first base, leaning and longing to steal second, rattled every pitcher.

As I became older, I realized that his courage on the field was part of the way he lived his life. He was a symbol of hopes and dreams, not only for African Americans, but even for me. I cheered him with all my girl power as hard as I could…until I was hoarse. When I met my husband eight years later, a major impediment was that he was—perish the thought!—a *Yankees* fan. To this day, more than fifty-five years later, it's still a sore spot.

But there I was, already feeling the stirrings of the civil rights movement in my heart. How could anyone want to harm Jackie? How could anyone be treated like a second-class citizen?

In 1950, when my mother was released from the hospital (after the stay that inspired my letter to the doctor), she was told to go to Florida for doses of sun. Sitting in the sun all day was thought to be good for your health back then, and the doctor also felt that after all her tests, she needed to rest in a warm setting.

Knowing that I would be miserable without her, my parents decided I should go with her. I was not happy at that prospect because I had to miss a week of school. I just wanted Mom home to be *there* for me. But the doctor won again and there I was, miles away from Brooklyn, surrounded by heated swimming pools with the ocean across the street.

Despite these amenities, I was grumpy, so after the sun and rest seemed to work, and Mom started to feel better, she said, "Let's go to the movies!" I jumped at the chance and grabbed her hand as we headed for the bus stop. Leaving the hotel grounds and gliding down Collins Avenue where the bright light bounced off spanking-new hotels, I felt free and happy. We stepped onto a bus and the unexpected happened...something that would stay with me for the rest of my life.

It was very crowded, but we were able to find seats side by side. The bus went to the next stop. An elderly black woman got on and I jumped up to give her my seat as I'd had been taught to do since forever.

"No, but thank you," the woman said. I tried to insist, but she walked past us to the back. I was hurt...I didn't understand why she refused the courtesy. I looked at my mother, who bent toward me and whispered, "This is the South, honey. She has to go to the back of the bus because of the color of her skin."

"What?" I was so surprised. "Why?"

"That's the way it is here. Segregated."

So there was my mom, far from Brooklyn, away from my dad, whose college and law degrees she helped make possible with her support, love, and sacrifice, alone with me and face-to-face with racial prejudice. She could have ignored it, said it was none of our business, let it go, and allowed the moment to pass. But Mom saw this moment as a key one for me and I've loved her for that ever since.

"Follow me," she said, grabbing my hand.

She led me to the back of the bus. Since there were no seats left, we stood next to a pole near the rear exit. My mom held on to the pole. I held on to my mom. I felt like the other passengers were staring at us, some maybe even glaring. At that point, I knew we were somehow behaving differently and we were doing it on purpose. Mom explained what was happening by whispering in my ear, and I felt grown up, part of her team.

But I was a little unsettled. Then Mom did what she often did when I needed comforting. She rubbed my back with her strong fingers, up and down my spine, across my shoulders, as the bus rolled slowly down the boulevard, making stops, letting people on and off. At one stop the elderly black lady gave me a little smile and descended the steps. I wanted to say something to her, but I noticed that Mom was silent, so I followed suit.

My mom never knew that one day, as a United States senator, her daughter would meet Rosa Parks, the woman who changed the bus craziness, and sit in the Capitol rotunda as a statue of Ms. Parks was dedicated. She didn't know I would also co-sponsor a law to honor Jackie Robinson with a Congressional Gold Medal in 2003. She didn't know that single gesture on the bus would mold me. Or did she?

6. *It's better to be strong on an issue, even if you turn out to be wrong.*
My parents were always clear and bold in their beliefs, never wishy-washy. It's the same thing Bill Clinton told many of us the first time in 1991, when he was running for president:

"It's what the voters want," he said to a group of House members in Washington with his usual good-humored generosity of spirit. "And you'll see...It's what your constituents will want. They'll forgive you some mistakes, but won't vote for you again if you're a wimp."

I quote this advice to anyone seeking a life of public service. One of my mentors, former congressman John Burton, said it another way: "Always go with your gut."

It's important to know what you believe and to stand up for it. It is not only respect that you will show yourself but it also shows respect for those you wish to represent, or serve with, by not pandering or flattering them if it goes against your true opinion.

I cannot overstate the importance of this principle. If you are not strong when you make your case to your staff, your colleagues, and your constituents, and, most important, to yourself, you might as well "hang up your cleats," "fold up your cards," "give up the ship," or whatever colloquialism you might use.

All of my mentors lived by this principle and I have as well—particularly when the votes I cast went contrary to popular opinion.

Whether it was "Don't ask, don't tell," the war in Iraq, gay marriage, bloated defense budgets, bank regulation, or holding up bills that were being touted as bipartisan, or even objecting to an election I thought was rigged, if I felt the policies were dangerous and wrong, I stood up—sometimes alone. In these cases, I was willing to lose my seat over these views, but I was taught to be strong. If you are wrong in the voters' eyes, they will forgive you if they see your passion, your conviction, and your courage.

7. *Sing. Sing? Yes, sing!*

Music was a major part of my family life. My mom had a beautiful singing voice and my dad could play a mean piano. He could sight-read anything from sheet music: show tunes, movie tunes. In the forties we stood around an old upright in our tiny living room and sang songs from the forties, thirties, and twenties. In those years of singing with my parents, I learned to love the clever, funny, and romantic lyrics to many songs. In the fifties we sang music from *My Fair Lady*. We sang songs by Irving Berlin, like "How Deep Is the Ocean," and "Getting to Know You" by Rodgers and Hammerstein, and songs from *Porgy and Bess* by George and Ira Gershwin and DuBose Heyward.

There was real value in a piece of sheet music. In 1956, "Sleepy Time Gal" cost thirty-five cents and three songs from *My Fair Lady* cost eighty-five cents. I still have the old sheet music and keep it in my piano bench. It's fraying but in good shape. When I'm alone at home, I pull out these songs and play them, but I'm not even close to my father's skill. Scientists say that our brains are wired to connect music with our long-term memory. All I know is that as I look back on my life, music has been a way for me to forget the troubles of the world and focus on the good things of life.

Right before I entered high school in 1954, Dad wrote me a beautiful note.

To my daughter Babs:

Now that the elementary school door has closed behind you, you're about to enter the larger halls of high school with all its additional responsibility. Through it all, however, please continue to dance and never let the song escape from your heart.

Dad

In grade school, high school, and summer camp I took part in organized music: choruses, plays, and performances. My diva moment was playing Liza Doolittle in *My Fair Lady*.

As an adult, singing and music continued to play a major role as relaxation and distraction from the stress and pressure of my political life. In raising our children, my husband, Stewart, and I made sure they too appreciated music. We bought a used piano from a twenty-year-old who wanted to exchange it for a "hi-fi." Lucky for us, it was a 1906 Steinway Baby Grand and it remains one of our most prized possessions.

Later, singing and a new skill I developed writing lyrics to fit famous melodies became an interesting part of my political life. After I was sworn in for my first term in the House of Representatives in 1983, singing actually changed a discriminatory policy forbidding women representatives from using the House gym.

Incredible. I couldn't believe it.

The men had a fully equipped gym with a large selection of weight training equipment, a big area of massage tables, and lavish shower rooms. We "girls" were consigned to a tiny room with a couple of showers and five huge hair dryers, the old-fashioned kind that they still have at hair salons, with big hoods that slide over your head. There was no exercise equipment, and hardly any space to even do stretches. It was like segregation: separate and unequal, clearly a gym in name only. As a Californian I was much offended at this, since in our state we had a workout sensibility for everyone, not just men.

An aerobic lesson I tried to run with my friend Claudette for the House women changed everything.

Congresswomen Geraldine Ferraro and Olympia Snowe walked in, looking like they could have stepped out of *Vogue* magazine. Their outfits were casual elegance—expensive t-shirts and jogging suits, all in perfect spandex. The rest of us wore "lived-in" attire. Several other friends were there as well. I'll never forget my House colleague Barbara Mikulski, who was about to make history by becoming the first Democratic woman ever elected in her own right to the United States Senate.

After Claudette said, "Hands on hips, bend at the waist" to the six of us, Barbara yelled out: "Look, if I had a waist, I wouldn't be here!" Everyone cracked up, but we also realized that this tiny space was impossible. We couldn't even stretch our arms out to the sides without hitting one another.

We tried everything we could to integrate the gym but struck out. Finally, lyrics won the day. I was so frustrated, I sat down and wrote new words to the song "Five Foot Two, Eyes of Blue." I showed them to my fellow female representatives Marcy Kaptur and Mary Rose Oakar, both of whom could carry a tune. We sang it to our Democratic Congressional Campaign Committee chairman Tony Coelho, who suggested we sing it to the entire Democratic caucus. He truly thought it would bring a smile and a change of heart and policy.

We knew we needed to get it just right if this was to work. We were very nervous before the performance. Everyone kept saying "no" to our simple request to use the gym. The powerful Dan Rostenkowski complained that if we got into the facility, he would have to empty out his stash of shampoo that he kept there.

Huh? As if a group of congresswomen were going to steal beauty products out of the lockers?

I called our singing group into a huddle.

"Smile, above all else," I said. "We don't want to come off as angry."

God forbid women who wanted equal rights should be seen as angry. We should have been! But I remembered the lessons I had learned: Smile and be nice while being tough.

"And," I added, "*Enunciate*. It does no good if they don't understand the words."

With that, we let it rip.

Exercise, glamorize, where to go, will you advise?
Can't everybody use your gym?
Equal rights, we'll wear tights,
Let's avoid those macho fights.
Can't everybody use your gym?
We're not slim, we're not trim.
Can't we make it hers and him?
Can't everybody use your gym?
We're only asking… can't everybody use your gym?
(Big finish)

Our male colleagues loved it. By the way, there were 413 of them and 22 of us then. It worked. They finally let us use the gym. First they suggested special hours, but we fought it and said no. Then they tried other tricks such as just opening the gym to women on weekends. We said no again. Finally the gym was opened for everyone, period.

Over the years I have used homemade lyrics and rhymes to vent my feelings, with humor, irony, and, yes, on occasion, bitterness. I can't say they've ever changed a policy as easily as the House gym song did, but I can say that my rhymes and lyrics have brought smiles where there were frowns. Sometimes they underscored that the fight was worth it, and in a way I never thought they would, they document my years dealing with issues and personalities, challenges and priorities. (I have sprinkled some examples of my rhymes throughout the book and in the Appendix.)

In the House I named our singing group the Red, White and Blues. In the Senate I named it DA DEMS. It consisted of Lucy Calautti, a good friend and wife of my former colleague Kent Conrad, Liz Tankersley, who was my first legislative director, and Senator Debbie Stabenow, who did some cabaret singing in her early years. Barbara Levin, Senator Carl Levin's wife, sang with us from time to time. Special appearances were made over the years by colleagues Byron Dorgan, Tom Daschle, and Dan Akaka. Saving the day was our guitarist Kent Ashcraft, who used to play in the Marine band. Yes, men too. No segregation here!

Not every verse I wrote was performed, but many were, usually at Democratic retreats and meetings. They were a light break from all the serious conversation.

8. *Go for your dreams.*

It is hard to remember just how difficult it was for girls in the fifties to dream big. Certain careers were wide open for you—secretary, teacher, nurse, telephone operator. Outside of that, it was slim pickings.

I credit my dad for getting me to think very differently. Looking back on it, I wonder if it was because he never had a son. Mom and Dad had suffered a miscarriage and lost twin boys. I don't know if that had anything to do with it. What I do know is that in addition to taking me to Dodger games and gangster movies, Dad also shared his love of the stock market with me and always took me outside to play catch with a pink little ball we called "a Spalding," named after the company that made it.

He got such a kick out of throwing the ball above my head and watching me jump high to catch it—which I became pretty good at. But at the end of the day, my dad himself was really a role model at dreaming big. He went to City College at night after a full day's work to earn his degree in accounting and become a CPA. Then, when he was over forty years old, he graduated from Brooklyn Law School after four years of night school. He dreamed of becoming a true American, and was aware of all issues and responsibilities of citizenship. So education was everything to him and he put out an extraordinary effort for himself and his family.

In my life I never followed the traditional path for a woman. I majored in economics, worked on Wall Street, and went into politics. I did marry at the traditional age of twenty-one and we had our two children before we hit our thirties. But if I hadn't followed my dreams, this book would be vastly different.

9. *Never settle for less than love.*

My mother taught me that it wasn't important to have a huge number of "friends" around you.

"If you have only one friend, and she or he is truly a friend, count yourself lucky," she said. "What's important is to make sure those you confide in, those you spend your time with, those you care about, truly care about you too."

I remember a particular case in point. In high school I was stuck on this guy named Oscar. He was an unusual choice for me: a foreign-born student from Eastern Europe. I knew that he had a very troubled life and that somehow was appealing to me. So I asked my parents if I could invite my new "boyfriend" over for dinner.

"Mom," I said, "I don't think he's ever eaten steak in his life!"

Food was always a way to show affection for my family and my mother was pleased to share our bounty. My father was less enthusiastic, but he always was when I told him I had a boyfriend.

Let me be clear: we were far from rich or even in the middle of the middle class. Anyway, Oscar started to come over on a regular basis and began eating us out of house and home. I loved it until he started acting weird. He became jealous if I even talked to another boy and made fun of the fact that I was co-chairman of the Boosters, a group that cheered on our not-so-winning high school basketball team.

"Why do you care about this silliness?" he said. "You are spoiled rotten by your parents."

Now maybe he was right, but my life was warm and I was surrounded by love, and I didn't understand why he felt that I was being spoiled. I began to doubt myself and was having a very hard time dealing with his criticism and cynicism. Through it all I still liked him, but wound up confused and mad at myself. So, you guessed it, I took it to my mom.

She had a simple solution.

"If any person in your life doesn't really care about you, hurts you, especially if you have shown them love, then walk away and walk away fast," she said. "Why do you need it? What good does it do you? I know you feel bad for Oscar because his life isn't as good as yours, but if your warm family life makes him jealous, well, that's his problem. He doesn't understand that there's a big difference between being spoiled and being loved."

There she was again: giving me advice I would have had to pay an analyst thousands for if I couldn't follow her wisdom. I told Oscar we should break up because I was too young to have just one boyfriend. He didn't argue, just looked sullen, as if he expected it. He walked away. As he did, I felt as if an enormous weight had been lifted from me. Maybe it was lifted from him too.

So, yes, find good people who truly care about you, give them your love and support, give them respect, but expect it back. Otherwise, take a hike. Get away. Find real love, real friendship.

No wonder when I was eleven I wrote the following rhyme to my mother. I found it in her jewel box after she died:

I'll always love my mother.
She is so dear to me.
And when a good thing happens
She's always there to see.
She makes delicious suppers
That I just love to eat
And when she tucks me in at night
It really is a treat.

And so when you give out medals
My mom deserves the prize.
She is a wonderful person
In everybody's eyes.

So that's the legacy of my childhood, the core values I've carried with me throughout all of my political career. Each time I encountered tough personalities—both those who agreed with me and those who opposed—these lessons have served me well.

Chapter Two

Love, California, and the War That Changed Everything

———— ◆ ————

I was born on November 11, 1940, to Sophie (née Silvershein; born in Austria) and Ira Levy, on a big holiday that was then called Armistice Day, the official American celebration of the cease-fire in World War I, the war that they thought at the time was the "war to end all wars." My mother always reminded me of this. It didn't turn out that way, of course, which is why it's now called Veterans Day, and honors those who fought and sacrificed in the wars that have happened since then.

In addition to my American name, Barbara Levy, my parents gave me a Hebrew name, which was traditional for Jewish families. Mine was *barucha shalomis*, which means "blessing of peace." Turned out this fit me well, as I devoted so much of my life as a young mother trying to end the Vietnam War, and so much of my life as a grandmother trying to end the war in Iraq. However, it never described my personality.

There were many, many Jewish refugees in my neighborhood in Brooklyn who'd come over from the "old country." Shopping on Nostrand Avenue with my mother after the war ended, I asked her why so many of the store owners and workers had little tattooed numbers on their arms.

"They were in concentration camps, sweetheart...Auschwitz, Ravensbrück,

Treblinka. They escaped or survived, but millions of others were killed in the Holocaust."

The Holocaust. It seemed like it was always on my parents' minds. They'd each lost dozens of relatives to the Nazis. It made me wonder why someone would want to kill me, not because I was doing something bad to him, but just because I was me. Seemed unbelievable to me. Crazy. Wrong.

The pervasive shadow of the Holocaust over my family, friends, and neighbors and what it revealed about the potential danger in the world beyond Brooklyn—people wanting to kill us just for being us—had a profound and lasting impact on my life. I read Anne Frank's *Diary of a Young Girl* and thought how easily that could have been me, if my grandparents hadn't left the old country when they did. When I was eighteen years old and visited Amsterdam for the first time, I saw the tiny space Anne Frank inhabited to hide from the Nazis, only to be discovered right before the liberation. I've been back to visit that space three times since.

I cannot overstate the impact of the Holocaust on me. It was far from the only example of man's inhumanity to man, and whether it turns up in America in the form of prejudice or around the world in the form of genocide, it always arouses emotions within me and I have to act.

Education was everything to my father; my mother shared his fervor. Not one of Dad's siblings, all born in Russia, was able to pursue a college degree. They had to work all the time to survive. Some of my uncles were entrepreneurial; one become a successful manufacturer of light fixtures, another manufactured children's clothes, and one of my favorite uncles was Uncle Phil, who ran a diner which was referred to in those days as a "candy store."

All of the siblings looked at my dad as the "true American" and he made them proud when he obtained his bachelor's degree from City College of New York. He became a CPA, helping small businesses keep their books straight. Then Mom supported Dad's goal of going to law school. She was so proud of him, she set aside her education dreams for him. He worked by day and went to school by night at Brooklyn Law School.

When Dad became a lawyer in the 1950s, it was the beginning of the

McCarthy era, named after Joseph R. McCarthy, the junior senator from Wisconsin. Along with the House Un-American Activities Committee (HUAC), J. Edgar Hoover's FBI, the Hollywood Black List, Red Channels, and other crazy hate groups, McCarthy created a terrible plague of accusations of treason and espionage, without proof or basis in reality, against thousands of innocent American citizens.

McCarthyism inflicted severe damage to many State Department and other government employees as well as celebrities including Pete Seeger, Leonard Bernstein, Dorothy Parker, and Gypsy Rose Lee. It even threatened my own father. When my dad took the bar, in those years they had an oral exam before a committee. He was asked by them whether he was a communist and had read Karl Marx. It was outrageous. But somehow Dad managed to convince the committee that he was a loyal American and he got his license. Maybe it was because he was such a big Dodgers fan.

When he passed the bar exam, my mom was so excited, she flung open the kitchen window of our fifth-floor apartment and yelled out to me:

"DAD PASSED THE BAR! DAD PASSED THE BAR!"

I was confused by her excitement. As I ran up the stairs, I was thinking, *Of course Dad would pass by a bar.* He never drank much except on holidays and sometimes a little when company came over. Sometimes I took things a little too literally.

President Dwight David "Ike" Eisenhower was a big hero to my father, even though the famous World War II hero was a Republican, while my father was a lifelong Democrat. Dad was grateful that Ike had led the Allies during World War II to defeat Hitler, who was trying to kill all the Jews in the world and nearly succeeded. A lot of Jews in America worried that the Nazis would win and then come across to the Atlantic to put them too in a gas chamber. No kidding. This was not a paranoid fantasy. From 1938 to 1943, Hitler appeared to be winning.

Ike prevailed, though, the war ended, and we were all safe—and eager to fulfill our American Dream.

Education was a big part of the American Dream. It was the way a first-generation immigrant could do better than their foreign-born parents, rising up the social and economic ladder. Education was therefore the most important thing to my parents. I was the eager beneficiary of their priorities.

One of my mother's biggest regrets when she grew old was her lack of a high school and college degree. In her time, education was a much higher priority for men. So she kept putting it off, and frankly, she lacked encouragement. She had gone to business (secretarial) school and when she was sixteen, she went to work, very skilled at typing and stenography.

After I was married in the sixties, Mom studied hard for the high school equivalency test. By that time, she was in her late fifties. I can't remember her ever taking it, but I do know this: degree or no degree, she knew her stuff and she taught us well. And she made sure her daughters had the opportunity for all the education they wanted, and we got it.

I am proud that I went to public school from kindergarten through college. I loved school, especially high school—George W. Wingate, a new high school in Brooklyn whose claim to fame was that it was shaped like a banjo and appropriately nicknamed "The Banjo School."

I was in Wingate's very first graduating class. All of our sport teams were called the Generals (after Wingate's rank in the army). There were no girls' sports in the fifties, so my best friend Juliette and I decided to be the first girl "coaches" of the boys' baseball team. This caused enough of a stir because of its unprecedented nature to rate a story in the *Brooklyn Eagle*, and the first "Barbara" clipping my mom cut out and put in her memory drawer. Maybe that was the start of my going against the usual stereotype of a girl's path at that time. However, the rest of my high school years were not particularly groundbreaking.

I sang in the chorus and was also the head of the Wingate Boosters, which turned out to be great training for my days as a cheerleader for the hard-working but hapless basketball team at Brooklyn College. Going to college wasn't a choice. It was the way it was supposed to be, and of course it would be free. Only when the cost per semester went up to about eighteen dollars did my dad say it was getting really expensive, what with all the textbooks that I had to buy and all. Those were the days.

But we found a way. I majored in economics with a minor in political science, an unusual combination for college girls, 90 percent of whom majored in education so they could get one of the few good jobs open to women when they graduated. My dad gave me a sense of excitement about the stock market, so I went a different way. While he was supportive and proud, it was entirely my decision.

Another major event happened during my freshman year at Brooklyn College: I met Stewart Boxer.

I was sitting in the gym balcony watching a group of basketball players having a practice game. I'd never seen Stewart before, but what I was attracted to were his graceful jump shot and passing skills. It was wonderful to watch.

Lucky for me, he never looked up at the balcony, since what he'd have seen on that day was a silly-looking freshman sorority pledge in a ridiculous beanie and a bow. Who would ever take such a girl seriously?

I couldn't get Stewart off my mind, so by asking around I found out that "Stewie," as he was called, was two years older than me, a political science major and very popular. He belonged to Lord House, a fraternity-like organization, but only for athletes. I learned quickly where the Lord House brothers sat in the cafeteria and began to make frequent trips past his table, hoping he would notice me, but being very careful not to make any eye contact.

But soon after, a miracle happened. I was playing tennis as part of my physical education class when, as usual, I made a wild swing and the ball went soaring. Who happened to be walking just a few feet from where that tennis ball landed? Walking alone too. You guessed it.

Stewart retrieved the ball and took a good look at me, as if he were seeing me for the first time. Then, to my amazement, he tossed the ball back to my court and yelled at me.

"Are you going to the SING?"—so named because it was a singing contest between sororities where we made up lyrics about school set to Broadway tunes. We took it seriously and practiced for weeks on end. All of us sat around and crafted words about classes and teachers and things that made us laugh but had no other redeeming qualities.

"Of course," I managed to reply. "I sure am."

"Maybe I'll see you there," Mr. Cool said back. That was our first date. He suffered through the performance and then took me out for a soda at Wolfie's, a popular diner for Brooklyn College kids. I had dated a few boys before this, but I felt different about Stewart, right from the start. He was both athletic and smart. He was generous on the basketball court, passing to others rather than hogging the ball. Where other guys dressed sloppily, he always looked very collegiate with his pressed khaki pants, button-down shirts, and, most of the time, a corduroy blazer.

I liked his dark black hair, which was buzz cut on top and long on the sides, and his black horn-rimmed glasses seemed cool to me. I liked that he would teach me about jazz. I liked his choice of hot dogs—Nathan's in Coney Island. He would take me there for "dinner," telling me, "Watch the way they handle those dogs over the fire! And notice how they cut the french fries and they add just the right amount of salt."

I loved that he held a job after school to help out his mom, who had been widowed many years before. He worked as a shoe salesman at a chain store called National Shoes. He would ask me to meet him there occasionally. At the time, I wore a size 4B shoe, entitling me to buy sample shoes at ninety-nine cents each. Enough to make Imelda Marcos jealous.

I also like that Stewart was very poor. Does that sound crazy? I found it romantic, and it made me admire him so much, because it never made him down. It only fueled his dreams to become a successful lawyer. I also was moved that he had a special needs brother, whom he always looked out for.

I was smitten, but also leery of becoming "exclusive" with a guy when I was only eighteen years old. Several months after we met, as the summer of 1959 approached, I decided to take a three-month trip to Europe. Our first argument ensued, as he didn't want me to go. But I did.

It was an amazing trip. I had a summer fling with a student musician I met on a student ship that transported us to Amsterdam. When I returned, I realized it was Stewart that I wanted. Unfortunately when I told him that, *he* wasn't ready for an exclusive relationship.

I was heartbroken and couldn't shake it. My grades left the "A" range and other guys were not the answer. I don't remember how we got back together, but I know during this separation, we remained friends. Once he took the friendship too far, and I had to employ the art of tough. He asked to borrow my car to take out another girl in the Bronx. Boy, did I tell him off.

To this day, I cannot believe he asked for that car. In any case, we got back together soon enough, and on my nineteenth birthday, Stew gave me a beautiful Florentine gold watch with the inscription, "Together Forever." It was a serious birthday gift, and we discussed marrying "someday." I admonished him for spending so much. He admitted it was a lot—seventy-five dollars—but he wanted me to have it. When Mom saw the watch, she said, "This must be serious." We said, "Yes it is." So she took matters into her own hands and announced our "engagement." We laughed so hard about it and still do.

We went along with it, and Mom threw an engagement party at our now much nicer apartment in Flatbush. We got married two years later. I often joke that Stew married Debbie Reynolds and woke up with Golda Meir. He has never refuted that.

Six months after we were married, we took our belated honeymoon to Europe, using the popular new guidebook called *Europe on Five Dollars a Day*. But there was one thing we splurged on: we bought a brand new Volkswagen Bug for nine hundred dollars and used it to take us to all the cities we longed to see, including Paris, Amsterdam, Vienna, and Rome. Paris has remained our favorite European city ever since—especially the Left Bank, with its vibrant students, artists, and cafés, serving croissants straight from heaven.

So there we were, home again after our honeymoon celebration. Two youngsters, really. I was twenty-one and my husband was twenty-three. Stewart ended his job as a social worker to focus entirely on the tough job of going to law school, so as soon as I graduated from Brooklyn College, I marched out, hoping to use my degree in economics to get a job working on Wall Street and pay the rent for a new one-room studio on Ocean Parkway in Brooklyn.

Our little place was in the back of the building, so the rent would be cheaper, only ninety dollars a month. The landlord promised us he'd fix up the lobby, which had a useless fountain in the center, but no paint or carpet, so everyone tracked cement dust into their apartments. Months went by and still no action from the landlord, so, feeling a rising tide of outrage, I typed up a petition and got everyone in the building to sign. There were at least a hundred doors in our building, and I knocked on every one of them.

We got the carpet. Maybe it seemed like a small matter to the landlord, but he was wrong. I knew if all the renters stood up for our rights, we would win. And we did. I think that petition organizing was an important moment in my political education, but I didn't know it at the time. Later, I wouldn't understand why the Republicans would make fun of President Obama because he was a "community organizer." Organizing people to fight for their rights is a tough job that needs strong leaders, and he was one for sure. I'll bet that if I'm ever put away in some nursing home for demented old politicians, I'll be the one organizing for better tapioca pudding.

Nevertheless, for all my organizing skills, I couldn't get a job as a stockbroker on Wall Street. They wouldn't even let me into their training programs. Firm after firm told me "women aren't stockbrokers." The male college grads landed spots, but I had to settle for being a secretary, while I studied for the stockbroker's exam on my own.

I worked at an old-line firm for Elizabeth Ellsworth Cook, one of the few women on Wall Street at the time, who was an expert in municipal bonds. Elizabeth put out a famous weekly newsletter on the municipal bond market, but always signed her name "E. E. Cook."

"If men on the street ever knew my newsletter was written by a woman," she explained, "they'd never buy it."

This kind of discrimination was considered ordinary—fine and dandy. Elizabeth Cook didn't complain about it and neither did I. In retrospect, that was as bad as the prejudice and discrimination itself. Racial discrimination was being attacked in the early sixties, but it took a few more years before women woke up to realize the injustices aimed at them.

When I finally passed my stockbroker's exam and got my license, the bosses weren't impressed. They didn't even ask Elizabeth about me, and since she wanted to stay employed, she could only show me sympathy. No chance I could be a full-scale broker for them, no, none at all. I wasted no time: I left the same day and found a different firm that understood that my earning a commission meant dollars for them too. The firm was called J. R. Williston and Beane. I earned a small salary and commission, allowing us to move to a tiny and affordable apartment in Manhattan.

The 1960 presidential election had been the first presidential election Stewart voted in. I wasn't twenty-one yet, alas, but we both had seen John F. Kennedy at a rally in Lincoln Center in New York and thought he was completely terrific. He was so youthful, handsome, charming, and energetic. JFK made us feel hopeful about our country and its huge problems. He made us feel that we could do it, stand up, be tough but compassionate, and change the world. When he was assassinated in 1963, it was a horrific blow. Devastating. Awful. Everyone remembers where they were at the moment they heard, and we were heartbroken, then and now.

JFK's assassination was a turning point in my life. My determination to make money as a stockbroker began to fade and fall away. What an empty, hollow way to make money, one commission at a time, buying and selling! Suddenly, I wanted to get away, leave New York and escape the pressure to earn lots of money because it was so expensive to live there. We decided to move to San Francisco after we visited my sister, who had moved there several years earlier.

My sister is six and a half years older than me, and always led the way in terms of testing the limits of independence. She paved the way for me with my parents, who became more lenient about stuff like curfews and foreign travel after she proved it was okay. She was an extraordinary student and poet. (She's also a very private person, so I won't mention her name.) My mother saved my sister's poems about the tragedy of war, some of which were printed in local newspapers. She had earned multiple master's degrees, and without her having moved to California, I'm not sure we would have ever wound up there.

Anyway, while we stayed at my sister's home in Marin County, we fell in love with the clear skies, the slower pace, and the gorgeous San Francisco Bay. The city itself reminded us of the neighborhoods we had seen in Europe. So when I asked Stew if we could pick up and move to San Francisco after law school, he agreed.

"Why not?" But he added, "I'll have to get a job at least a year in advance."

Fate played a role there too.

One day, tired of waiting for the bus, Stew hitched a ride over the Golden Gate Bridge. The guy who picked him up turned out to be a successful lawyer who advised him to go straight to the state courthouse, where Stew got several offers. In short order, he had a good job and we would soon be moving to California to pursue our dreams.

Stew was still immersed in classes and exams, so I quit my job on Wall Street and flew out alone to San Francisco to find us a place to live. I was also pregnant, but the baby wasn't due for two more months, so I thought there would be plenty of time to find somewhere to live.

Wrong! Our son Doug decided it was time for him to emerge the day after I arrived in San Francisco—May 21, 1965. I was spending the first night of my arrival at my sister's home in Marin County when something scary happened. My water broke. That wasn't supposed to happen eight weeks before the due date. My sister and her husband took me to the ob-gyn, and my new doctor rushed me to the delivery room. The first thing I thought was how I would get through this without my husband. There were no cell phones then, so we had to call the Fordham law school, where he was a student, and ask them to tell Stew what had happened. Stew never forgot that moment. He pleaded with Fordham to let him miss one final so he could be with me for the birth, but they said no way. If he left, he wouldn't graduate. They said no to an honor student and a member of their law review. So much for family values.

I can never forget the birth of both my children, especially Doug's, which was so dangerous. My doctor, John Kerner, who was one of the most beloved and respected ob-gyns in San Francisco at the time, stayed with me every minute. He didn't want me to have too much anesthetic, so I'd be alert throughout the birth. If anything went wrong, it would be much worse for the baby. So he talked to me the entire time, told me when to push and when to rest. In those years no relatives could be in the room, so I kept my eyes on my doctor and only wished that I had the opportunity to know him better before this ordeal. Doug was clearly in a rush and couldn't wait to see our new home state. When he was born, Dr. Kerner moved him as fast as he could right into the incubator, which was next to my gurney. He didn't even take the time to wash the baby. He told me he wanted to create a warm and calm environment for our newborn.

In those days, they didn't have much in the way of preemie neonatal technology except an incubator. They told me our firstborn son had only a fifty-fifty chance of surviving, and it would cost a thousand dollars a day for the special care he needed. Oh, my God! They might have well said a million dollars a day. I was transferred to a ward at Mount Zion Hospital and given charitable care. Bless them. The doctor said that every day Doug hung on, he would increase his chances by 10 percent. Our whole family hung on with Doug.

Becoming a mother for the first time in most cases is not as complicated as it was for me. My joy for this nearly four-pound baby was indescribable, but so was my fear about the possibility of losing him. I didn't have Stew with me for this poignant moment, but I never shed a tear because I knew in my heart that Doug would fight and make it—and he did.

About a week after Doug's birth, after he finished his last exam at Fordham Law, Stew flew out from New York.

Doug was strong and came home after thirty days in the hospital. He has been strong ever since. His traumatic birth brought home what it's like to be frightened to death about a loved one and then on top of that to have no health insurance. I've been fighting for universal health coverage ever since. And when male colleagues come onto the Senate floor to lecture American women about how they should accept government interference in their reproductive health care, and then go into what it's like to give birth, I and the women I serve with roll our eyes. They don't have the foggiest idea what they are talking about.

I remind them on the Senate floor quite often: "Keep government out of our private lives and instead make sure our families have the health care they need."

After Doug was born, and with Stew's law degree in hand, we moved into a small apartment in San Francisco. In 1967 our daughter, Nicole, was born, again prematurely but not as early, so she only had to stay in the hospital for a couple of weeks. By then we had insurance, since Stewart was working as a law clerk for Justice Byrl R. Salsman of the California Court of Appeals.

Stewart and I were very focused on raising our family. But we also opposed the escalating war in Vietnam and wanted to do something to help stop it. I remember our first peace march in 1966. Doug was an infant in his blanket and oblivious to the whole thing. Stew and I passed him back and forth, carrying him, so excited to be with other parents and children as part of the "parents' brigade."

We marched from the Richmond District to Golden Gate Park. Everyone was holding handmade peace signs and shouting slogans. I wore a large pendant that had these words on it:

"War is not healthy for children and other living things."

When we arrived at Golden Gate Park, it was a real scene. Speaker after speaker called on President Lyndon Johnson to end the war now. One unpleasant memory I have are small groups of anarchists trying to distort our message to suit the one they had, which was something like "down with America." They had it wrong. It wasn't about "down with America," it was about wanting to save America. We were there to end the disastrous war. So there were some altercations as some of these radicals tried to push Maoist literature on the rest of us. I thought then that I would defend their right to do what they were doing as long as they were peaceful, but really, it was so counterproductive.

In 1968, we moved across the Golden Gate Bridge to a beautiful little community in Marin County called Greenbrae. We bought our small three-bedroom American dream house for forty thousand dollars with a monthly mortgage payment of $156. Everything was going so well. We both were involved in presidential campaigns. Stew was for Robert Kennedy and I was for Eugene McCarthy. We spent the night of the California primary watching the election results with friends. Stew supported the winning candidate, as I was licking my wounds. After we paid the babysitter, Stew left to drive her home and I sat down to watch the news. What I saw was the horror of the live assassination on TV, as another Kennedy hero fell to bullets. As I sat there alone I was devastated.

I was stunned, frightened, a twenty-seven-year old mother with two small children. America had lost JFK, RFK, and Martin Luther King, Jr.—all assassinated. What was happening? Our country seemed to be in chaos with a new kind of horrible violence aimed precisely at those great leaders who were urging us toward our better angels. Having grown up in the sheltered America of the 1950s, I wondered how our kids would view a world where strong leaders were blown away, one by one, and the foolish, unwinnable war in Vietnam continued to escalate.

How could I sit back and do nothing? I had two choices: either withdraw into a psychological bomb shelter and pretend everything in our little bubble was safe and secure, protected from pain...or reach out and try to change things.

Not a difficult choice, and I haven't stopped reaching out since. Overnight our home started to feel like Grand Central Station, with stacks of envelopes being stuffed, addressed, and stamped that spilled across the dining room table as the kids played around its edges.

I began to help organize community efforts to end the war in Vietnam, save the beauty of Marin County, help low-income teenage dropouts get job training, and other local causes. I worked with other young moms who were yanked out of their traditional lives by events beyond their control, but impossible to ignore. In retrospect, this was really the beginning of the political revolution of the women in America, the so-called "women's liberation" movement, but no one knew that at the time.

We fought on, placing a peace initiative on the ballot in 1970. Nobody thought we'd win—it was thought to be just a gesture, since Marin was a Republican county in those days, and tended to support Richard Nixon and what was now his expanded war in Vietnam and Cambodia.

We were all volunteers. I did the publicity for the peace initiative campaign. And to everyone's surprise and delight we won! A message was sent from Republican Marin County to Richard Nixon: end the war!

This first big victory inspired me to increase my nonstop political activity. I helped launch Marin Alternative, a progressive grassroots political organization, and a support group called Women's Way, and helped found the Kentfield After School Child Care Center, The Education Corps, and Marin Community Video. I was most often the catalyst who stepped aside once the project had developed a life of its own.

In 1972, elections were being held for the Marin County Board of Supervisors. There were many exciting issues at the local level, including land use planning to preserve the beauty of our county, the need to address pockets of poverty, and human rights. Our kids needed after-school activities and care; our roads and overpasses needed attention. And above all, it was a platform to bring ideas forward. Stew and I decided one of us had to run. Our first choice was, logically, *him*. Why? Because he was a man, a lawyer, and therefore more electable. No woman had been on the Board of Supervisors for twenty years, when the amazing Vera Schultz had been instrumental in professionalizing Marin's county government, creating the positions of county administrator, public works commissioner, and county counsel. She was most beloved for helping start the Marin General Hospital, and was the biggest powerhouse behind getting the world-renowned architect Frank Lloyd Wright to design the landmark Marin County Civic Center.

But Stew backed out. There was no way we could pay the mortgage and take care of our family on the eleven-thousand-dollar-a-year county supervisor's salary.

So I ran.

One of the first people I told about my plans, hoping to get her to volunteer for my campaign, was my next-door neighbor, a well-regarded teacher and cordial friend. We sat down over coffee in her kitchen and I went into my spiel about the issues—preserving Marin's natural beauty, opening up county board meetings, safe school crossings for our kids, after-school activities—while she remained totally silent. *Uh-oh*, I thought to myself. This wasn't going well.

Finally she cleared her throat and spoke:

"I don't think you should do this, Barbara. Your kids are young and it doesn't seem right."

I was stunned. She was a working woman who was divorced with two small kids. Hadn't we made any progress since the fifties? Were we all doomed to be like Lucille Ball's character on *I Love Lucy*, trying to be a professional performer like her husband, but falling on her face every chance she tried?

I said thanks to my neighbor and went home with tears in my eyes. I had learned a valuable lesson at the start-up of my first campaign and never cried again. The fact is, if you run for public office, if you put yourself out there, you will get hurt by a lot of people. So just expect it and toughen up. So I started without this neighbor's support and never knew, actually, if she voted for me.

My first and only losing campaign was very exciting. Everyone volunteered, since we had a very low budget. I was so nervous asking people for money that every written appeal I made asked for just two dollars. I clearly remember sitting in our tiny headquarters on Sir Francis Drake Boulevard in Kentfield. It was a tiny room next door to a tiny dress shop. We waited for the mail to come in every day and ripped open the envelopes. Someone spotted an envelope with the return address of one of the biggest donors in the country, who had been an important part of the national Democratic Party finance operation. We couldn't wait to see the size of the check she had written. Several of us stood around the desk and there it was... *two dollars*.

Later she told me, "Barbara, you get what you ask for." A good lesson I never, ever forgot after that.

Everyone in our operation worked gratis and we were really running on adrenaline. We used whatever money we had for postage, sending out as much snail mail as we could, and taking tiny ads in the local newspapers.

The focus of our message was the environment, but women's rights and education played a role. My opponent, Peter Arrigoni, was a very nice person—the nicest I've ever run against—and he was caught off guard by the strength of our challenge. Our slogan was so over-the-top, I'm embarrassed to even mention it, but here goes.

SAVE MARIN: VOTE FOR BARBARA

Yes, that was our slogan. It related to my stand against unbridled development, which many feared would destroy the beauty of our county.

I had to learn by doing. I remember the first debate between Peter and me. I was so nervous that I went completely dry. It's hard to talk when that happens. Luckily, I found a Life Saver in my purse and managed to get through it.

There was so much prejudice against women candidates then. There were times when it felt like I had won a few votes, when people in the audience didn't ask me how old my kids were or whether my husband was supporting my running for office. But there were plenty of days when the old assumptions and prejudices prevailed.

At one luncheon, held at a community hall, the room was packed with more than two hundred women who agreed with me that we should control commercial development and preserve our environment. I was feeling great, when suddenly a voice from the back of the room piped up.

"So, tell me, Barbara," a woman said, "when do you have time to do your dishes?"

I was surprised, but naïve. These were older women who probably didn't have careers and couldn't understand me wanting one. So I made a mistake. I tried humor.

"We use paper plates," I wisecracked.

No one laughed.

Later, I thought it had also been a mistake to tell an environmental crowd that I used paper plates.

Dauntless, I began to go door-to-door, using old-fashioned "retail politics," where you try to meet people in their homes and talk them into voting for you.

Knock-knock.

"Who's there?"

"Barbara Boxer. I'm running for supervisor. Can I come in for a minute?"

The door opened a crack.

"I didn't think you'd be so short...You're the one with four kids under school age."

"No," I said, hoping to get to the issues. "I have two children."

"Oh, no, you have four kids. They told me."

At this point I had the feeling this woman wouldn't vote for me if I stopped a guided missile barehanded from crashing into her house.

"Lady, giving birth is something you never forget, and I only did it twice!"

The door slammed. She probably thought I left two of my children in the woods, and without bread crumbs.

My mom and dad were thrilled that I was running, but in some parts of my own family, the idea of a woman running for elected office was hard to understand.

"Isn't Stew making an excellent living as an attorney?" my mother-in-law asked me. It was embarrassing that I would even want to work at all.

"Of course he is, Mom," I said. "But I can't just sit around and watch our country escalate a war in Vietnam and ignore the real problems we're having at home. I want things to be better for your grandchildren."

I don't think this changed her mind, but later I found out she had saved clippings from the race, which my mother had sent her. I kept going, and our campaign must have been doing pretty well, since one night Dr. William Filante, the other candidate challenging the incumbent, came over to see me.

"Barbara," he said to me and Stewart as he leaned back on the couch in our living room, "I have a great idea."

Stewart and I said nothing, waiting to hear what it was.

"You should drop out of the race."

"Huh?" I was surprised but tried to remain calm and friendly. "I'm doing really well, Bill. Why would I ever do that?"

"I know you're a good candidate, Barbara, and you've run a good campaign. But"—he paused for a moment and stared straight at me—"your candidacy and potential victory would be bad for women, and I'm sure you wouldn't want to be responsible for that kind of damage."

"What?" I was flabbergasted. "How can you say that?" Was this guy nuts?

"Only the oppressor can free the oppressed, Barbara. Women are oppressed by men, so don't you see? Men have to free you." He alluded to his wife, who was a doctor too. I thought, *What? Did you take her exams for her?* "If you win," he said, "you'll actually be hurting the cause of equal rights for women."

I was stunned, and could see Stew was too, by this intellectual gobbledygook and his insane line of reasoning. But the time to step up and be tough had arrived.

"Excuse me, Bill, but this conversation is over."

I stood and escorted him to the door. No way I was going to listen to any more of this garbage.

"You're the one who should drop out," I said, as I closed the door behind him. To be honest, I slammed the door behind him.

He wound up coming in third in that race, and I was first. But in the required runoff, he endorsed the incumbent, so I lost by a slender margin.

The next morning I phoned the kids, who'd been staying with their aunt and uncle. I was worried for Doug that his classmates might make fun of him about his mom losing. At five, Nicole probably wouldn't get anything like that.

"Doug," I said when he came on the phone. "Mommy tried to win but lost by a little bit. If anyone says anything about it, don't you worry, it's all okay." I went on and on.

There were a few moments of silence while I wondered what kind of trauma I'd visited upon this poor child. Finally he spoke.

"Mom, can you make me a peanut butter and jelly sandwich for lunch today?"

Thank God for my kids. Without them I'd never have been grounded enough in real life to have made it in politics.

But we'd lost. It was disappointing. We'd spent a lot of time and money, fought hard, and almost won. But, bottom line: we lost.

So... how does the old song go, it's one of my favorites: "Pick yourself up, dust yourself off, start all over again." Jerome Kern wrote the melody and Dorothy Fields the terrific lyrics. Years later, in his 2009 inaugural address, Barack Obama used the same lyrics, changing the end to "...and begin the work of remaking America."

Steve McNamara, publisher of the local Marin County newspaper, the *Pacific Sun*, approached me after my loss. Apparently he had really appreciated some of the progressive and spunky things I said during the campaign.

"You know so much about local government now," he said, "it would be a shame not to use it. Come and work for me."

When I told him I had no training in writing, although I really liked to write and had done press for several of the campaigns I'd worked on, he said, "Can you make a good speech? Yes. Then just put the paper in the typewriter and talk to it. Don't get hung up."

It turned out very well. I was delighted to receive two awards for my writing from the San Francisco Press Club and the Press Bar Award—one for my in-depth story on the California Supreme Court and one for a story on a beautiful elderly lady who lost her home in a bank scam in which she faced a balloon payment on her mortgage that she never really understood.

While I was working for the *Pacific Sun*, I was approached by California state assemblyman John Burton, who was running for Congress in a district that included Marin County. He pretty much had San Francisco locked, since he and his brother, Phil, were very popular there, but he was relatively unknown in my home county. He asked me to join the staff of his campaign. It was a big decision to leave the *Sun*. I truly enjoyed my colleagues there, the team approach to producing the newspaper, and the fact that my stories were having an impact. Because the *Sun* had a progressive point of view, my stories were shaping public opinion in the county, calling attention to everything from local environmental challenges to the war in Vietnam, where soldiers were deploying in increasing numbers from Hamilton Air Force Base in the county.

I was proud to be a reporter. My two years with the *Sun* went flying by, but I was eager to get back into a political campaign and John was a great candidate. By this time I was known as a good writer and I took over the press operation for Marin County. I also had many contacts from the county supervisor campaign and so I called everyone I knew and organized many house parties.

These house parties were not frivolous. They were basically small community meetings where John would show up, lay out his platform, and take as many questions as he could. Then our staff would sign people up, give everyone a bumper sticker, and ask if we could actually place it on their car. John's opponent was Roger Boas, a San Francisco supervisor who had many connections in the city but not in Marin. We moved so fast that Roger simply couldn't keep up with us as we systematically nailed down the key people in Marin we had targeted.

In any case, John won and hired me in 1974 to staff his Marin County office with a terrific team. My job was to continue to do press for him in the county and help put together his schedule and appointments when he was home from Washington.

John became a mentor. I learned so much working for him. One time when he cast an unpopular vote, I asked him if he was nervous about the reaction.

"Remember always after you vote," he said, "you still have to look at yourself in the mirror the next morning." That said a lot in a simple way.

John also never led you astray. Once, after a gathering, a constituent asked him how things were going. He said, "Lousy." When pressed, he went on.

"Nobody cares about poor people and my pleas are falling on deaf ears."

And he had a dry sense of humor. I'll never forget when John introduced a bill making it a crime to be poor, with appropriate punishment. Many people didn't get it. He always said what he thought and was completely fearless. I was lucky to see how someone like John could survive in public life.

One day I called John and told him he had been invited to San Quentin Prison for the Inmates Council dinner. These were the leaders in the prison—prisoners and community leaders as well as the prison administrators. John had another event in San Francisco that night, and he suggested that I stand in for him.

I was proud to do so and appeared as scheduled, though I have to admit I was a little unsettled when I heard disconcerting shouts from behind the forbidding walls as I walked from my car into the prison.

I don't honestly know what I was thinking when I sat down—maybe I was just a little nervous—but I asked the guy sitting next to me why he was at San Quentin.

"Murder," he said. Then, noting the look on my face he added: "But that was a long time ago."

Okay. Now what? I decided to ask him about prison conditions, and my heart rate slowed down as I took copious notes. Some of the things this inmate told me were awful. How little exercise they got; how hard it was to get books; how dangerous it was.

The purpose of the dinner was simply to expose the honor prisoners—those whom the warden and guards trusted—to the community. There were no speeches, just small discussions at the tables that were organized to facilitate the give-and-take. The next morning I called John and asked if I could put out a press release about the event and told him he should write a letter to the warden. John was nice about it, as always, but said,

"I don't really want to do that, Babs. It's a state issue. I'm glad you went, but I think we'll leave it at that." When John said "leave it at that," the door was closed. He was the boss and I worked for him.

It was at that very moment that I realized I had to try one more run for office. It wasn't fair for me to assume that John, or any other "boss," would see things my way, or do things my way. No, I had to run again if I wanted to really make a difference in the things I cared about. It wasn't that prison conditions were number one on my list, but I still felt it was something that could be addressed with a simple conversation with the warden.

It helped that I had recently read an article in *Ms.* magazine pointing out that women take defeat too personally, whereas men try two and three times. So I told John I was going to try for the supervisor seat one more time. The seat opened in 1976, so if I was going to run, I'd have to leave his staff soon. He was very supportive.

In 1976 I ran again for the Marin County Board of Supervisors...and I won. It was my first victory as a political candidate, and I was thrilled. I had learned from my mistakes and ran a much more effective campaign. I was more of a known quantity, and with a solid platform. People had read my newspaper articles and learned to trust me. I wasn't afraid of debates, I had a long list of endorsers, and I knew how to raise the necessary funds. In 1972 I was outspent by about ten to one; this time I was competitive, because John helped with the donors who had given to his campaign. He said the word and they were more than willing to support his choice for county supervisor. We won by about two thousand votes against a strong female candidate, June Weden, who was quite conservative.

When I took my seat as a board member, the nuclear arms race was in full swing. I used my bully pulpit to point out the futility of "preparing" for nuclear war. If a bomb actually dropped in San Francisco, our little county, just a few miles away, didn't have a chance. Believe it or not, the federal government gave us a grant to put in place a plan to evacuate Marin County, moving our people to Napa County to get away from the nuclear fallout. With my leadership the county supervisors decided instead to use the funds to print a booklet that we sent out to every resident explaining that the best way to move forward was a nuclear freeze with the Soviet Union. I still have a copy of that booklet. It was a proud moment to see Republican and Democratic supervisors agree on this strategy.

My happiness was short-lived when a year into my term I lost a hero, an idol: my dad. It broke my heart. And it was a premature death, in my opinion.

Dad had a dear family friend, a doctor at New York University Medical School, who had always been on the cutting edge of research. In retrospect, however, he evidently went too far out on the ledge. In those years there was a theory that large doses of aspirin a day would ward off heart attacks. Dad went on this regimen of six aspirins a day. Not baby aspirin. Full-dose aspirin. Dad was afraid of having a heart attack and was glad to be doing something his friend thought would prevent it. I don't know how long he was on that huge aspirin dose, but one day, suddenly out of the blue, Dad died of a massive stroke.

Years later we learned that aspirin has benefits in *very* small doses for people at risk for heart attacks. My dad was sixty-nine and much of his family lived well into their eighties. To this day I believe I lost my dad because he was a guinea pig in a failed experiment.

For many years, I tried hard not to think about it. But I missed him so much. He was an inspiration and a pal. I wasn't a kid. I was thirty-seven when he died, but I still needed him. I realized then how it hurts to lose someone we love, no matter when it happens. This personal loss and other experiences in my life made me committed to guaranteeing the right to know both the potential benefits and toxic side effects of medical treatments, as well as of the food we eat. Dad did see me handle many issues close to my heart as a county supervisor, such as working with colleagues to preserve the beauty of west Marin, supporting a transportation system that included ferries, and working to clean up the air. I was an advocate for stop signs to protect our kids walking to school and also strongly supported a program to use our extra dollars to assist organizations that helped the homeless, the helpless, and the addicted.

My fight as an elected official had begun.

Chapter Three

At Home in the House

———————

In 1982, about two months before the filing deadline for John's congressional seat, he called me. After I had settled into my county supervisor role, I rarely spoke with my great mentor because we were both so active in our jobs. "Babs," he said, "are you sitting down?"

"What is it?" I said. "Are you okay?"

"No, but I will be. I'm calling you from a rehab facility in Arizona, and I am determined to save my life and get off my addiction to drugs and alcohol."

Before I could catch my breath and get out a word, John calmly added, "I want you to run for my seat."

My mind froze. I had already decided to leave elected life at the end of my two-term stint as a county supervisor two years later. I planned to either go back to journalism or continue a new career I had started as a radio talk show host at KGO radio in San Francisco. I could only work in the middle of the night, so they gave me that terrible slot during the wee hours of the morning. But I was convinced I could move up.

This call from John was so unexpected, so out of the blue, that, uncharacteristically, I could find no other words than, "Are you sure, John?"

"As sure as I've ever been about anything."

And then he said again with total conviction, "I want to save my life."

"I'll talk to Stew and the kids. We have such a short time frame to decide."

As soon as I hung up the phone, I ran downstairs to tell Stew. He was as stunned as I. "We'll discuss it with Doug and Nicole tonight." They were teenagers then.

Five minutes later, John's brother, the all-powerful Congressman Phil Burton, called. He and I hardly knew each other. When John hired me to run his Marin campaign for Congress, Phil was opposed. He thought I was too much of a novice. John told me he stood up to Phil and said this was his campaign and I was in.

Since John had succeeded and gave me a good deal of credit, I guess Phil was won over. That was too much to hope for, though, as he said, "I'm calling you to ask you to run for John's seat in Congress. But you are not my first choice. Art Agnos [an assemblyman and then later mayor of San Francisco] is, but he turned me down."

So Phil didn't exactly give me a ringing endorsement, but nevertheless it was an endorsement. He also said he would raise most of my campaign funds, but that didn't happen because unfortunately for me, Phil found himself in a tough race against State Senator Milton Marks. The rap on Milton was that he'd "show up for the opening of an envelope" and I guess he did, because Phil had a hard race, but he won it. It also took a huge toll on him.

When Stew and I organized our family meeting later that night, everyone said, "Go for it." We all realized openings like this come rarely. We were in.

The district six election that year would be won by whoever was the Democratic candidate, so my first and only serious hurdle was winning the primary against a wonderful woman named Louise Renne. We were both popular county supervisors, she from San Francisco, me from Marin, but had very different approaches to the battles that lay ahead in Washington, including a recession that caused increasing unemployment and the nuclear arms buildup that was creating such high anxiety in our district.

Louise was always very gentle. We had some very pleasant debates.

"When I get to Washington, I'm going to knock their socks off," she told the audience in one of our debates.

I thought this was a little soft. So our campaign decided to riff off that difference in our styles and my slogan became: "Barbara Boxer gives a damn. Ronald Reagan doesn't."

Looking back, I can't believe we actually had that slogan on posters all over the district. But I was determined to let the voters know that I wasn't going to Washington to be soft or gentle. The issues were too profound and the people hurting too much. So I basically ran against Ronald Reagan instead of Louise, whom I really liked. I won that primary handily.

Ronald Reagan had started out as a liberal pro-union movie actor and spokesperson for General Electric. But he changed. Radically. As a political candidate he veered to the right and shortly after being elected, he became a hero to the conservative movement by firing more than eleven thousand striking air traffic controllers on August 5, 1981, decertifying their union and imposing a ban on rehiring any of the strikers for life. Wow! Talk about taking no prisoners. It made me furious because he was so tough on working people who actually held the life and death of millions of people in their hands. (Five years later, some air traffic controllers were allowed to reapply.)

So it was actually President Ronald Reagan who put the wind at my back—not that he wanted to, but he did. I won the primary.

But the general election race in November was tough. My opponent, Dennis McQuaid, was a smart lawyer, very articulate, and he found an issue.

District six had been gerrymandered by Phil Burton to benefit his brother, John. Phil had made the district very blue-collar and included in it the city of Vallejo, which proudly hosted Mare Island Naval Shipyard. That was a perfect demographic for John, but for me, it was problematic, to put it mildly. The construction workers and machinists were a bit taken aback by a total environmentalist women's rights advocate and a peacenik to boot. I had to get over there and press the flesh—hard and often.

John did his best to help when he was well enough, as did Congressmen Vic Fazio and George Miller. I hired a great local Democrat named Wyman Riley who knew Vallejo inside and out.

While my ace team in Marin kept things going there, the rest of my team stepped up the pace in San Francisco, where I knocked on house doors, stood at factory gates, and went everywhere accompanied by my gay and straight supporters. We went into bars and meetings where they vouched for me.

By the time of the November general election in 1982, the deep recession had caused Reagan's popularity to plummet in my district. His image had become someone who didn't care about the majority of the people, but rather someone who believed in a notoriously disproven conservative theory of "trickle-down economics" that provided big tax cuts for the rich that would theoretically benefit everyone. The tax cuts didn't benefit anyone but the rich, of course. Nothing was trickling down, except economic hardship for the middle and working class citizens. It didn't work then and it still doesn't work.

But it worked for me politically. I told the voters I was going to Washington for *them,* not for the wealthy few. I told them that I would fight for them. Hard. I worked night and day, meeting the voters wherever they were—all in my high heels. My ad showing me in a boxing ring worked very well in the blue-collar areas I needed to convince.

On election night I won and was on my way to the House of Representatives. My head was spinning. As a mom, a local elected official, and then as a candidate for Congress, I railed against the injustice of an unfair tax system, and an economy in trouble, and proclaimed the absolute imperative of a nuclear freeze. Now, thanks to the voters, I would actually have a forum to do something about all of it.

Only about eleven thousand people have served in the House of Representatives since it was organized in 1789. Now I was one of them, the fortunate daughter of an immigrant mom.

The term of a House member is two years, and every two years the Speaker of the House swears in all 435 members for that Congress. I was elected to the 98th Congress and took the oath in 1983. After the mass swearing in, those who wanted a photo with their families and the speaker got a number and were ushered into a waiting room off the speaker's lobby, next to the House floor. When your number was called you had to get in there, pronto.

I was one of those new members who definitely wanted a photo with the speaker and my family. I was so excited. This was going to be one of the most memorable photos of my life, celebrating my first campaign for national office that touched on every issue I carried in my heart.

I had Stew, Doug, Nicole, and my mother with me. Sophie had moved out of New York in the late seventies to live near us after we lost Dad. I was waiting breathlessly for our number to be called when Stewart said he *had* to run to the men's room and would be right back.

Our number was called.

I tried to stall for a moment, but was told that no delay would be tolerated, there was a long line, it was now or never. So we all ran up to pose with Speaker Thomas P. "Tip" O'Neill and Stewart missed the official photo.

Somehow the press got word of this comedy of errors. I don't know why it was so significant to them. Must have been an otherwise slow news day. But that evening the papers wrote that new Congresswoman Barbara Boxer's family photo was "the greatest leak since Watergate." Thank God my husband has a sense of humor. And the wonderful Tip did another photo with Stew in it at the end of his long photo session later that day.

When I was sworn into the House of Representatives, I was forty-two years old. Tip was seventy, one year younger than my mother. I think my mother was more excited about meeting Tip O'Neill as he swore me in than she was about me becoming a member of the House. She never dreamed she would ever meet this hero of hers.

I found out later that my mom was quite representative of Democratic women of her age. When Tip came to the San Francisco Bay Area to do an event for me, it was as if Frank Sinatra or FDR showed up. It was a giant female senior citizen swoon.

Not that it was limited to senior citizens. I loved Tip O'Neill. Everyone did. I was fortunate to serve under him for the last four years of his tenure. I don't think I have ever met a warmer person than Tip, who made it a point to know even the lowliest freshman in the House.

One time, early in my first term, Stewart and I were going to Cape Cod for a vacation weekend.

I happened to mention it to Tip as we were passing in the hall. It turned out that, like most Bostonians, Tip spent some time there.

"Great! Millie and I will take you out to dinner. We'll pick you up."

I figured that was just something nice to say, but to my surprise Tip's office called me with a date for dinner in Chatham while we'd be there. Really? Wow!

On the appointed day, Tip pulled up in front of the hotel bigger than life as he exited this big fancy American car, his white, full head of hair a bit windblown. His wife, Millie, was sitting in the front passenger seat. No driver for Mr. Speaker? Okay! We hopped in the back and off we went with Tip O'Neill, second in line to the presidency, as our man at the wheel.

What a ride we had. As we made our way toward the restaurant, it seemed like everyone on the street called out to him. Tip was well known for saying "all politics is local" and we saw it in action. He knew everyone and everyone knew him.

"Tip...over here!"

"Tip...remember my family?"

"How are ya? How are the kids?"

I swear Millie must have told "Thomas" ten times to pay attention to the road as he swerved to make appropriate eye contact. I could tell from that drive how Millie kept his feet on the ground if not his hands on the wheel. That's why families are so important to an elected person. We got such a kick out of seeing them together in that car, but by the time we got to the restaurant our hands were red from squeezing so hard. We were very happy that we lived to tell the tale.

The author William Novak joined us for dinner. He was helping Tip write his memoirs. It was a memorable time.

When I got to the House we had a huge freshman class. Reagan was president; the economy was terrible. Tip had a large Democratic majority in the House, but he knew how many votes he could lose on important bills and still deliver legislation.

Tip came over to me a couple of times to say something like: "Do what you have to do on this. We have enough votes."

That kind of thing made Tip beloved. He respected each of us. He made it easy. He knew that from time to time our constituents' interests prevented us from voting with him and in those cases he never pressured us. That earned him loyalty, deep loyalty.

On one occasion, for example, there was a big bill funding the military. I felt there were already far too many destabilizing nuclear weapons and tons of other military spending waste. When I told Tip that I would vote no, he was concerned, not so much for the final vote count but for my local California politics.

"Are you sure you should do that? You have a lot of defense contractors and military bases in California."

"Ending the arms race was a central part of my platform," I explained to him. "It's what I believe, so I hope you don't need my vote for this one."

"Okay. Of course," he said. "Do what you need to do to stay true to your promises...and yourself."

That was a very important bill for Tip to get through the House, but he knew exactly why I couldn't be with him.

As the Democratic majority leader, Republicans tried to demonize him in an election in the eighties. They put out ads in which Tip looked unhealthy, bloated, and angry. We all have photos like that. They tried to turn his amazing ability to govern for the people against him. Ronald Reagan was known to say we don't have to look for the problem because "government is the problem," so they tried to make Tip the symbol of big spending and pork barrel politics—in short a symbol of "the problem"—but it didn't work.

Tip was re-elected by his usual large majority.

I met President Ronald Reagan at a White House reception for new members of Congress shortly after my swearing in. At that time presidents held a formal dinner at the White House for the freshman members of the House. I realized immediately how personable and charismatic he was, with Nancy never leaving his side. But with the nation's economic problems, I felt a bit uncomfortable being in that opulent setting all gussied up in my best gown. In fact I felt like a hypocrite and began talking to the waiters, telling them quietly that I was going to work for them, to fight hard for an economy that worked for working people.

They looked at me in a way that said, "Sure, lady, that's great, but don't talk about it now, please." It was naïve of me to bring it up, I realized in hindsight, which is always, as they say, twenty-twenty.

During my terms in the House of Representatives I fought Reagan's policies at every level. I supported a nuclear freeze, going to the Nevada test site to protest along with colleagues like Tom Downey and Leon Panetta, and actor Martin Sheen. I worked to save the National Endowment for the Arts and environmental protection. I tried to get the equal rights amendment through the House that first year of my term, but we fell six votes short, and it's never been voted on since. Reagan's view was that it wasn't necessary, and I'm convinced that's why we failed.

Sometimes we beat him. Sometimes we didn't.

Reagan was the first president I served with, and because of our deep differences, including his never uttering the word "AIDS" for years, I learned more about the art of tough. I had to.

I wrote a song about Ronald Reagan and the arms buildup for my singing group, the Red, White and Blues. We sang it to the tune of "Ballin' the Jack" for our colleagues at a retreat. I would love to think it made a difference, but can't really claim it had anything to do with Reagan eventually reaching out years later to Mikhail Gorbachev and easing the tensions that had so impacted the people affected by the nuclear arms race. Good for him on that. But in the early Reagan years? We were on the brink.

The deep anxiety that surrounded all of us at that time was crystallized by sixteen-year-old Ursell Austin in front of the Select Committee on Children, Youth and Families, chaired by Congressman George Miller.

Sitting in front of a committee of lawmakers, she said, "I think about the bomb every day now. It makes me sad and depressed to think about a bomb ever being dropped. I hope I'm with my family. I don't want to die alone. I think about it most on sunny days, when I'm having a good time. I think—it could happen right now...I also used to think about it when I was at a school that was built on two levels—an upper level and an underground level. When I was in the classrooms underground, I'd think about the building crashing down on me and suffocating me if the bomb dropped. I'd think about all the air being sucked out of me and I burned up under the rubble... I want to live longer, but at least I've lived this long. I feel the worse for little children. It's not their fault that governments cannot find a way to solve their problems...I think the arms race has gone too far. I hope you will open your eyes and your minds and stop the arms race before it is too late for us."

All the Republicans could say after that amazing testimony was that Miller was misusing the committee. It was in fact a perfect use of the committee—trying to understand the impact of the nuclear arms buildup on our children.

Peace activist Helen Caldecott said there was "missile envy" between the United States and the Soviet Union, and that was a great way to put it.

At the same time I was opposing Reagan on the nuclear arms buildup and other issues, there were a few things we actually agreed on. Ronald Reagan spoke out often about not playing games with the debt ceiling. He helped save Social Security. He took executive action on immigration. What I came to respect about President Reagan was that he fought for what he believed in, but whether he won or lost, he moved on.

During my first year in the House, I learned that you can't predict which issues will become yours. You can think as I did, for example, that I'd become the voice of children's rights, or women's rights, or workers' rights, and when you get into the arena, those issues are "taken." So some freshmen in Congress become frustrated, while others find a niche nobody has occupied, or they work with the leaders on overall strategy.

I took the "niche" approach. I told my staff to reach out to the respected nonprofit, community-minded organizations that were working on issues I cared about. Thanks to my then chief of staff Sam Chapman, who stayed with me for more than twenty years, that outreach paid off. Sam had also been a county supervisor in Napa County. He knew that everything we did in D.C. had to be communicated to the people in our district. He was a great writer and he had another quality I needed. His temperament was the opposite of mine. Mine was hot, his was cool. He was cautious, caring, careful, and a wonderful example for our staff.

Groups started to come to us with their issues. On the ERA, women's organizations asked if I could gather a large number of co-sponsors before the issue came to a vote. I loved that assignment and took it happily. Co-sponsors are those members of the House or Senate who actually put their names on a piece of legislation, giving that legislation a boost before it gets to the floor for an actual vote.

As I went around the overwhelmingly male House of Representatives gathering these signatures, I got to know many of my colleagues and, believe me, personal relationships matter tremendously. If a colleague couldn't go so far as to put his name on the legislation, I didn't push, but asked him if he would consider voting for us when the time came. It was very fortunate that I was able to get acquainted and form friendships from the get-go, because I had many important moments ahead when I would need support for my very own bills.

That became part two of my approach to legislating in the House: get the support of colleagues, because there is no scenario in which you can succeed without a coalition.

I had run on a platform that pledged to reduce the size and priorities of the military budget. There were reports of cost overruns on missiles, planes, and other big-ticket items, but I had none of the details, and it would be daunting to take this to the people without them. How could we get some legislation that could be understood and meaningful to regular people who had nothing to do with intimidating things like rockets, bombers, and nuclear submarines?

Then our relationship with smart "outside" groups paid off.

A woman named Dina Rasor came to us in mid 1983 from an organization called the Project on Military Procurement. She was working on waste in the Pentagon budget and told Sam that her organization was going to expose their "Catalog of Spare Parts." Her theory, and I totally agreed with it, was that if we could show the American people the absolute rip-offs going on with purchases they could understand, they would connect the dots and realize how bloated that defense budget was.

She told Sam about the $640 toilet seat, the $7,600 coffeepot, the $436 hammers, and other egregious examples of this scam. She explained that the problem existed because the Pentagon didn't require that its spare parts requirements be put out for competitive bids to small business. Large defense contractors were making these parts in house and charging a fortune. It took Dina's organization to smoke this out by examining the fine print in contract after contract.

"How about some good old American competition?" I said to Dina and Sam when they laid this out for me.

"Yes, that should be the plan," Dina agreed.

So we worked with Dina, and Donna Martin on her staff, and with Sam and Bernie Ward on our staff, and wrote the provision of a bill I called the Small Business and Federal Procurement Competition Enhancement Act. It was a mouthful, but I wanted to make the point that we were offering a pro–small business and a pro-competition bill. The actual bill language was written by the legislative counsel, as is the case in almost all bills, because no matter how good a bill may be, if it is incorrectly written, there can be unintended consequences.

We introduced our bill on October 25, 1983. I still have the photos of me holding up a drawing of the coffeepot. And for months, I wore an ordinary bracket on a chain around my neck that should have cost a few dollars rather than the hundreds of dollars the Pentagon was paying on a regular basis. It was a great way to bring attention to the subject.

Our bill was referred to the House Small Business Committee where the chairman, a wonderful man named Berkley Bedell from Iowa, passed it out of the committee and allowed me to keep my name on it. Just so you understand how generous he was...that hardly ever happens. Most chairmen take the bill and put their own name on it or attach it to a larger bill they authored. But my named stayed on the bill, which had to be approved by the full House and then by the Senate. Eventually the bill became Public Law Number 98–577. Thank you, Berkley Bedell, for your generosity of spirit.

Another friend of my bill was Senator Chuck Grassley, who held a hearing on the general subject of procurement reform and invited me to speak. Members of the House do testify from time to time before a Senate committee and I considered it a great honor. The day after I testified, my picture appeared above the fold of the *Washington Post* holding a photo of the $7,600 coffeepot. The caption was a quote from me:

"It [the coffeepot] might as well be made of gold."

Another funny thing happened while I was fighting hard to pass this military procurement reform. I went home to Marin County to talk about my bill at a community meeting and point out the absurdity of the spare parts prices, when suddenly a woman in the back jumped up.

"A six-hundred-dollar toilet seat?...Really?" she exclaimed. "Where can I get one of those?"

That was in the rich part of my district.

On October 30, 1984, one month after I testified before Senator Grassley's committee, the bill was passed by the Senate and became law. There was a hiccup right before my bill passed the Senate, though. Senator Dan Quayle had doubts about the bill, and that could have held things up, but fortunately my friend Congressman Marty Russo of Illinois swung into action, and addressed Quayle's questions. That's how I learned that just one senator can hold up a bill and even kill it. Later, I used that power as a senator myself from time to time.

Marty and our dear friend George Miller, the congressman from Martinez, California, were so important helping me out in the early days of my career. They were part of a "Tuesday night dinner" crowd. At the time, not one woman was part of this Tuesday group. George and Marty as well as

Tom Downey decided it was time to change things, so I was invited. I guess I passed the initiation, because I was invited back and pretty soon was joined by Nancy Pelosi and Anna Eshoo. The glass ceiling—or at least the restaurant ceiling—was broken.

At these dinners, usually held in a Chinese restaurant, colleagues would talk about their families, their latest political challenges, and their priorities. A highlight of every dinner was telling stories from earlier times involving exciting victories or agonizing defeats.

A recurring theme centered around the importance of your word. When you give it, you must keep it. But you had to listen very *carefully*. If you were trying to get on a committee or handling a committee assignment, you had to ask each colleague for his or her vote. If they said something like "You are the greatest and I wish you nothing but success," you couldn't put them down as a yes. Nope. You had to listen for the words "yes, you have my vote." Everything else was fluff.

I learned that the hard way. I once asked a colleague if he would vote to put me on the Appropriations Committee.

"Barbara, we really need a woman and you would be great," he said.

I was flying high. But when I told Congressman Phil Burton, who was trying to help me get on that committee, he frowned.

"He's a no, Barbara."

I didn't understand, but Phil was right. I missed getting on Appropriations by one vote. Lesson learned.

Clearly it was important to build friendship and trust, and breaking bread with colleagues is a great way to do it. Dan Rostenkowski, the all-powerful chairman of the House Ways and Means Committee, which made all tax policy, was always at the Tuesday night dinner. We had northerners, southerners, east coasters, and west coasters. We were usually all Democrats but very diverse in our views, and every so often a brave Republican would wander in to join us. I look back fondly on the kind of camaraderie we had in those days, since it's fallen by the wayside in the Congress today.

After Marty retired, and other members left office voluntarily or involuntarily, I kept the group together, even after I got to the Senate in 1993. Not once a week but every few months, particularly when Stewart would come to D.C., I would book that local Chinese restaurant close to the Capitol.

I was figuring it out, learning all the time from both successes and mistakes. With more and more colleagues helping and advising me, and with the assistance of respected outside sources and a good publicity plan, my legislative strategy was taking shape. Add a great staff and I was able to become an active and involved member of the House, and actually get something done.

One dimension of my legislative strategy became to add whenever possible a dedicated Republican to the mix. I learned that when I teamed up with Chuck Grassley on our spare parts bill. He and I teamed up again on the Military Whistleblower Protection Act, which we introduced in 1985 to guarantee that military personnel who blew the whistle on waste and fraud weren't fired. Senator Grassley helped me get it through the House, but it didn't make it into law until 1988. Sometimes you need to be patient. Correction: you *always* need to be patient.

Another extremely important bill I was proud to carry while in the House was the Violence Against Women Act (VAWA). It was brought to me by the dynamic senator from Delaware, Joe Biden. I was so excited that Joe had asked me to carry the House bill. Whenever there was a major idea like this, a good legislator wants a bill in the Senate and in the House. It builds more momentum and it usually guarantees hearings will be held in both bodies. The bills are usually identical.

Joe and I had developed a good relationship over the years. I had been impressed with him in 1986 when he criticized then Secretary of State George Schultz for the Reagan administration's support of South Africa, which was still in the depth of its system of apartheid. So when Joe decided to run in the Democratic presidential primary, I participated in his campaign.

He thought I would be the right person to organize women supporters, so he sent his talented sister, Valerie Biden, to see me. We bonded immediately and brainstormed about how I would start to work in Iowa. Joe had made a very energetic and compelling speech in May of 1987, when he talked about "reclaiming the idea of America as a community" and the need to "restore America's soul." He was truly on his way and I was happy to help.

My plane trip into Iowa never got off the ground due to terrible storms. I was frustrated by the delay but far more distressed when Joe was accused in the media of plagiarizing a speech by Neil Kinnock, leader of the British Labor Party. Phrase for phrase.

Joe called a meeting with all of his congressional supporters. Joe wanted our views. Most of us felt the issue was hurting him far too deeply to continue, but we thought he should get out on the campaign trail to see if the public and the media would overlook his gaffe. I'm quoted in the *Washington Post* as saying: "If people get to know Joe and hear his ideas about the country, he has a chance, but if everywhere he goes, the only thing he can talk about is this [the charges of plagiarism], he won't have the chance."

Unfortunately for Joe, his campaign never recovered from the charges, which continued to dominate his every appearance. He dropped out of the race on September 23, 1987. He said his candidacy had been destroyed by "the exaggerated shadow" of his mistakes.

In February 1988, he had his first brain aneurysm, which kept him away from the Senate for months. I wasn't the only one who wondered if his aneurysm might have been fatal if he'd continued to campaign. Who knows.

In any case, Joe was very kind and grateful to supporters like me in the years after his recovery and return to the Senate. I was really happy that he'd asked me to carry the Violence Against Women Act. As Joe said at the time we needed to put the spotlight on this "quiet" epidemic. He was so right. Even the name "domestic" violence was a misnomer, he said. It reminded him of women being thought of as household pets. I remember we both pointed out that at that time there were more shelters for animals than for battered women. That is still true today.

Joe and I made a great team on this. We built the case for it early on, as I was able to get some small provisions through as part of the Higher Education Act of 1992 that dealt with rape prevention on college campuses, an issue that continues to plague us to this day.

Carrying Joe's bill launched me on the path of being a legislative leader when it came to protecting women. I will always treasure the words he said in the Senate on June 21, 1994, after I'd been elected to the Senate myself and, after five years, the VAWA was finally on the brink of passage:

"This bill...did not move until my friend from California came to the U.S. Senate. When the distinguished senator from California came and made the case with the passion and urgency that she does, things began to move."

I learned there and then how important it is to thank colleagues, to share credit, to be gracious in victory. And of course I learned once again how long it sometimes takes to get things done. If you want instant gratification, this isn't the job for you.

On September of that year the Violence Against Women Act was signed into law by President Bill Clinton.

An interesting postscript: In 2000 the Supreme Court overturned one section of VAWA which gave women the chance at a federal cause of action if the crime against them could be proven to be a crime of hate due to their gender. It was a five-to-four vote. In the same year, a bill I authored called The Driver Privacy Protection Act that Joe helped me enact during the VAWA debate was upheld unanimously. That law protected all of us from having the personal information we use to obtain our driver's licenses sold to the public. My bill gained traction when it was reported that a stalker followed a young California actress in her car, wrote down her license number, and then bought information including her address from the state motor vehicle bureau. He tracked her down and murdered her. I was sick at heart. (I thank my then administrative assistant Drew Littman and my chief of staff Laura Schiller for their extraordinary work on this bill that was passed in my freshman year as a senator.)

I highlight this information about the Supreme Court to point out how getting your bill across the finish line may not be the end of the story. The Supreme Court may decide in response to a case that your law is unconstitutional. In the case of keeping driver's license information from going on sale, we won. Joe also played a major role in saving dolphins from extermination, and for that I give most of the credit to his then eight-year-old daughter, Ashley. I had a bill in the House to protect the dolphins, which were dying by the thousands due to something called "purse seining on dolphin." This is a lethal method in which tuna fishermen surround the dolphins because tuna swim right beneath them. Then they throw a huge net around tuna and dolphins and, sadly, dolphins become an "incidental catch."

There was a boycott of tuna sandwiches and schoolchildren like Ashley demanded action. She was determined that her dad help me pass this bill.

This issue was one I believed in. Dolphins are smart, beautiful creatures that need protection. Outside groups like Earth Island Institute really deserve credit for the bill becoming law. Activist Sam LaBudde's video showed the hapless dolphins dying in the chase or in the nets. And there I was, in the Congress of the United States, realizing that a simple label on a can of tuna fish would let consumers know if the tuna in the can they were purchasing had been caught in a way that brought harm to dolphins.

We had many supporters in the House. What member could turn away from all those schoolchildren who were leading the tuna sandwich boycott? We had a great legislator in the Senate. Joe Biden wanted more than anything to show his daughter that her father could come through.

Feeling the pressure, in 1990 large tuna canners said they would voluntarily place the label on their cans, and the fight for the legislation became easier. It passed in 1992, and it's estimated that because of our bill tens of thousands of dolphins have been saved every year.

Very few freshman members of the House of Representatives are well known nationally when they first arrive in Washington. I certainly wasn't. A real exception to this, however, was Congressman John Lewis, who was elected in 1987.

John Lewis had been one of the key leaders of the 1960s civil rights movement, known for his incredible courage and his deep belief in reconciliation in the face of the ugliest racism. Lewis organized the original nonviolent sit-ins at segregated lunch counters in Nashville. He was one of the thirteen original Freedom Riders, and coordinated the famous Mississippi Freedom Summer. Just before Martin Luther King, Jr.'s incredible "I Have a Dream" speech in Washington, D.C. in August 1963, John gave a memorable address; my favorite line was: "By the force of our demands, our determination, and our numbers, we shall splinter the segregated South into a thousand pieces and put them together in the image of God and democracy."

By the time Lewis was elected chairman of the Student Nonviolent Coordinating Committee, he had been arrested more than twenty times. On March 7, 1965—known as "Bloody Sunday"—Lewis and other activists marched with six hundred others across the Edmund Pettus Bridge in Selma, Alabama. There, he was beaten and his skull was fractured. He still bears the scars from that terrible, turbulent time as he serves his fourteenth consecutive term as the congressman from Georgia's fifth district.

Despite the misery that he saw, the hatred he stared down, the wounds that he received, John is one of the most positive people I've ever met or worked with. John's compassion, understanding, and willingness to walk in someone else's shoes, even though his own shoes were tough enough, became evident to me in a most unexpected way. Back in 1988, then Majority Whip Tony Coelho led a fifteen-member delegation from the House of Representatives to the Middle East that included both me and the newly elected John Lewis. It was the time of the first intifada and tensions between Israelis and Palestinians were increasing dangerously, with violence and suffering all around.

We did what we could in Israel to help get the parties back to the peace table, and then went to Morocco, one of Israel's best friends in the region. I was particularly eager to meet with King Hassan II, the reigning monarch of the country, and seek his help figuring out the best way to ease tensions between Israel and the Palestinians.

John was the only African American in our delegation and I was the only woman and also the only Jewish member. There was much fuss and preparation before our meeting with the king at one of his many palaces in Marrakesh, a fascinating old city I wish we'd had more time to see. We were told to enter and wait in an arena-sized reception area that was decorated with beautiful posh couches and tables, as if twenty-five separate living rooms were arranged in the cavernous space.

Then we were summoned into an opulent meeting room. I remember leather-bound notebooks and pens for each of us and men with curlicue ballerina shoes walking in and out of the room with tea and exotic treats to eat. I've been in some beautiful meeting rooms over the years, but never one as majestic. It's good to be the king.

When King Hassan arrived, everyone was quite cordial, but when the conversation got around to our trip to Israel, he suddenly became angry and went on a tirade. We had been talking about Israel's strong push to end the intifada and how the situation was evolving into a dangerous atmosphere for both sides.

"If that's the Jewish mind, we are all in trouble," the king said.

As he continued to use the phrase "the Jewish mind," he became angrier and angrier. I realized I couldn't bear to be in that room with him.

So I stood up.

My heart was beating so fast that I dared not speak. It was just awful to hear the king keep referring to "the Jewish mind." I looked at Tony to convey my discomfort. Tony knew me well, so he stood up too. He got it.

"This meeting is over," he said.

One by one, our delegation of fifteen stood up and everyone walked out silently, which I could tell shocked the king and all of his party. I guess getting walked out on wasn't something that had ever happened to Hassan before.

We went to the bus that had brought us to the palace. As we entered, everyone was very quiet until one of my colleagues broke the silence.

"Barbara, you really overreacted to that comment by the king. He didn't mean anything by it."

I was shocked.

"You don't say 'the Jewish mind.' That's indicative of someone who has a deep prejudice," I insisted, "and a discriminatory attitude toward an entire religion."

But then a couple of others who agreed I had made a big mistake chimed in. They too thought I'd ruined the whole occasion. Things were looking bad for my popularity rating, but suddenly, a deep, authoritative voice came—ironically—from the back of the van.

"Barbara's right," the voice said. "I know prejudice when I hear it."

It was John Lewis, putting an end to the discussion. It was over. Every person in that van respected and accepted John's view. As a new member of the House, it would have been easy for him to go along with the sentiment that had started to spread in that van, but he didn't do that. He spoke his own mind without equivocation and the entire atmosphere changed. I loved him so much at that moment and I still do.

After that, Tony Coelho handled the matter in a very diplomatic and quiet way by having a meeting with the king later in the evening. I don't know what was said, but feelings were soothed. It could have been an international incident at a delicate time in the Middle East. But he took care of it.

The next morning as we were preparing to fly out of Morocco, there was suddenly a hold on the plane. We didn't know what to think. Then, through the narrow plane door, two men wearing those curlicue ballerina shoes marched in, carrying a gigantic hand-painted box of chocolates that King Hassan had sent us. We took it as a peace offering.

For me, the trip to Morocco was a moment of truth. I'm usually as thick-skinned as you have to be in the world of politics, but the king's remarks were not about one person; they were about the Jewish people, and they came from someone who I had thought was a friend of Israel.

In hindsight, what I think deeply affected me was how difficult it is for Israel in that region, when even her friends would desert her. And that hurt me tremendously, as I lost a whole wing of our family during World War II simply because they were Jewish. Israel was supposed to be the safe place for a people who had struggled so hard to survive.

Israel needs friends. Friends like John Lewis. The problems between Israel and the Palestinians have gotten steadily worse since 1988. I wish I could figure out how to solve them. When I worked as a reporter for the *Pacific Sun* in

1973, I sat across from a very bright writer whose name was Ira Kamen. The news then was filled with trouble in the Middle East, and the Yom Kippur War had broken out between Israel and Egypt. I was down in the dumps about it and so was Ira.

In a moment of levity, he said: "Maybe Israel and Cuba should trade places. This way Cuba will be near their friends and Israel will be closer to Miami!"

Having a sense of humor helps when you're dealing with apparently intractable problems.

My whole career was about fighting for issues that affected many people. Sometimes I was involved in issues that affected just *one* person.

In 1984 I received a letter from a woman named Margot Hogan, who wrote that she was about to be deported. She was an Australian who married an American who had served in World War II. They had both spent some terrible time in a Japanese prison camp. When they returned after the war to live in the United States, she thought she'd earned American citizenship simply by being his spouse.

But no. Margot, over sixty by then, said that as soon as her husband had died, she'd been notified that she was about to be deported back to Australia.

"I have a heart condition and no relatives to care for me in Australia," she told me.

That's when you needed to have the support of the leadership and your colleagues. Obviously these "private" bills could be abused and no doubt some were. But the only thing that could save her was a private bill. It was called A Bill for the Relief of Margot Hogan. It became law on October 19, 1984. I got it done because members of the House trusted my judgment on this. I was so grateful that Mrs. Hogan could stay in America. I was also grateful to serve in the House—a rowdy place even then, but a place where we did many good things for the people during my time there.

Chapter Four

An Unsettling Time: AIDS, Sexual Harassment, and the Senate

—————◆—————

I really didn't expect a gargantuan issue that would impact the world would fall on my shoulders when I was sworn into the House in 1983. When AIDS first came into my consciousness, I didn't know what it was, how you got it, not even what it was called.

Early one morning in 1982 I was walking a path with my friend Carolynn alongside a restored marshland, my first successful effort as an environmental organizer. She grew uncharacteristically sad. When I asked her what was wrong, Carolynn, a professor of music at San Francisco State, told me her writing partner was suffering from what he was first told was pneumonia in a San Francisco hospital.

When I offered my cheery assessment that pneumonia shouldn't be such a big problem for a young, healthy man, she told me that she thought that too, but somehow this was different. He wasn't responding to medication, just getting weaker.

"He's kind of wasting away, Barbara," she told me. "And they don't know why."

That was the first time I heard the phrase "wasting away," but by the time

I was sworn into the House in 1983, I had learned that this "wasting away" was caused by a virus now called HIV, Human Immunodeficiency Virus, which led to a disease called AIDS, Acquired Immune Deficiency Syndrome. AIDS was becoming a huge and devastating epidemic that seemed to be cutting down people all around me, and at that point it seemed that the victims were all gay men.

My colleague Congressman Phil Burton, a true powerhouse in the House when I got there, was one of the first members to acknowledge and understand the dire need for AIDS research and he pushed hard for AIDS research funds. When he died unexpectedly from an aneurysm just months after I was sworn into the House, I was forced to step up and shout from the rooftops to get help. So I railed about the lack of attention AIDS was getting from the Reagan administration. Sometimes I was not polite.

"Anyone who knows how to stop the transmission of AIDS and refuses to talk about it," I said, "is guilty of murder!"

In retrospect, that was not an overstatement, but at the time I got more dirty looks than I care to remember. I also took a gamble and sent out very graphic mailings to the vulnerable parts of my district. The explicit nature of the information raised eyebrows, but I was desperate. I really was.

When Phil's wife, Sala Burton, was elected to his seat after his death, she had the most intense AIDS burden: not only because she had to help build coalitions in Congress to obtain the needed funding for research and treatment, but also because she kept losing friends, supporters, and staff to the disease. Then, after Sala's death from colon cancer in 1987, a new congresswoman, Nancy Pelosi, brought her considerable energy to the fight. Phil, Sala, and Nancy represented most of San Francisco. I represented about a quarter of it, as most of my district was in Marin County.

In 1982, President Reagan had appointed Dr. C. Everett Koop as Surgeon General of the United States. Many people in the Reagan administration—like Gary Bauer, a key advisor and future leader in the Family Research Council, whom many called a gay basher—were opposed to spending any money on the "gay disease." But even though he came from a conservative religious background, Koop approached the disease as a doctor, not a reactionary politician. To him AIDS was a tragic disease that had to be prevented and controlled. By this time the Centers for Disease Control and Prevention (CDC) had reported ten thousand confirmed cases. It was becoming a true disaster. And I believe if Dr. Koop hadn't been so frequently stifled until 1986 by his bosses in the Reagan administration, many fewer Americans would have died.

In 1988, Koop created a controversy when he mailed AIDS information pamphlets to every American family. Religious activists were upset, calling for Koop to be fired. The battle got more intense when Koop suggested sex education in the early grades.

Nevertheless AIDS continued to spread like wildfire. What could we do? We needed answers. When we learned from the CDC that AIDS was sexually transmitted and a condom could stop that transmission, I wanted that simple, easy-to-understand and enormously useful information distributed far and wide in my district. Dr. Koop's mailing was great, but I knew a barrage of communication would be necessary in my home district to break through the wall of fear and denial.

I had to get over my innate embarrassment in order to talk about risky sexual behaviors and how to stop AIDS. Of course, Reagan was still refusing to even say the word "AIDS." His conservative backers claimed that the "gay disease" was caused by immorality and in their narrow minds it was a "choice to be gay"—an incredible inaccurate lie that now, thank God, is beginning to be a dark shadow of past history.

Back then, however, we were still under the shadow, so I believed it was incumbent upon every member of Congress who had a threatened constituency to be strong and assertive. Reagan had the biggest bully pulpit in the world, but he wouldn't talk about anything that had to do with AIDS, and still never used the word himself.

Nevertheless, I had to talk about condoms. After all, we had information that could save lives. If I didn't get that information out there, *that*, in my mind, would be immoral—I would be guilty of a crime. I couldn't shy away from what I knew. I was also grieving the loss of many gay activists I knew personally, many of whom had helped me in my campaign for Congress.

In 1985, I was appointed to the House Budget Committee, a six-year assignment I had coveted because I wanted to have a say in AIDS funding. Without that type of position, I would have been consigned to begging.

Not that I hadn't been begging already. Early on I had gone to William Natcher, a longtime Member of Congress from Kentucky. He was then chairman of the Health Subcommittee of Appropriations. I visited his office, explaining this "mysterious disease" that had hit San Francisco and other cities that had large gay populations. People were getting skin diseases, had breathing problems, and were wasting away. We didn't know exactly how it worked yet and we needed research funds. I was distraught and worried that Congressman Natcher, who was seventy-six at the time, had probably never met a self-identified gay person in his life.

"Mr. Natcher," I said, "I know you don't have a large gay population in your district, but among the voters I represent, AIDS is killing people every day."

To my immense relief, this southern gentleman couldn't have been more wonderful to me. I was a novice, and he certainly wasn't used to women members of Congress.

"I see you are upset, and that you care a great deal. If people are sick then we must help," he said in a soft southern drawl.

That was the second year of specific AIDS funding, and it increased by 50 percent from the year before to twelve million dollars, all because of Bill Natcher. The last presidential budget request I saw for AIDS was thirty billion dollars for domestic and global AIDS funding. Who knew then what twelve million would become? But that twelve million dollars gave us all hope.

I still wanted to assert more leadership so I asked Budget Chairman William Gray if we could set up an AIDS Task Force on the committee and I asked to chair it. Bill said yes and I was most grateful to him.

I remember when Elizabeth Taylor came to testify before the full Budget Committee. She was eloquent and compassionate, and she used her celebrity in the fight against AIDS as much as she could. Some other notable celebrities

I've worked with include Ted Danson, Carole King, Robert Redford, Leonardo DiCaprio, Ed Begley, Bonnie Raitt, Jackson Browne, and Pierce Brosnan on the environment; Martin Sheen, Sally Field, Angelina Jolie, Ben Affleck, and Joanne Woodward on foreign policy and the arms race; Jimmy Smits and Geena Davis on fairness in films; Elizabeth Taylor, Barbra Streisand, Fran Drescher, and Christine Lahti on health issues; Barry Manilow on music education, and Paul Newman on children. Over the years, Oscar-winning lyricists Alan and Marilyn Bergman have been by my side on a range of progressive issues as have Julia Louis-Dreyfus, Lilly Tomlin, A&M Records legend Jerry Moss and his wife, Ann, as well as music entrepreneur Clarence Avant and his wife, Jackie, and actor Paul Reiser and his wife, Paula. They all leveraged their influence to help bring attention to issues and they helped me every time I ran.

When Rock Hudson, a longtime friend of Ronald Reagan's, died of AIDS in 1985, it must have changed Reagan's attitude, because in 1986 he ordered Dr. Koop to write a new AIDS report and things began to change. How sad that since its inception in 1983, Dr. Koop had been directly excluded from the Executive Task Force on AIDS, which did next to nothing except back a small number of research grants.

After 1986, however, the new Koop report treated AIDS not as a moral issue but as a health issue. Dr. Koop and Dr. Anthony Fauci of the National Institutes of Health led the charge to treat AIDS as a chronic condition, not a death sentence. Finally, a blood test was developed to detect HIV.

I admired Dr. Koop when he was ripped apart by social conservatives and responded:

"My entire career has been dedicated to prolonging lives, especially lives of people who were weak and powerless...who need an advocate."

Fauci continued his stellar career in public health and is also a hero of mine.

When scientists determined that HIV could be transmitted from mother to child and that risk had to be addressed, I was depressed by the tragic news. We already had our hands full dealing with adults, but this required immediate attention. When I met a remarkable human being name Elizabeth Glaser, my spirits lifted.

Elizabeth was a mother fighting with every fiber of her body for the life of her son, Jake, after she and her husband, Paul, lost their daughter, Ariel, to AIDS.

Ariel was born in 1981 and died in 1988, only seven years old. Here's why.

Elizabeth had received what was thought to be a routine transfusion during childbirth. Four years later, she learned that the blood was tainted with the HIV virus. Ariel had been infected with the disease through breast-feeding. Their son Jake was born in 1984, and the virus was passed on to him as well, *in utero*—from the tainted blood. Until then, nobody thought Elizabeth was anything but healthy.

When I met Elizabeth, she had one mission only: a pediatric AIDS initiative in America. She teamed up with two friends, Susie Zeegen and Susan DeLaurentis, and there was nothing, and I mean nothing, stopping these three women. I have met numerous activists on many issues over the years but never, ever, had I seen a team like this. They *never* stopped. They were out to save lives and prevent illness and there wasn't a second to waste. Their determination was contagious. I saw firsthand the magic they performed on Democratic and Republican members of Congress.

Elizabeth's husband, Paul Michael Glaser, is a well-known actor and director. He and Elizabeth had many friends, who had many friends, who had many more friends. Famous friends, rich friends, not-so-rich friends. That's how the Pediatric AIDS Foundation started and has continued ever since. It is now called The Elizabeth Glaser Pediatric AIDS Foundation.

Soon after the foundation started, Elizabeth and Paul testified, upon my request, at the House Budget Committee. The hearings, held in March 1990, were extremely emotional. We heard Elizabeth's story and saw her courage. She explained to us that children with AIDS can't be treated clinically in the same way as adults. She fought for testing protocols for kids. She suggested that there must be a way to stop the transmission from mother to child, which was the biggest problem raging in Africa. She and Paul woke us up and changed minds. One thing Elizabeth made sure of: she would never, ever, pit children's needs against the gay AIDS community. Never. She taught us that we must *all* stand with each other and help each other. She was an angel—truly.

She was now fighting not just for Jake but for all the children in America and the world who were infected with the disease or who were HIV-positive. When you spoke to her, you knew there was going to be a time when scientists would learn how to stop the transmission of the virus from mother to child and how to treat AIDS in a way to prolong life. She was absolutely right.

The foundation kept fund-raising and the funds went directly to research. She and her amazing group asked sports figures like Sandy Koufax to attend these fund-raisers and it paid off. Millions were raised. Elizabeth's theory was that scientists needed to collaborate more, so the foundation made sure they were constantly networking, sharing information, no longer working in isolation.

Elizabeth died in 1994. All the advances came too late to save her. Miraculously, Jake exhibits no symptoms of AIDS. He's healthy today, and has the same amazing power of his parents to persuade and keep the focus on a cure and a vaccine. He's contributing to American AIDS leadership in the world that has been carried out by every president of both parties, for which we all should be very grateful. It is one of the few issues that has united us across party lines.

The Pediatric AIDS Foundation is one of the reasons for this bipartisan approach to AIDS. Another is the work of the singer Bono, who has been unrelenting and who won over none other than that bulwark of conservatism, Senator Jesse Helms. In the early 2000s Helms expressed regret that he didn't do more to combat AIDS early on. "I'm so ashamed that I've done so little," he said after being persuaded by Bono, proving that miracles do happen.

But I still can't forget the argument I had with Helms during the Senate debate over President Bill Clinton's nominee to become Assistant Secretary of Housing, Roberta Achtenberg, the first openly lesbian nominee ever to be confirmed by the United States Senate. We really went at it. Dianne Feinstein and I were new senators, but since Roberta was a San Francisco supervisor, and we were proud she was from our state, we were moving her nomination forward. Helms called Roberta "that damn lesbian" and a "militantly activist lesbian." I said, "This confirmation was as ugly as it gets on the floor of the United States Senate."

Helms slowed the confirmation process down, insulted Roberta on the Senate floor over and over again, and tried to rally a majority against her. After Roberta won her vote 58 to 31, I spoke to the National Women's Political Caucus and reminded them that Helms had said, wagging his finger: "This vote will be remembered." I told the group it will be remembered because we stood up and we won.

Elizabeth Glaser had a profound effect on me. We had a special connection. I remember a phone conversation as she was resting in a Washington hotel room after a vigorous day speaking to a broad array of senators and House members. I called to tell her I had just read her book, *In the Absence of Angels*, and learned that we were born on the same day. Perhaps it explained our instant ability to get to the heart of what we both knew we had to do together. I helped introduce her to the political world and she won them over. She taught me so much about toughness, about how to focus, focus, focus, even when the task was daunting.

The second issue that drove my run for the Senate was Anita Hill's testimony and subsequent vilification at the Senate confirmation hearings of Clarence Thomas.

I was still in the House of Representatives on July 1, 1991, when President George H. W. Bush nominated Clarence Thomas to the Supreme Court to replace Thurgood Marshall, who had announced his retirement. Such a nomination had to go through the Senate Judiciary Committee, where Joe Biden was the chairman.

The nomination hearings were intensely contentious from the outset. Even before they began, many women's and civil rights groups opposed replacing Thurgood Marshall, a liberal icon, with Thomas, a man who had previously expressed his strict opposition to abortion. These groups worried that he would want to reverse *Roe v. Wade*. Thomas was also against affirmative action, even though he himself was an African American who had benefited greatly from such policies.

I watched the hearings on TV with increasing disbelief and dismay. I was appalled when, after the customary evaluation by a committee of the American Bar Association, twelve ABA members voted that Thomas was not "well qualified" but only "qualified," two voted that he was "not qualified," and one abstained, for an overall vote that was one of the lowest ratings in history for a Supreme Court nominee and an embarrassment to the Bush administration.

Then things became even more dramatic. After the hearing was officially concluded, National Public Radio Supreme Court correspondent Nina Totenberg received a leaked confidential Judiciary Committee/FBI report. The report stated that Anita Hill, a professor at the University of Oklahoma Law School, had been interviewed and had stated that Thomas made inappropriate sexual comments when they worked together at the Department of Education and again later when she worked for him at the Equal Employment Opportunity Commission.

This leak created a frenzy in print and broadcast media. The coverage brought pressure to reopen the hearings on Thomas, but the committee stalled. The hearings were not reopening. So Congresswoman Pat Schroeder suggested that a few of us march over to the Senate, where we knew that Senate Majority Leader George Mitchell was having lunch with all the Democratic senators. We wanted to present the case to our Democratic colleagues that Anita Hill's charges were serious and hearings on the Thomas nomination, still being stalled by the committee, should be reopened.

I rounded up Congresswomen Eleanor Holmes-Norton, Louise Slaughter, and Jolene Unsoeld. Pat got Nita Lowey and Patsy Mink, and the seven of us marched over to the Senate and up the stairs at the Senate side of the Capitol. We had no idea that there would be so many cameras facing us as we moved up the Senate steps: still photographers, TV cameras, tape recorders, hand mikes, boom mikes, and flashbulbs.

"Where are you going?" someone shouted at us.

"To speak to the senators."

"What do you want them to do?"

"Slow down and look at the charges."

"Is Thomas guilty?"

"We don't know. We just think the charges are serious and deserve to be discussed."

That now famous walk was captured in a photo that catapulted the issue of women's rights into the American consciousness. In my case it was a run. If you examine that photo (see the photo insert), you'll see yours truly in the lead. Not because this was my idea—it was Congresswoman Pat Schroeder's—but because I was from California and running was part of my workout. I hung that photo in two different places of honor in my Senate office as a constant reminder of the fight for equality for all who view it.

Once we got the media behind us and went through the doors, there was a small but stern group of staff people lined up in front of a set of large closed mahogany doors. We asked them to stand aside and we knocked on the doors. One opened a crack.

"You can't come in," we heard a female voice, a senior staffer, say.

"Why not?"

Then we heard a very odd phrase flung at us from the same woman—Senator Mitchell's gatekeeper.

"We don't allow strangers in the Senate," she said.

"Strangers?" we shouted right back. "Are you kidding? We're your Democratic colleagues from the House!"

She explained that any non-senator was technically called "a stranger" and we shouldn't take it personally.

Weird to be called a stranger. It looked hopeless. Then I made one more try.

"Listen, there are about a hundred cameras out there and they all took our picture coming up the steps. They know why we came here and they'll want to know what happened, so if we don't at least meet with the majority leader..." My voice trailed off with what I hoped was an ominous tone.

That's when she got it.

"One moment," she said. "Wait here."

We waited. She came back in a moment.

"Okay," she said. "The majority leader will see you in the side room now."

During the meeting we argued that Professor Anita Hill was credible and believable and to ignore her was wrong. New hearings were scheduled.

Now that I know my way around the Senate, I would bet that Mitchell told my pal Joe Biden to open the hearings and let Anita Hill be heard. That would quiet us. Then, he told Joe, shut the hearings down and vote. Let me be clear, I don't know that for sure, but that's what I think happened. We women of the House were a giant nuisance to the senators. We had to be mollified and then it would be back to business as usual.

We thought Hill's testimony would change the course of the confirmation. It didn't turn out that way, for sexist, unfair reasons that were kept secret and far beyond our control.

That's what I believe. She was heard, the hearings were shut down, and the vote was fast, just four days after her extraordinary testimony.

Nevertheless, what those hearings achieved was monumental in terms of changing the makeup of the Senate forever. At the time there were only two women in the Senate and absolutely none on the Senate Judiciary Committee. The people of the country were shocked on both counts. After this "obligatory" hearing, the good old Senate "Boys' Club" inevitably did what they should *not* have done, namely, they confirmed Thomas on October 15, 1991. But the election of 1992 shook everything up, tripling the number of women in the Senate, leading to the passage of the Violence against Women Act, and finally getting a woman, none other than California's Senator Dianne Feinstein, on that committee. (For that, I do credit Joe Biden. He literally recruited her.)

Anita Hill was a very attractive, calm, and dignified woman. Obviously an expert on legal matters, she made it clear from the outset that she was testifying as to Thomas's character and fitness, not about the legality of his actions. Professor Hill was treated with disdain and disrespect by the committee, but she pressed on fearlessly with her testimony:

"He spoke about acts that he had seen in pornographic films, involving such matters as women having sex with animals, and films showing group sex or rape scenes...On several occasions, Thomas told me graphically of his own sexual prowess."

She went on to describe one occasion when "Thomas was drinking a Coke in his office, got up from the table at which we were working, went over to his desk to get the Coke, looked at the can and asked 'Who has put pubic hair on my Coke?'"

This Coke can story became notorious. Oddly, however, the men on the Judiciary Committee didn't seem to take it seriously. Some scoffed, others claimed she had to be lying. Thomas cleverly played the race card and accused Professor Hill and the media of committing a "high-tech lynching."

Oh, my God, I thought. What a slick twist.

And it didn't end there. When you read the transcripts of the Thomas hearing, you see him presenting himself as the victim. The women in the country didn't buy it, but the senators did. Senators asked questions of Anita Hill like: "Are you a scorned woman? Do you have a martyr complex?"

Women in America couldn't believe it. But then again they could. They were living through these things in the workplace. Professor Hill's testimony pushed women's buttons. It was familiar. It had happened in one way or another to many of them. They all could have been Anita Hill, and many of them had even worse stories to tell.

It had happened even to me, in the most unexpected situation and by the most unexpected perpetrator: my beloved economics professor at Brooklyn College.

Except for one semester during which my grades fell because of my romantic troubles with Stew, I always got good grades. So when I got a C-minus in my senior year from this professor, I called the economics department and spoke to him. He told me the problem was my final exam; that startled me, because I thought I had aced it. He said he couldn't change the grade unless we went over the final together and I should meet him at the office the next day. I said fine.

By then I was married and living around the corner from campus. Stew walked me over and waited for me outside the building. Determined and still perplexed, I knocked on the professor's door. Classes had ended—it was almost graduation day—and the halls were empty.

"Come on in!" the professor said, and he motioned to the long conference table. I sat across from him and noticed he had no papers in his hand, and the table was completely clear.

"Where's my test?" I asked. "I thought we were going over it together."

"No, we just need to talk," he said, looking intently at me.

My spirits were lifted. Maybe he had had second thoughts about my test and would give me the good news.

"Look, Barbara, I have so enjoyed you in my class. You were so perky and you participate so well."

"So why did I get this terrible grade? It pulled down my average."

"Because I like you so much, I had to bend over backwards the other way."

This made no sense. I got up to leave, exasperated, and he jumped up, blocking the door with his body.

"I need to go!" I said.

"Just give me a good-bye kiss."

He leaned over and put his wet lips somewhere on my face. It was disgusting.

"I need to go somewhere right now. My husband is waiting for me." That must have scared him, because he stepped away from the closed door.

Thank God for Stew! I ran out of there shaking.

I was stunned and outraged, but reported nothing. I was twenty-one years old and ready to graduate. The C-minus he gave me really bothered me, because in economics, my major, I had never gotten less than a B-plus. In retrospect, of course, that was his plan . . . to get me into his office alone. Sure, he had a great reputation as a loving father of several children and that gave him a trustworthy aura. I don't know if he had other victims, but it was hard to believe I was the only one.

I remember this incident as if it were yesterday. Stewart was there for me and helped me work through it. We wanted to report him at the time, but

Stew and I knew he could hold up my graduation and I already had a job waiting for me on Wall Street that I desperately needed, since Stew was starting law school full-time. So Stew was the only one in the world who knew about it, as was the case with so many women in those days, until Anita Hill told her story, and I told mine.

I blame myself for not focusing more on what was happening behind the scenes after we had marched up the steps of the Senate. I might have learned in real time what I learned later—that the committee had refused to allow the testimony of two women, Angela Wright and Rose Jourdain, both of whom were prepared to say that Thomas had made unsolicited sexual advances.

Wright, who'd worked for Thomas at the EEOC until he fired her, said he had pressured her for dates, asked about the size of her breasts, and made similar comments about other women. Jourdain also said Thomas was always commenting on her body, and Sukari Hardnett, another former Thomas assistant, told the Judiciary staff that "if you were young, black, female, reasonably attractive and worked directly for Clarence Thomas, you knew full well you were being inspected and auditioned as a female."

In May of 1993, moreover, an article in the *New Yorker* by Jane Mayer and Jill Abramson stated that Joe Biden had abdicated control of the Thomas confirmation hearings and didn't call four women who'd traveled to Washington to corroborate Anita Hill's claims, including Wright and Jourdain.

They also claimed that Thomas had lied under oath, since they had seen video rental records showing Thomas's interest in and use of pornography to a far greater extent than the public had been led to believe. Mayer and Abramson wrote a book, *Strange Justice: The Selling of Clarence Thomas*, which was a finalist for the National Book Award and was also made into a movie for TV.

Looking back, I failed to do the follow-through. I failed big time. Not that it would have been easy. We women of the House were seen as the enemy. We really were…enemies of the status quo, of the way things were, of the *gentlemanly* way things were. I believe that even my buddy Joe Biden had to succumb to the vast majority of his committee members on both sides.

It's a long, sad story and there's even more. In 2010 Clarence Thomas's wife, Virginia, left a voice mail message on Anita Hill's office phone at Brandeis University over a weekend, demanding that the professor say she was sorry for accusing her husband of sexually harassing her.

"I would love you to consider an apology sometime and some full explanation of why you did what you did with my husband," the voice mail said in part, according to NBC News. "So give it some thought and certainly pray about this and come to understand why you did what you did."

Incredible, isn't it?

Professor Hill called the message "inappropriate," and reported it to her employer's security department, who in turn reported it to the FBI. Further, Professor Hill said she has no reason to atone.

"I have no intention of apologizing because I testified truthfully about my experience and I stand by that testimony," she said in a statement to NBC News.

Anita Hill's story touched the hearts of women and caring men across the nation.

I definitely rode that wave. It was a rough wave and very high, but I hope you can understand now why the Anita Hill case translated into victories for women. Anita Hill is an icon who went through hell for coming forward, and I hope she knows what a difference she made, even though Clarence Thomas got confirmed.

Major federal laws were passed to address sexual harassment and violence against women, and the long march to get more women elected to Congress was kicked into high gear. All because of her courage, her ability to be tough under extraordinary pressure.

I was one of those women who benefited from her particular art of tough.

The pull of this issue of respect for women was tugging at me. It was one more reason to try to get into the Senate, in which women made up a dismal 2 percent of that "august" body.

Chapter Five

From an Asterisk in the Polls to Senator

W hy would I ever give up a safe seat in the House of Representatives where I was helping to make a difference on important issues and enjoying the camaraderie of that raucous Democratic caucus? How did I ever think I could win a race for the United States Senate in 1992, running as a liberal in a purple state that had never elected a woman to the Senate?

Believe me, there was *nobody*... not one pundit, Democratic or Republican, not one person, who thought it was a bet worth making.

"It's impossible, Barbara. I can't stand the thought of your losing a platform for national issues. Please don't run."

That was what one of my best political friends, Joyce Linker, told me. Joyce was the mastermind behind my Women Making History fund-raisers, luncheons honoring women trailblazers, a tradition I kept for more than thirty years. Her blunt assessment was a sentiment shared by countless supporters.

But winning was not my original reason for running. I knew the United States Senate was the brass ring, the impossible dream for me. I also knew that just running a good, visible campaign would give me a megaphone that I had never had before. I couldn't and wouldn't run for another term in the

House. I had to get away from there, and the person most responsible for that compelling impulse was a guy named Newton Leroy Gingrich.

Newt Gingrich was an assistant professor at the University of West Georgia who had been denied tenure and was twice defeated before being elected to the House of Representatives in 1978 on the Republican ticket. Therefore, he was on the minority side of the aisle and had already been building his power base among the most conservative members of Congress for four years by the time I arrived. At the same time I started my House tenure as part of the largest Democratic freshman class since Watergate, Gingrich founded the Conservative Opportunity Society. Ronald Reagan endorsed the COS ideas in his 1984 presidential re-election campaign, including their goals on crime, social issues, economic growth, and education, none of which he'd ever mentioned during his first term as president. Then, in 1989, Newt became the House Minority Whip and announced that he was going to "build a much more aggressive, activist party."

Although Newt always tried to sound high-minded, it was clear to me from the outset that he was really into the politics of personal destruction. I think he started the modern chapter of that down-low, tough technique. For example, he went after the Democratic speaker, Jim Wright, which led to Jim's resignation in 1989. Newt's charge was that Wright was enriching himself, because the speaker's supporters were buying copies of Wright's book in bulk. Of course, years later Newt took a four-million-dollar advance on his own book from his biggest supporter, Rupert Murdoch, who owned the company that published his book, and Newt never gave it a moment's thought. Selective ethics. But eventually, as we say in politics, what goes around comes around, and Newt resigned. Later the House Ethics Committee concluded that he had intentionally and recklessly provided false information on the tax-exempt status of a college course he was running for political purposes.

Wright, an eloquent speaker, had a few things to say about Gingrich, including the "mindless cannibalism" and "seeds of hate sown" by Gingrich in the House. Add to that this summation: "Newt Gingrich's tendency to outrageous verbal abuse and reckless accusations against anyone who stands in the way of his personal ambition has fatally flawed any chance to achieve a degree of harmonious reconciliation necessary for an effective Congress."

I myself would have put it this way: "Newt, you wrecked the House for me. Really. Forever."

Shortly after he disposed of Wright, in 1990, Gingrich distributed a notorious memo called "Language, a Key Mechanism of Control" that urged his followers in the Republican Party to "speak like Newt," using negative words like "radical…sick traitors" when attacking the Democrats and positive words like "opportunity…courage…and principled" when describing Republicans. He wasn't mentioning my name, but he was calling me, and my Democratic colleagues, traitors. Jim Wright had compared Newt to Joe McCarthy and he was right. Yes, Joe McCarthy reborn and with a high-pitched, irritating voice to boot.

It was appalling. I hated it. This was a kind of tough that was down so low, I couldn't believe it. Newt had a take-no-prisoners attitude and it made me recoil. He was steadily converting the House of Representatives from a functional legislative pillar of democracy to a polarized fistfight.

I never had a direct run-in with Gingrich. I stayed out of his way and I was much too small a fish in that large pond to become a target for him. But knowing my tendency to confront, I knew it was only a matter of time before I came up against him and his minions, and I wanted no part of it. When you join someone in the gutter, it's not pretty for anybody.

I had to leave the House.

In 1990, California's veteran Democratic Senator Alan Cranston decided not to run for re-election in 1992. Then, in a once-in-a-lifetime happenstance, the second California Senate seat came up for election in 1992 as Senator Pete Wilson left the Senate to become Governor Pete Wilson. Wilson had appointed John Seymour to the seat temporarily, but Seymour would have to face the voters in 1992 for the right to complete Wilson's term, which went until 1994. So the Cranston seat was a six-year seat; the Seymour seat was a two-year seat. The possibilities for my running began to look more interesting because I knew Dianne Feinstein was interested as well, and there was a path for us not to have to run against each other.

Newt was the ill wind at my back, unbeknownst to him, pushing me out of the House and toward a long-shot Senate race. But the next person to influence my decision in a very different way was my dear friend and former colleague, Senator Barbara Mikulski.

Barbara had welcomed me to the House and for a couple of years I served with her there, before she made history by becoming the very first Democratic woman elected in her own right to the United States Senate. Before Barbara, all of the handful of Democratic women had been appointed to the Senate, usually after their husbands died.

Barbara had been in that first aerobic class that led to our integrating women into the previously all-male House of Representatives gym back in 1983. We were buddies. So I phoned her to make an appointment and tell her about my considering a run to join her in the Senate.

"Come right over to my office, Babs," she said.

I already loved her for that "Babs," because that's what my dad always called me, and that's what Barbara calls me to this day. It never fails to make me smile, even if the news she has isn't good.

"Do it," she said, after I'd explained to her I was considering running. "Even as a freshman senator, you'll have more power than you do over there in the House."

"There could be a tough primary fight, Barbara," I explained. "I've heard about other Democrats who want to run and they're raising tons of money from the kind of political base that I don't have."

I told her that it appeared that I would have at least two very strong opponents in the Democratic primary: Lieutenant Governor Leo McCarthy from the Bay Area, and Congressman Mel Levine of Los Angeles. I also told her that our initial polling showed that in a three-way match-up, Leo was over 50 percent, Mel hovered around 15 percent. And me? I was an asterisk, meaning I didn't even reach 1 percent.

"That's okay. Go for it, Babs," she said with a smile. "Look what happened to me. I had two guys too. They thought I was so unimportant that they ignored me in the primary, attacked each other like mad, and I kind of walked through the middle unscathed. How's that for a strategy?"

"That might be my only strategy, given where I am in the polls." I laughed.

"I don't want to minimize my primary," Barbara went on. "It was rough and when I won, I had to face Ronald Reagan's assistant for public liaison, Linda Chavez, in the election for senator. We went earring to earring."

What she didn't say, being smart and discreet, is that Chavez had attacked Barbara for being a "San Francisco-style, George McGovern liberal" who hung out with an "anti-male…radical feminist" friend.

Talk about the perversion of the art of tough. Tough doesn't mean this kind of stuff. No, in this kind of situation, being tough means you don't respond to your opponent's garbage by slinging it back even harder.

So Barbara took the high road. She never responded to these nasty innuendos or tried to defend herself. Barbara campaigned strictly as a fighting populist from Baltimore, and it paid off. She beat Chavez with 61 percent of the vote. In addition, anyone who knows Barbara knows she's no anti-male radical feminist. They know instead how collegial she is with male colleagues, often calling them "Sir Galahads." When Barbara tutors new female senators, she always teaches us that coalition building is the name of the game.

You have to love her. She has a wonderful sense of humor and a great way with words. One of my Mikulski favorites is: "It's not about macroeconomics, it's about macaroni and cheese economics." Another: When former senator from Massachusetts Scott Brown tried to make a comeback race for the Senate in 2014 after he lost his seat to that fighter for the middle class Elizabeth Warren in 2012, he decided to run against the marvelous Senator Jeanne Shaheen from New Hampshire. Barbara said: "The constitution says that every state is entitled to two senators, not that every senator is entitled to two states." I've always felt that Jeanne would have won by an even bigger margin if she'd used that more.

Later, when Barbara worked until exhaustion on a huge 2015 appropriations bill, which had things in it she knew would cause fallout, Barbara said: "I made them swallow a porcupine and then I had to swallow one too."

To me, Barbara is what it should be all about, a senator who fights for the people, a woman who helps other women, and a negotiator who gets almost everything she wants. When she announced that she would not be running for re-election in 2016, joining me in that decision, I wrote a rhyme in her honor. This jingle has no particular melody, just words.

Ode to the Women's Dean
Before Mikulski won the day
A guy would have to pass away
And then his wife would take his place
Finally a woman in a senate space
But Barb she got there in her own right
First Democratic gal to win that fight
She won the race and joined the misters
But finally NOW she has nineteen sisters!

After my encouraging meeting with Barbara—who by the way is one of the few senators I can literally see eye to eye with, due to our both standing barely five feet tall—I told my husband, Stewart, about her words of wisdom.

"Good advice. And what's the worst thing that can happen?" he said. "If you lose, you'll come home to California," and we looked at each other with great big smiles. Actually, we laughed out loud.

We decided to take an overnight retreat at a small rustic hotel in Sonoma with my strong supporters and friends to discuss the Senate bid.

There were about ten of us, including Congressman George Miller and his wife, Cynthia, and my former boss John Burton, whose passion for politics and those without a voice was infectious. Rooting us on from New York were our childhood friends Gloria and Paul Littman, who have never left my side. I would have loved to have our two savvy grownup children there, but Doug, who had graduated from the University of San Francisco Law School, was being overworked at his first lawyer job at Hanson, Bridgett and Marcus, while Nicole, having graduated from the New York University film school, was similarly engrossed in working as a production assistant on her first films, the uplifting *Rudy* and the dark comedy *So I Married an Axe Murderer* with Mike Myers.

In any case, the talk turned quickly to whether or not I should run for the Senate. We discussed the opportunity. Should I run for the retiring Alan Cranston's six-year seat or go for the two-year seat being vacated by Republican Pete Wilson? This was an easy decision for our group. Running for a two-year seat would mean raising enough money to run in 1992 and again in 1994, an exhausting task. I had to go for the six-year Cranston seat.

We knew through the grapevine that Dianne Feinstein was willing to run for the old Wilson seat. I don't know all of her thinking, but I do believe her team thought the appointed incumbent, John Seymour, a former state senator and the chosen candidate to run for the rest of Wilson's term, wouldn't be that difficult to beat. They were right. Although Wilson beat Dianne for governor in 1990, she turned around in 1992 and replaced his hand-picked successor, beating him by a whopping sixteen-point margin.

We also talked about Gingrich, and his slimy creep of destructive influence on my beloved House. All agreed it would only get worse.

And, of course, I brought up Barbara Mikulski, my role model, who was being so supportive and encouraging and who laid out a path to victory in the primary.

We were very clear-eyed about the size of the mountain to climb. We knew what we faced in the primary and then in the general election against a Republican. California was far from a blue state at that time. There was agreement on the enormity of the challenge, but then George summed it up for the group this way:

"If this were a horse race, our horse would be the long shot. But I believe she can go the distance."

No more comments after that. There was a consensus.

I would continue to move toward that Senate run.

Okay. I was somewhat well known in the San Francisco Bay Area, active in local politics since the early 1970s and elected twice to the Marin County

Board of Supervisors and five times by my district to the House. But I was a complete unknown in southern California, where most of the people lived.

Luckily for me, I had developed a warm friendship with two couples from Los Angeles who dedicated themselves to my campaign: songwriters Alan and Marilyn Bergman and businessman Sim Farar and his educator wife, Debbie. So I jumped right in to start campaigning on issues like reproductive choice, equal rights, environmental protection, health care, sensible gun laws, reducing military spending, and digging out of the recession.

But campaigning for the Senate in a state as big as California, which is larger than many entire countries, has to qualify as one of life's most abnormal experiences. Campaigning felt like it had been designed to be a living hell, a way to make sure the winner will be tough enough never to crack under pressure in the job itself. This first senatorial campaign turned out to be a supreme test of my ability to sustain the art of tough.

And I almost failed the test.

I had to continue as an active member of the House of Representatives, flying back and forth to Washington, D.C., most weeks. Every time I was late or missed a critical vote, my opponents gloated publicly at the failure. Every time I couldn't stay in California and campaign, my staff and supporters would be upset with me. The red-eye overnight transcontinental flights ruled and I developed a case of permanent jet lag. Friends and family asked how I was coping with that.

"My body feels like it is in the middle of the country at all times," I'd say.

I had to raise money, and lots of it. Sometimes I felt like I'd choke if I had to ask one more person for a donation. But my chief fund-raisers, Suone Cotner and Nancy Kirschner, made it very (very) clear that I had to sit down in our Los Angeles campaign headquarters three or four times a week and start "dialing for dollars." I hated it! I could do it for other candidates and causes I believe in, but getting on my knees and begging for myself...Ugh! The scope of this was way different from any of my previous campaigns. Thousands of dollars a day had to be raised.

But I had to do it, so I came up with a slant on President George Herbert Walker Bush's "Thousand Points of Light," the name of a very successful charity that he had promoted in both his 1989 inaugural address and 1991 State of the Union address. I started a program we called "A Thousand Points of Loot," representing a thousand parties that each raise a thousand dollars to get us to our first one million dollars.

It worked.

We scheduled close to a thousand small events with the goal of raising a thousand dollars at each one.

"If you want to have one couple over for a gourmet dinner and charge them five hundred dollars each, that's fine," I said. "Or you can have a hundred people at a beach party for ten dollars a person. That's fine too."

This program was wildly successful. Since I couldn't go to all those parties, my friend Pat Mitchell, who eventually became the CEO of PBS, produced a wonderful video that was essentially an uplifting infomercial. It was a collage of my years in politics, on the stump, at meetings, with kids, seniors—all shot in California's beautiful environment. All with me, just looking at the camera and speaking ad lib. All with a convincing announcer whose mission was to tell everyone watching how high the stakes were.

And they *were* exceedingly high. The Cranston seat had been a progressive one for twenty-four years. That tradition could be won or lost in this Senate election. The video had drama, forward momentum, and a sense of urgency. We used it over and over again at these house parties, which were in locations far and wide. At each event we also sold our famous "Boxer shorts," which were, well... boxer shorts—underwear. But they were one of a kind, made of heavy black cotton with a pattern of the words "Boxer for Senate." They were actually so ugly they were almost cute. And they were a big hit. We actually sold thousands of them for about twelve dollars each.

Another favorite was my Boxer nightshirt—a long T-shirt with the words "Boxer for Senate: You'll sleep better at night."

Sometimes I would phone in to the larger events on the speakerphone and recruit the attendees to put on their own parties. We asked hosts to display all the different merchandise on a clothesline. Item by item, the goods were sold, and it all added up.

It was working and it was fun. It was different. No contribution was too small. I was flying beneath the radar and Leo and Mel didn't seem to notice I was gaining on them. The Mikulski strategy of "covert operations" was working.

Then in March of 1991 came the "march of the Congresswomen" to protest the treatment of Anita Hill; that too gave my campaign a boost.

But I had to deal with an often adversarial press that kept hammering on questions about "how can you possibly win?" despite my best efforts to stick to the big issues at every appearance and press conference. Then Leo and Mel, though still ahead of me in the polls, began bombarding me with expensive and inaccurate negative ads about the House Bank scandal.

Ah, the House Bank scandal. Here's the true story of this not-so-scandalous brouhaha in a nutshell. It was early 1992 and in those days the House Bank took five days to post members' paychecks. Unfortunately, we members of the House didn't know that. Therefore many members, including me, would write checks thinking the funds were in the account when they actually weren't. No checks ever bounced. Essentially the House Bank gave you overdraft protection, without charge and without any notice. What great friends they were!

When the "scandal" broke, every member was investigated by the FBI. Oh my God! There they were—two FBI officers, in a then-secret location (actually my tiny D.C. headquarters on Capitol Hill), who were both kind of embarrassed, asking me about my checking account. All I could think about during their questioning was how many con men and murderers were getting away without being investigated, as not one but two agents bore down on me.

Soon after they "interviewed" me, I received a letter of clearance. I was exonerated. But not in the minds of the press or my two opponents. The press demanded to see my checks. I remember telling them they had no right to see how much I spent at the cleaners or in the grocery store. They were incensed at my attempt to retain some personal privacy and got even more hostile. One of my opponents' campaign commercials showed me bouncing all over the screen.

Pretty good. Subtle.

The nastiness of the attacks increased exponentially. And the press was still convinced that I had no chance, no business being in the race at all. At the same time, Dianne Feinstein, who was running for the two-year seat, had been a popular and successful mayor for San Francisco after the horrible assassination of Mayor George Moscone and City Supervisor Harvey Milk by a crazed former city supervisor, Dan White.

"Boxer no, Feinstein yes," the press figured, but in addition the question was raised more than once: "How can two Jewish women be elected from California in one election?"

Dianne and I had totally different supporters in the Democratic Party and very different styles, but I'll never forget how she threw her enthusiastic support my way when I was struggling and my poll numbers were moving in the wrong direction due to the effective attacks aimed at me.

"Let's campaign together!" she said.

From then on whenever she spoke at rallies and campaign conferences, she'd say, "Two percent may be fine for the fat content of milk, but it is not fine that only two percent of the senators are women."

Everyone loved it.

And when I was asked how California would send two Jewish women to Washington, I answered, "It's just what the Senate needs, a double dose of chicken soup."

Privately, however, it made me mad that no one ever thought it was a problem to elect two Protestant men.

With the negativity I was facing every day—awful ads against me on TV and in newspapers, bumper stickers that read "Barbara Bouncer," with all the embarrassment that comes with people thinking your checkbook is a mess— coming home to California permanently was looking better and better to me. One day in March of 1992, I phoned Stew and told him I wanted out.

"I'm quitting," I said. "I don't like it. I don't want it. I'm dropping out of the race."

All this three months before the primary election.

I was surprised when he didn't respond with enthusiasm, since he'd been worried about the incredible stress and all the aggravation. I thought he'd encourage me to quit right away, but he didn't.

"Let's talk about it when you get home," he said.

Okay. I had just one more stop to make before I could see him—a Democratic Party dinner for women to watch an episode of *60 Minutes* that had been filmed weeks before. The show focused on two female senatorial candidates—Geraldine Ferraro and me. They had a great film clip I could hardly recognize of me campaigning months ago, when I was eager and full of enthusiastic energy.

All the women watching the show with me were ecstatic.

"Barbara," one said, "we're so proud of you for your courage!" Little did they know that my courage was suffering from a severe malady: the loss of tough.

"Thank you," I said and left, finally pulling into my driveway at about ten p.m. I was surprised to find my kids, Doug and Nicole, waiting for me. Their father must have called them over from San Francisco, where they both had apartments.

"Where's your dad?" I asked.

"I'm watching a ball game," Stew's voice came from upstairs. "Go ahead and start without me."

"Sit down, Mom," Nicole said.

Doug handed me a book by Dr. Seuss, one of our family's favorite authors, called *Oh, the Places You'll Go*. I must have read them *Green Eggs and Ham* and *One Fish, Two Fish, Red Fish, Blue Fish* thousands of times as they were growing up.

"Read it aloud, Mom," Doug said. "And think about what it's telling you."

I smiled. All those years I had read to them and now they wanted me to read again. So I began. It was about the ups and down of life—in poetry, of course. It was about the wonders of life—"great sights...high heights..." that are possible. Then, as I read aloud, the scene changed to the downside, the disappointments that happen to everyone.

Wherever you go
you'll top all the rest.
Except when you don't
Because sometimes you won't.

I paused at this.

"Mom," Nicole said, "this election isn't about you. There's no way you can drop out. What will that tell the world about women? That we can't take the heat? That we let the polls and the press push us out?"

I was deeply moved as she went on.

"You may not win, Mom," she said, "but you can't drop out. If people see you hanging in there despite all the stress and opposition, they'll relate to you. We all have to fight sometime in our lives. They need to see your grit. They need to know you're fighting for them and their kids. But, Mom, you have to start by fighting for yourself."

"It's only ninety days to the primary," Doug said. "Just give it all you have and see what happens. You can't quit."

Out of the mouths of babes. Doug at twenty-seven and Nicole at twenty-five were smart young adults who knew me so well . . . and I knew they were right. I had to continue, no matter how crazy it was. The great *60 Minutes* show, my devoted, hard-working staff, everything Nicole had said about women counting on me—I had to dig deeper. So what if none of the pundits thought I could win. When was the last time I listened to them anyway?

As I reflect back at this extraordinary moment in my life, when my children acted like adults while I acted like a child, I also know that it isn't easy being the child of someone who holds a national office. My kids tell me they take the heat when I take a controversial stand. They are often asked to explain my positions, which aren't always theirs, and worst of all, a child of a politician is often compared to either an idealized version of their parent by fans or a dumber than dumb version by detractors.

The baseball game ended and Stew came downstairs.

"The kids are keeping me in the race," I told him, certain he'd planned all this with them and knew what would happen.

"It's only three more months," was all he said, but from that night on, he took time off from his busy law practice and traveled with me more.

Meanwhile, the negative spots continued to run. One night we fell asleep with the TV on and I suddenly sat up straight in bed, frightened as a booming voice on one of my opponents' commercials was attacking me.

Stew woke up too, looking alarmed.

"It's okay," I told him. "But, God, we can't ever get away from this!"

We couldn't yet start our TV commercials because we didn't have the funds to run them until just ten days before the election. My opponents had way deeper pockets. After all, they were favored to beat me, so the smart money went to them in droves.

But the campaign had beautiful moments too. People sent in small contributions, saying, "We believe in you." Thousands of supporters bought my yellow-and-black "Boxer shorts" at house parties. Schoolchildren wanted to hold my hand. Seniors in nursing homes never wanted me to leave. People with AIDS urged me to keep fighting on for a cure. Small-business people wanted me to help them recover from the recession. Veterans needed me too, as they were a large percentage of the homeless population in our California cities.

They were all looking for me to do something. Me—a very average human person. Maybe that's what they saw in me and appreciated. I'm average. My mother never graduated from high school. I went to public school, from kindergarten through college. I worked to put my husband through law school. I had trouble finding childcare for my kids. I cleaned house, I shopped, I cooked. My checkbook was imperfect and so were my closets. If I could do it, they could do it.

Those were the thoughts and images in my mind every night when I crawled into bed with sore feet and a voice that croaked like a frog.

Lights out.

Then it's six-thirty a.m., and "oh, the places I had to go!"

*   *   *

Doug and Nicole were right. I won the primary election and became the official Democratic Party nominee, with a good lead at the polls when the campaign began.

I wanted the election to be a debate about the issues, but my Republican opponent, conservative TV talk show commentator Bruce Herschensohn, felt differently. It was attack after attack. I was a "selfish, out-of-touch politician."

Meanwhile, I had a great message on the heels of the Anita Hill–Clarence Thomas debacle. The Senate voted to confirm Clarence Thomas in October 1991 and it was fresh in everybody's mind; the look of the Senate was in their minds too. People saw with their own eyes that the Senate didn't look like a democratic forum. It looked like a men-only country club. They were truly shocked. It seemed that nobody ever noticed before that there were ninety-eight men and only two women in the Senate.

We began to see that this was working in our favor, driving key donors to our side—Sol Price, for example, the founder of the Price Club, which is now Costco. Sol was supporting Dianne for the other Senate seat from the start. He had given me the brush-off when I went to San Diego to meet with him a few months before the Anita Hill issue broke.

"Do you really think two broads can win both seats?" he told me in his famous crusty voice. "Two Jewish broads at that?" But after he saw the reality of the "Boys' Club" Senate, he called me back.

"Okay, Barbara. I'll support two broads. It's outrageous up there on Capitol Hill!"

Sol was one of a kind and when he passed away in 2009 at ninety years of age it left a real void. How many people of means call senators and ask them to raise their taxes so we can do more for kids? That was Sol. He was a super successful guy who always cared about everyone else.

"Let's shake up the Senate by electing Barbara Boxer" and "The Senate should be about running the country, not running a country club." That's what we said over and over to prospective voters and donors alike.

*   *   *

My biggest exposure on the national stage after winning the primary was attending and speaking at the Democratic National Convention in August of 1992. Four thousand two hundred and one delegates packed New York City's Madison Square Garden when Ann Richards, the governor of Texas, introduced the only female Democratic senator, my dear friend Barbara Mikulski, for a special speech and presentation.

Barbara wasted no time getting to the point.

"This is the *Year of the Woman*," she began.

"Bill Clinton has said it's time for a change after twelve years of Republicans in the White House, and we women agree because *we are the change.*

"This year we have many women candidates for the Senate who are going to be elected and join me in the Senate, bringing a new vitality...heart... spirit...a different way of doing business...a different perspective... Women in high office will never be a novelty again."

She concluded by referring to Anita Hill without mentioning her name.

"Never again, when a woman comes forward to tell her story to a committee of the United States Senate, will she be assaulted for telling the truth...Never again!"

Then she introduced Carol Moseley Braun, the African-American candidate for the Senate from Illinois (she won that November), who spoke beautifully.

Then me.

I was exultant. We candidates weren't at the speaker's rostrum but had decided to speak from the middle of our state delegations, surrounded by supporters, and with our own platforms and microphone so we could be easily seen and heard. All around me placards and banners were waving that said BARBARA BOXER and ELECT WOMEN NOW. My daughter, Nicole, was close at my side and son, Doug, right next to her. What a scene.

I spoke. And thinking back now, I realize that the issues I hammered on were exactly what I've been doing ever since.

"Back in 1968," I said, "I began to worry about the future of my children. So I decided to fight for my dream and haven't stopped since..." I told the crowd that I wanted to do everything I could to fulfill the dream that built America but was now in danger. I was worried about our country's economic security, about California's 10 percent rate of unemployment, about why our country ranked twenty-first in world education, about the cost of my children's college education and their grandmother's medical care. How could middle-class people like us make ends meet?

I was also upset that the U.S. was still spending 150 billion dollars a year to defend Europe and Japan. I felt those dollars should be brought home and invested in our children, in health research, in caring for our environment and creating hundreds of thousands of new jobs.

And I was very concerned about our government getting in the middle of our most personal decisions and planned to continue my fight to "protect a woman's right to choose!"

There was a huge round of appreciation for that. Since we only were supposed to take a few minutes each, I got to the heart of it.

"I will stand up against anyone who will take us back to the days of darkness, whether it's Jesse Helms, Strom Thurmond, or Orrin Hatch. I will fight anyone who will take us back to those dark days.

"We women candidates will crack open the doors of the United States Senate, open them wide, and *start running a country, not a country club!*

"Thank you."

Wow. What a moment.

Right after the convention Nicole, Doug, Stewart, and I went to a Bill Clinton fund-raiser in East Hampton, Long Island, about two hours east of New York City on the Atlantic Ocean. There were about three hundred people there, a big fund-raiser to say farewell and good luck to Bill and Al Gore right before they went out on their mega campaign bus trip. It was absolutely great.

Liz Robbins, who organized the event, introduced me to Paul Newman, and we began what turned out to be a long association. He'd visit my office to explain the amazing charitable work he was doing, for children in particular. We admired each other's efforts and shared a lot of views about the country's neglected priorities. I worked with his wife, Joanne Woodward, on nuclear arms reduction and the two of them were wonderful to me, even hosting a very successful fund-raiser for me at their New York home.

After the party Doug had to get back to law school and Nicole to her job. Stew and I went back to my campaign for the Senate in California. After the experience and inspiration of the Democratic convention, I felt I just had to win, and knew it was going to be an intense fight to the finish.

Meanwhile, the state Democratic Senatorial Campaign Committee assumed I could hold my lead and sent their limited dollars to support other Democrats in other races. In California's expensive media market even a thirty-second spot cost $25,000 back then, so I couldn't afford to go on television until right before the November election.

I had a fantastic campaign team headed by Rose Kapolczynski with my pollster Mark Mellman following every up and down tick and my TV maven Jim Margolis producing great spots. But they were all suffering mightily because we could only afford to air our good material at the last minute. So what most of the voters in the state knew about me for crucial weeks was what they heard night and day from the hostile, totally inaccurate stuff Herschensohn's campaign was putting out.

It began to work for my opponent. I started slipping, slowly but steadily. My margin over Herschensohn shrunk to 3 percent, and was now a statistical toss-up, too close to call. My supporters were becoming extremely nervous and begged me to "go on TV. Even a short spot would help." But we knew that was a recipe for failure. You couldn't spend early and then go dark right before you really needed to advertise.

We finally started running our ads about three weeks before the election. The bleeding stopped and pollster Mark told us we were edging up; then Democratic political operative Bob Mulholland interrupted a Herschensohn campaign appearance holding a large poster advertising a strip club.

"Should the voters of California elect someone who travels the strip joints of Hollywood?" he shouted before being hastily escorted out.

Herschensohn was forced to admit that he'd been to a strip club with his girlfriend and another couple "once." After that he tried to ignore the problem and keep attacking me, but despite all his efforts, he wound up spending the last few days of the campaign denying a series of related charges. Even his horrible mailer saying I was immoral because I was pro-choice wasn't working.

We never changed our strategy and stuck to the issues in all of our commercials. I refused to comment on "strip club gate" because to me, the election wasn't about that. It was about the stark differences between a progressive mainstream candidate and a far right extreme candidate.

On election night I won by five points. Dianne also won and was sworn in as a senator as soon as the election was certified in November. I had to wait until the expiration of Cranston's term in January of 1993. So I joined her two months later and she became California's senior senator and I the junior, titles we would hold forever. I never minded being junior senator to Dianne, especially when I became a senior citizen.

We'd done it. Dianne and I became the first ever all-woman Senate delegation in the history of the country. We were going to the Senate to represent the largest state in the union—joining Barbara Mikulski, who was re-elected that year, Patty Murray of Washington, and Carol Moseley Braun of Illinois. The year 1992 did indeed become the Year of the Woman. We wound up with only six women in the Senate, but we had tripled our numbers. And then after she won a special election in June of 1993, we were joined by Texas Republican Kay Bailey Hutchison.

What had become quite apparent is that in presidential election years, Democratic candidates on the ticket do much better than in non-presidential years. Democrats turn out in large numbers for presidential elections, but tend to stay home in off-year elections, a bad thing. Dianne and I were very fortunate to be running the same year as Bill Clinton and Al Gore. Bill and Al were the first Democrats to win the presidential delegates from California since Lyndon Johnson in 1964. They won because of their youth and energy, and they offered hope from a bruising recession. The enthusiasm they generated was so important for achieving a large voter turnout that helped all the rest of us on the ticket.

Clinton beat George H. W. Bush in California by fourteen points in 1992, and California has voted blue in every presidential election since then.

I won. I was the junior senator from California. Sometimes I couldn't believe it and had to pinch myself. Me? Barbara Boxer, born Levy, a first-generation American on my mother's side, the product of a public education from a Brooklyn kindergarten class to Brooklyn College, was now representing the huge Golden State of California in the United States Senate.

Election night was still a thrilling blur in my mind. But I did remember when my Republican opponent Bruce Herschensohn phoned our suite to concede at about two a.m., and how Marilyn Bergman, Gloria Littman, Shelley List, and I were starving and tried to order some food from room service that never arrived. We called and called, and room service swore they had sent it, but nope, nothing, no food ever came up to our suite.

Later we found out that the food had been delivered by mistake to the *other* new Democratic senator and big winner Dianne Feinstein's suite, where her people were pleasantly surprised by the unexpected present from unknown friends. I don't think they ever knew who ordered that food originally. But that was okay. Being hungry was good for us.

Chapter Six

Crashing the Old Boys' Club

On November 8, just five days after the election, I took the red-eye to Washington, D.C., for freshman orientation on Senate procedures and committee assignments.

Two months before I was sworn in, the venerable Senator Robert Byrd of West Virginia invited all the new women senators to sit down and listen to him talk about the history and traditions, the formal and informal protocol of being a member of the United States Senate.

We all showed up, the four of us—Dianne, Patty Murray, Carole Moseley Braun, and me. It was the very first time in history so many women came at once, pundits had called it the "Year of the Woman" and the very chivalrous Robert Byrd wanted to help "the ladies" in a special way.

He explained how to understand the archaic ways of the Senate, like what is a filibuster, what is a cloture vote, what the rules are, the way to behave when you are presiding in the Senate, all the things that no one in their right mind would ever understand. And by the way, even with this kind of orientation, it took me five or six years to truly understand it, but by then I was altered for life because it's so crazy.

Byrd was seventy-five years old at the time and certainly knew what he was talking about. Nobody came close to Robert in understanding the way the Senate worked and, in my view, nobody came close to Robert in knowing the history of democracies starting from the ancient Greeks. He constantly quoted from those Greek leaders, usually members of the Greek Senate explaining their democracy. He also wrote books about them.

He extolled and demonstrated often the simple elegance and beauty of our Constitution. Robert always had a copy of that revered document in his jacket pocket and was known for hauling it out in the middle of a speech, waving that little pocket copy around when he thought its lofty ideals were needed to win a debate.

He was tough, tough, tough. Once, on the Senate floor, he took on Republican Senator Rick Santorum, chastising Santorum's recent remarks. Santorum had railed against President Clinton using words like "lies." He also kept referring to the president as "that guy" and held up a poster that read "Where's Bill?" This was a clear assault on the dignity of the United States Senate and Byrd was truly angry.

Byrd said Santorum was "juvenile, reckless and vengeful." In his summation, which rated a story in the *New York Times*, Byrd said: "There have been giants in the Senate and I have seen some of them. Little did I know…I would live to see pygmies stride like Colossuses while marveling, like Aesop's fly sitting on the axle of a chariot, 'My, what a dust I do raise.'"

Santorum knew he was not one of the giants Byrd had been talking about.

But what we also knew was that Robert Byrd was one of the original Dixiecrats, the breakaway faction of the Democratic Party in 1948. The Dixiecrats were adamantly opposed to Harry Truman's civil rights policies and wanted to preserve racial segregation, discrimination, and protect the "southern way of life." They had nominated Strom Thurmond for president and actually won five southern states. Not only that, in his twenties and thirties, Robert Byrd had been part of the Ku Klux Klan. We knew he had filibustered and voted against the Civil Rights Act of 1964.

But Robert Byrd had apologized "a thousand times" for joining the Klan and said he regretted filibustering the Civil Rights Act. Now he was anxious to be part of a new trend in 1992: mentoring a group of women senators that included an African American. I wanted to learn whatever I could from Robert Byrd, and I did. We all did.

One thing I've never forgotten. Byrd told us how important it was for every new senator to take a turn presiding over the Senate. Someone has to be in the seat up on the dais at all times, even though there may be nothing happening, when no one is speaking, and the members are all coming and going somewhere else.

According to the U.S. Constitution, the vice president is the president of the Senate, but the Senate must choose another president *pro tempore.* This is usually the most senior senator in the majority party at the time, but in reality, that senator is too important and busy to be there, so the job is rotated among junior senators to give them experience in parliamentary procedure.

Got it? But what Byrd really wanted to tell us was this:

"Never read a newspaper."

Yes, that's what he told us, and with a very straight face.

"Don't ever read a newspaper when you are sitting up there, because the TV camera is on you. Even if no one is speaking and nothing is happening, sit there without reading or working in any way. And the freshman with the best and longest number of days presiding," he said, "gets the Golden Gavel at the end of the session."

I never won the Golden Gavel, although I had my share of "chair duty." But I just couldn't win the gavel despite my competitive nature. I had to do other things. When you have a state the size of California, you have so many people visiting you, so many people calling you. More than most. I had said to the people of California: "Stay in touch," and they did. I got more mail than anyone else in the Senate. Still do, but most of it's e-mail these days.

The second orientation was more relaxed but quite serious. Barbara Mikulski held a special get-together for the women freshman Democrats only. Barbara gave us good advice, as usual.

She knew that each of us had our own agenda, the big issues we were concerned about and the Senate committees we wanted to get on because they focused on legislation to affect those issues.

"This is how you get on committees," she told us. "You have to go to George Mitchell." He was then the Senate majority leader. "You have to fight, to lobby for the committees that you want, make the case and convince people."

I knew what I wanted. My first choice was the Environment and Public Works Committee, since I'd always been a champion for the environment and for building our infrastructure, which is so important for a great nation and has the added dividend of creating good-paying jobs. My second choice was the Budget Committee, since I served on the House Budget Committee for years and felt that a nation's budget was a nation's priorities. Joe Biden helped me with a persuasive strategy with which to lobby Leader Mitchell. Joe said, "Make the case that you were a known environmentalist in the House and that you truly enjoyed the Budget Committee over there as well." He told me to give the leader some "slack" on the third pick, since it was really a hard task to balance all the requests and "George would be grateful for that."

I checked this strategy with Senator Mikulski and she gave me her approving look. I wasn't that excited about being put on the Banking Committee as my third committee, but they had openings that had to be filled, so I was a good sport about it and took one for the team. That's always appreciated in the Senate.

These committee assignments were made in the first month of my term, so by the end of January 1993 I was set and ready to go. My first choice was certainly the right choice. There weren't that many strong environmental leaders in the Senate except for a few, like the wonderful Republicans John Chafee and Jim Jeffords, and Democrats George Mitchell and Frank Lautenberg. Unlike other issues that had many more leaders, there was a clear opening for me on an issue I always carried in my heart.

To flash forward for a moment, I was right to be leery of the Banking Committee. There was such a direct link between our work and their daily profits that bankers were always banging on my door. I remember once when the bankers were really mad at me because I felt they were overcharging for the use of ATMs. I finally agreed to see them, and all those blue suits crowded into the conference room of my personal office looking really mad. I had to lighten it up.

"You know," I said, "I've never used an ATM." Which was true. "I use an SNB."

"What's that?" one of them asked.

"Stewart N. Boxer. I just yell, 'Hey, Stew, can you cash a check?'"

Some laughed and the others were humorless.

Later, in 1998, I was to trade the Banking Committee for the Foreign Relations Committee, which is an extraordinary committee in this crazy world we live in; I also traded the Budget Committee in 2001 for the Commerce Committee, a committee with very broad jurisdiction, from the FAA to the FCC to consumer protection. In 2007 I became chairman of the Ethics Committee. That has been a very important assignment that carries with it an enormous amount of trust. It says in the Constitution that Congress must police itself, and that's the critical responsibility of the Ethics Committee.

Barbara was great at our meeting. She always told it like it was, no frills or soft-pedaling. The press was staked out near her office, and when we all left, they asked Senator Mikulski how it went. She told them that this was one of her happiest days. "Some women look out the window waiting for Prince Charming but me? I'm looking for more women senators. And it has finally happened."

On January 4, 1993, I walked down the aisle of the beautiful Senate chamber situated at the center of the north wing of the United States Capitol building where the swearing-in took place. Escorted by Dianne Feinstein, the senior senator from California, I looked around in awe and wished my mom were still alive. She had passed away just before I won my Senate race. I pictured my mom and dad, sitting up there watching me from the visitor's gallery that overlooked the hundred Senate chairs on the tiered semicircular platform facing the raised rostrum of the presiding officer.

After the orientation from Barbara and the hustling to get on committees, I had a clear vision of what I'd do once I'd arrived in Washington, D.C., as one of the two senators from California. But you never know what's coming your way in life, and double that when you are in politics, where anything can happen and usually does. Surprising and uncontrollable events can take you off your neatly put-together legislative plan.

Two such events hit me right in the solar plexus right after I began my first term. The first was the Bob Packwood case.

I had followed Bob Packwood's career since he'd been elected to the Senate from the state of Oregon in 1968. He was only thirty-six years old then, the youngest man in the Senate at that time. Yes, he was a Republican, but he had a good voting record on a lot of issues I cared about. I had agreed with his support for restrictions on gun owners, liberal civil rights legislation, his pro-choice stance, and his vote against Clarence Thomas. He'd crossed party lines and was the first Republican to support Richard Nixon's impeachment. He was a conservationist who advocated solar energy, returnable bottles, and bike paths, and he seemed like a very progressive guy.

So I was shocked to read right after the election in 1992 a long front-page story in the *Washington Post* that documented allegations against Packwood by ten women, mostly former staff members and lobbyists, of unwanted sexual advances. I lost my breath. I couldn't believe it. But the reporter did an amazing job of citing her sources and providing direct quotes, not hearsay or rumors.

When I was sworn into the Senate that January, I assumed that the Ethics Committee would investigate these allegations and do the right thing. The committee had always been three Republicans and three Democrats, regardless of who was in the majority, so there couldn't be any partisan politics. And one of the Democrats happened to be Barbara Mikulski, so I had no doubt that they'd take the *Washington Post* story very seriously. Packwood himself had called for an investigation to clear himself.

But as time passed, he changed his mind and so did Republicans on the Ethics Committee. Nothing happened. And in the 1994 elections, Republicans won control of the Senate. Of course, that made it much harder to get the Clinton agenda passed. There would be no more sensible gun laws, no more talk of healthcare reform, and on the Packwood front, nothing continued to happen. It seemed to me unbelievable that months and months had gone by and still no public hearings. How could this happen, I asked everyone I knew on the committee. All I got were stares. But one stare gave me an answer.

Wait a minute. I learned later that the committee had deadlocked three to three, in a rare partisan vote, which allowed the Republicans to squash the public hearings. At that time the vote was unknown to members, since these votes are confidential.

I went to see Barbara Mikulski. Barbara was the vice chairman of the Ethics Committee, and Mitch McConnell the chairman, because Republicans were now in control of the chamber. I knew the committee had portions of Packwood's scandalous diaries and was alarmed that there wasn't any movement on calling for public hearings, even though more and more women were coming forward with complaints. When I confronted her, Barbara just looked at me when I asked her if I should keep up the push for public hearings. She never said a word because she was precluded from doing so by the Ethics Committee rules.

"Unless you say I'm wrong, I am going to force a vote on having a public hearing," I said.

Again, Barbara said nothing. But I knew her so well from our days in the House, and our friendship ever since, that I had my answer from the stoic look on her face. So I made my decision to become the prime mover in the Senate for an amendment that would force the Ethics Committee to have hearings. I knew that if I brought up a standalone bill to force open hearings, McConnell would never let it get to the floor or come up for a vote. That's the way it works. I made a sneak attack by adding my bill as an amendment to another bill. That's also the way it works, then and now.

The Republican response was fast and furious. McConnell had been cooperative when in the minority but now he definitely changed. He didn't want to lose that Oregon Senate seat and had no interest in going after the truth about Packwood. He decided to be Mr. Tough Guy with me, since I was only a very junior member of the Senate and, he probably thought, easily intimidated. So he told Barbara to deliver a message to me: If I didn't step back, if I kept on pushing for a vote on public hearings, he was going after Ted Kennedy for Chappaquiddick and Tom Daschle's wife for being a lobbyist, an unprecedented threat, and to me, quite unethical.

I was truly stunned, so during a vote on the Senate floor I confronted him. Standing close, and stretching to my greatest height, I looked up at him.

"Are you threatening me?" I asked.

"No. I am promising you," he said.

Wow. Talk about the perversion of power. Incredible. But those were fighting words. You don't get anywhere talking to someone who got to the Senate in large part because she was a woman fighting for equality, and you don't threaten a senator who was born in Brooklyn. I grew up very aware of my surroundings at all times, and I smelled something vile: a cover-up. Threats. Intimidation. Worst of all, I couldn't talk to my mentor, Barbara Mikulski, and get her advice. As a member of the Ethics Committee, she was gagged.

I was on my own. No matter that Mitch was threatening my colleagues so that we would all retreat and Packwood would only get a slap on the wrist for his disgusting behavior. I doubled down and kept forcing a vote on the amendment to hold open, public hearings on Packwood. I'd been elected on the promise to fight for women's rights and I was going to fulfill that promise.

Then I was rudely reminded that this was indeed the old boys' club Senate. The new Republican Senate majority leader, Bob Dole, came after me with full force, telling the press I was the most partisan senator he had ever worked with. I said to myself, *Who is the partisan?* A senator who wants an airing of the facts and the truth? Or someone who would stop justice because he didn't want to lose a senator from his own party—a senator who was engaging in behavior that had hurt at least twenty women and sullied the reputation of the Senate? At the same time, McConnell said my efforts to hold public hearings were a "frolic and a detour" and he was threatening my colleagues with ethics investigations. And all this after the Anita Hill circus.

I stayed the course and Republicans were forced to filibuster my amendment, killing it eventually on a vote of 52 to 48. We needed sixty. I'd lost the battle, but kept fighting the war.

The *New York Times* wrote an editorial on August 4, 1995.

"Rather than exposing Mr. Packwood's shame, the Senate decided to wrap itself in it. There have been few seedier legislative performances in recent years...Senator Boxer's reasonable resolution would have required public hearing in any case where the Ethics Committee finds 'substantial credible evidence' of senatorial wrongdoing...She introduced it after the committee's three Republican members, in keeping with Mr. Dole's wish, said no to public hearings, thereby blocking an open inquiry into the long string of sexual-harassment allegations against Mr. Packwood. All Ms. Boxer was trying to do was require the committee to follow its own longstanding procedures of holding open hearings in major ethics cases."

The *Times* rightly pointed out that my resolution won the support of three Republicans in the Senate: Specter, Cohen, and Snowe. I was grateful to them. But we still lost.

The *Times* also quoted another direct stab from Bob Dole at me.

"Why don't we turn [the policing of the Senate] over to the Senator from California?" Mr. Dole sneered.

The *Times* concluded that having me policing it would be better than leaving it in the hands of Dole and McConnell.

That made my day.

The turning point came when all of Packwood's diaries came to light. Ironically, he had deliberately made portions of his diaries available to the Ethics Committee in 1993 in an attempt to clear himself. According to William Raspberry of the *Washington Post*, Packwood wanted to use some of the pages to "show that there was contemporaneous exculpatory account [his] of events that constitute a part of the charges against him," which means, in plain language, that Packwood declared in his diaries that the sexual "encounters" were consensual. What a joke that turned out to be.

When the Ethics Committee asked for more of his diaries, Packwood claimed that the Fifth Amendment protected him against self-incrimination, so his diaries couldn't be subpoenaed by the Ethics Committee. That specious argument was rejected, so he turned over five thousand pages. Five thousand pages! And this was more than twenty years after the notorious White House tapes had blown open the Watergate hearings and led to Richard Nixon's impeachment—which Packwood had voted for! I guess he never thought he'd be the one in the scandal spotlight the next time around.

But it gets worse. On September 8, 1995, Packwood wrote: "Channel 2 said five more women are willing to come forward to say that they have been sexually abused by me or sexually harassed or something, including one in the early nineties. I've got my diary and I'd like to have Cathy change and retype my diary so it shows something different, but turns out the typeface is different and somebody could tell it."

My take: Isn't that called tampering with evidence?

Packwood then admitted to his lawyers that "there is some damaging stuff" that he had altered in his diary. When that was discovered, 3,200 missing pages were also subpoenaed. Now we're up to 8,200 pages of salacious and arrogant scribblings. By this time members of the committee, such as Senator Richard Bryan, had to admit that these revelations "raised questions about a possible violation of one or more laws, including criminal laws."

Here's one particularly damaging, widely reprinted example:

Grabbed Tracy Gorman behind the Xerox machine today and she got a little pissed. What's the big deal? I was smiling while I did it. She made this big stink about it and it took me about two hours and a couple of thousand dollars to calm her down. I have one question—if she didn't want me to feather her nest, why did she come into the Xerox room? Sure, she used that old excuse that she had to make copies of the Brady Bill, but if you believe that, I have a room full of radical feminists you can boff. She knew I was copying stuff in there. I had my jacket off and my sleeves rolled up, revealing the well-defined musculature of my sinewy arms which are always bulging with desire. I know what she wanted. This didn't require a lot of thought.

Here's another example that the *New York Times* reprinted from an entry Packwood made on November 3, 1989:

"Went down and took a hot tub ... just blew my hair ... I didn't use any gel on it at all." He goes on about his hair. What is it about politicians and hair? This guy had to be kidding. He barely had any hair, as far as I can remember. But the fact that he saw himself as some kind of Romeo is a look into his mindset. What woman could resist that hair? I read another excerpt in which he quoted a woman telling him that his hair was essentially irresistible.

One woman's deposition talked about her working at the Red Lion Inn in Oregon. She recalls Packwood following her into a closet in the early eighties after he had asked her to retrieve his luggage. There, he foisted himself on her. She expressed her deep embarrassment. Imagine a United States senator and a hotel worker.

Really. A fair fight, right?

In his quotes I see a sick human being who, while voting with feminists, secretly detested us. I guess he thought he would be "rewarded" for his votes.

At the end of the day it was the revelations from the diaries, pressure from his victims, and the presence of women members in the Senate that forced McConnell and Dole to back down. Packwood became a huge liability. Eventually the public would demand public hearings and the spectacle of so many women telling their Packwood stories was too much for his defenders to bear.

Packwood resigned on September 8, 1995, and went on to have a lucrative career as a consultant and political lobbyist. His successor, who still serves in the Senate, is the progressive member Ron Wyden. Once I saw Packwood in a restaurant in southern California in the early 2000s. I did a not-so-tough thing: I ducked behind Stew so Packwood wouldn't see me.

The Packwood case was so intense that it seared my soul—so much so that Mitch McConnell and I barely spoke a word for twenty years—twenty years! Then suddenly last year we became close collaborators and allies, in an effort to save the Highway Trust Fund and the transportation programs it supports.

Our sudden collegial relationship stunned all our colleagues, but most of all, it stunned the two of us.

As we developed a winning strategy for our bill, we also developed trust. The stereotypes we had of each other as hard-nosed ideologues melted away. We actually celebrated our teamwork at a Capitol Hill restaurant with our top staff. We exchanged gifts. He gave me a Louisville Slugger bat, and I gave him a tie with bridges all over it. He wrote me a lovely note and said it was "fun working with you." Now "fun" is not an adjective I have ever heard anyone use when they talk about Mitch McConnell, but we actually did have fun, because the whole thing was so unexpected. The best part was, we saved America's transportation program.

I can honestly say it was the strangest turn of events and, oddly, it is also a side of being tough. You have to forgive and be willing to take a risk. He did it too, and the risk for him was evident on the faces of his Republican colleagues. I'm sure they were thinking, "What has happened to our boy Mitch?"

On January 17, 1994, at the same time as the Packwood case was unraveling, my beloved home state of California suffered one of the worst natural disasters in recorded history: the Northridge earthquake.

We'd experienced earthquakes before, most notably the Loma Prieta in 1989, in which sixty-three people were killed and 3,757 injured. The epicenter of that quake was in Santa Cruz, but the damage extended far north to San Francisco and Oakland, where the double-decker Nimitz Freeway had collapsed, crushing forty-one people to death. I was in the House of Representatives then and couldn't believe how slowly FEMA, the Federal Emergency Management Agency, had responded. I was also dismayed by how long it took to get anything through the maze of city, county, and state bureaucracies, which all had different timetables and requirements. In fact, it wasn't until September of 2013 that the new eastern span of the Bay Bridge was officially opened.

But we'd learned a lot from the Loma Prieta about what not to do and how not to do it when an earthquake strikes. And now, as United States senators, both Dianne Feinstein and I had to shift our attention away from Washington, D.C., to focus quickly on the emergency as well as on long-term measures to recover from this devastating calamity.

The epicenter of the Northridge quake was in Reseda, just north of Los Angeles. The quake went on for ten to twenty seconds, and was felt as far away as Las Vegas, 220 miles to the east. Aftershocks went on for eleven hours. Fifty-seven people were killed and more than five thousand injured. At the time the Northridge earthquake broke all records in America in terms of cost.

The quake definitely caught us off guard. We had to drop a lot of other things and focus on getting FEMA to work out there. Luckily, President Clinton had picked James Lee Witt to be the new FEMA director when he took office in 1992 and they had really turned that agency around. Clinton and Witt also remembered the 1989 Loma Prieta earthquake and wanted to be sure the timing, quality, and pace of FEMA's response was much better this time.

I got particularly close with James Lee because he was almost a father figure to the people there. I went with him and saw him put out his arms to the victims in need, and Bill Clinton did the same. They were very warm and compassionate.

I made clear what we needed: a quick roadmap for affected residents to DACs—disaster area centers, where they could get the help they needed in one place. Help with their private insurance, temporary housing, unemployment insurance, access to advocates who would assist them if they were eligible for a number of federal rebuilding programs.

We had to change the "Anybody but California" attitude that had pervaded the Senate before we got there. The Golden State's image was that of an invincible, recession-proof state with the lion's share of defense dollars. But that was no longer true. That was changing and California needed attention. Yes, we were known for glamour, sunshine, Hollywood, and innovation. But our population was large and we had our share of every problem in the country, including unemployment and recession. Then came the earthquake and we had to make our case, convincing our colleagues that the billions needed from FEMA were absolutely justified and necessary, including eleven billion

Official Wingate High School Graduation photo of me— Barbara Levy—in 1958.

Me helping Geraldine Ferraro stay dry in San Francisco after she was named vice presidential candidate in 1985.

The "Red, White, and Blues" singing farewell to Speaker Tip O'Neill at the Capitol in 1986. Left to right: Congresswoman Marcy Kaptur, Congresswoman Mary Rose Oakar, me, and Speaker O'Neill with his wife, Millie (seated).

Here's the famous photo of women members of the House walking up the Senate steps in 1991 to demand Anita Hill be allowed to testify at the hearings to confirm Clarence Thomas to the Supreme Court. That's me at the top followed by Congresswomen Jolene Unsold, Pat Schroeder, Patsy Mink, Eleanor Holmes Norton, and Nita Lowey.

Me watching my opponent Bruce Herschensohn on the screen—on my victorious night, election night 1992.

With Senator Kennedy, one of my mentors, after our bill The FACE Act became law in 1994.

With Dianne Feinstein and the future speaker of the house, Nancy Pelosi, testifying at the House Resources Subcommittee on National Parks, Forests, and Lands in favor of turning the Presidio Army Base into a park in 1995.

With Vice President Gore in 1997 after a meeting about keeping my Dolphin Safe Tuna Label law safe from free-trade challenges.

Harry Reid wearing my Boxer hat during a trip to Iraq during war years.

During the 2010 battle for my fourth term, I had a radio debate with Carly Fiorina, the meanest and least-qualified candidate I ever ran against. It was very satisfying to beat her by 10 points.

With Lloyd Bridges in November 1989, supporting the The Ocean Protection Act, a campaign to keep California's coast safe from off-shore oil drilling.

Me and Elizabeth Taylor, who was a great fighter for AIDS funding in the early years of the disease, in 1990.

Receiving an award with Senator Dianne Feinstein, Gloria Steinem, and Faye Wattleton, then president of Planned Parenthood in the 1990s.

With Carole King in 1998, a great environmentalist who has used her talents to help so many of us.

Stewart and me with Barbra Streisand and James Brolin in 1998. Barbra cares deeply about electing those with a heart.

Jogging with President Clinton in 1994.

With Stewart and President Clinton in 1994 on the White House grounds.

Hillary campaigning for me in my first re-election to the Senate in 1998.

Celebrating our 50th anniversary. Left to right: Zain, Amy, Reyna, Doug, me, Stewart, Nicole, Zach, Sawyer, and Kevin.

for Los Angeles. I believe those rebuilding dollars saved our state's economy at the time, because the infusion of funds acted as a stimulus to the economy, bringing jobs and hope, and helped California out of the recession.

There were unexpected developments on the personal front too.

My daughter, Nicole, had met Hillary Clinton's youngest brother, Tony Rodham, at Paul Newman's big party in East Hampton right after the Democratic convention. After I'd won the election and was setting up my new Senate office in Washington, Tony called me to ask for Nicole's phone number. He wanted to take her to some of the inaugural balls.

I checked with her, of course, and she said okay. Next thing I knew, my daughter was dating the first lady's brother.

Meanwhile, I was assembling a staff and walking through Alan Cranston's big old office. I wanted to change the inner room where my office was to reflect my needs, so I started moving things around. It was so dark and gloomy with all this black leather. I got rid of all the furniture except for the big desk and turned the office into a very bright, peach-colored space. I put a big photo of my hero Jackie Robinson on the wall. Then I went to the Senate historian, who gave me photographs of every senator from California who had served before me, and I hung them up, all fifteen of them. I also found a great photograph of the Golden Gate Bridge and also some iconic Ansel Adams photographs of California's Yosemite National Park.

What a difference it made. When Cranston came to visit me to talk about nuclear arms control a few months later, I waited kind of nervously for his reaction to how I'd changed his office from a dark man cave to a bright living room style.

But he didn't say a word about the redecoration. Finally, just as he was leaving, I broke down and asked him.

"Alan, you didn't say anything about the office."

"Yeah, sure. Why did you move my desk out from the wall?"

That's all he noticed.

*   *   *

A few months later, on May 28, 1994, after a whirlwind romance, Nicole and Tony were married in the Rose Garden, the first wedding in the White House since Tricia Nixon married Edward Cox in 1971.

We kept it very private, with about 150 people invited, and as weddings go, it was easy to plan. How could you make the Rose Garden and the State Room any more beautiful? Nicole and Tony were not into the small details, just weighing in on the big decisions, particularly who sat where and what band to hire. First Lady Hillary Clinton gave us the best people to work with, and the wedding was truly magical. The Clintons were most gracious, standing next to Stewart and me on the receiving line, shaking hands with all the guests. We began outdoors in the early evening with both a Methodist minister and a Jewish friend of ours blessing the couple. There was a traditional Jewish *chuppa*, or arbor over the bride and groom, prayers were said in both English and Hebrew, and at the end Tony stomped on and broke a glass, another custom that we consider good luck. Then everyone said *mazultov*— congratulations—and we all went inside the White house for an evening of dancing and singing around the piano. Alan Bergman sang. President Clinton was around the piano singing along too.

It was a glorious time for everyone there.

Nicole and Tony's marriage brought the Clintons and the Boxers together in unusual ways. We were part of the family now, so Stewart and I joined Bill, Hillary, Nicole, and Tony at Camp David on several weekends.

I got to see firsthand why Camp David is such an important place for presidents and their families. In an hour drive, and just minutes by helicopter, our presidents have a true getaway from the White House, which, with all its grandeur, is still confining. There is ample outdoor space to walk, jog, ride horses, and think. It was built in 1935 as part of the WPA project during the Depression. Franklin Roosevelt named it Shangri-La, and in the 1950s President Eisenhower named it Camp David after his grandson.

I came to know Hillary Rodham Clinton as a powerful intellectual force with street smarts and a sense of humor that came at unexpected moments.

I also had a chance to discuss a range of issues directly with the president on long walks in the brisk air, and in front of crackling fireplaces with everyone gathered around. In one particularly memorable conversation he said, "Barbara, the economy is changing. No one is going to work for the same company in one career all of their lives then get a gold watch. Our working people are going to need constant learning, constant training. To be really successful, we need more and more formal education and our college graduates will strive to become mini-entrepreneurs with a distinctive skill set to offer in the marketplace."

I'm good at taking care of problems in the present, laying out a clear path to solve them, staying focused, but I have never been a futurist. When the cell phone came out, for instance, I said, "This is going to be the biggest flop." Good thing I wasn't the president of Apple! And Bill was right. When I look at my own kids now, they've morphed in several different directions.

Nicole and Tony had a son, Zachary, in June of 1995, our first grandchild. Nicole went into labor a month early. I was in Washington at work and Stew was at his law office, so we both rushed to Florida. Stew arrived in time for the birth, but Zach didn't wait for me. When I hurried into the hospital room, everyone was standing around this brand new baby crying tears of joy. I added mine, as I looked down at the most beautiful, smartest baby ever.

Our son, Doug, started dating Amy Lynch during this period as well. He asked if he could bring Amy to Camp David occasionally and Bill and Hillary said of course, since they were developing a serious relationship. On Thanksgiving Day 1999, Doug actually proposed to Amy at Camp David, creating more fond memories at that special place.

Sadly, Nicole and Tony divorced after about seven years of marriage. It was awful. They had this beautiful child, and the split was very painful for both of them—really, really, really hard. There were treasured times at the White House when Zach celebrated his early birthdays on the historic lawn with all his classmates. But the split was difficult for two strong families, united together and then blown apart, without a history of divorce on either side.

I just tried to completely seal it off from my job. And I believe Bill and

Hillary did the same thing. None of us let it get in the way of our public service, and our relationship became all work after the divorce, though Hillary and I would talk about what was best for Zach, as any aunt and grandmother would. Even so, it was awkward for my relationship with a president and first lady whose work I so admired, and whose friendship I cherish. We all experienced firsthand how utterly painful it is to watch a dream die. But this is what life brings, sadly, to many families.

As time went on, everyone from both sides of the family came to Zachary's games, from his soccer scrimmages as a child to his high school football contests. Hillary's mother, who was a loving grandmother to Zach, came; everyone came; even Bill when he was president, and Hillary when she was secretary of state. That's some pretty powerful cheerleading! After Tony and Nicole started new families and had more children, they all came to the games too. Everyone realized what matters most.

Chapter Seven

The Insanity of Impeachment, a Stolen Election, the Horrors of 9/11 and Iraq

————— • —————

My first term as a senator ended in January of 1999 and I never had a doubt I would seek re-election. I was getting to know the rules, the pace, and how to get things done. The economy was strong, the budget was in balance, and my prospects looked good. But on January 17, 1998, the news broke of a scandal involving the president and Monica Lewinsky. Everything got extremely complicated for me, as the nightmare effort by the Republicans to use this scandal to impeach President Bill Clinton began.

At first, my Democratic colleagues and I were skeptical that they would go through with impeachment. How could they make the case that a "high crime" had taken place, as required in the Constitution as a condition for impeachment?

I knew that the efforts to impeach Bill Clinton would present a real challenge to my re-election and might even up-end my plan to campaign against my Republican opponent, Matt Fong, the treasurer of California, on important issues like the economy, the environment, women's rights, AIDS, and education. With Bill Clinton as president, we had created millions of jobs, and we were doing great in California. So my slogan was, "Let's keep California moving in the right direction!"

But I couldn't keep my issues in play. All anyone wanted to hear about was the impeachment, a lethal gift to Republicans who saw an opportunity to paint me as a hypocrite and a partisan. My campaign was sidetracked by Impeachment Fever.

The issue tainted everything else, even the most innocuous events. I was invited by Alice Waters, the owner of Chez Panisse, who'd launched the healthy food movement in California cuisine, to visit a public school in Berkeley. She had a project that taught kids how to grow vegetables, harvest, and prepare food in a way that was good for them and also sustained their environment. The students made a lovely lunch that we all enjoyed together, and I had a wonderful time. I always supported good nutrition for our children and Alice had taken it to another level, using healthy food as a centerpiece of learning and socialization. I appreciated being there, since the event showed my ongoing concern for healthy, smart children. And let's face it: it was an opportunity to change the subject, to get away for a minute from answering questions about Monica Lewinsky.

Or so I thought. As the event concluded and I was speaking with some of the children, however, Hank Plante, a really sharp news reporter for KPIX-TV in San Francisco, came over and asked if he could do an interview.

"Sure," I said, thinking he was going to ask me about the students' healthy food project; since the children were gathered around me, I figured it would be a very nice visual for the camera crew.

"What do you think about the stain on the blue dress?" he asked.

I almost fainted.

"Hank," I said, "can we not talk about this right now with all the children around us? I'll say good-bye and meet you up on the street corner."

So I thanked Alice and the terrific bunch of kids and went up the street. *How could I answer his question about semen on the blue dress,* was all I could think about. It was awful. Hank kept hammering away on the blue dress, the scandals, the impeachment. That was his job, but I wanted to slug him.

"Hank," I said, "the president made a big mistake. His behavior was terribly wrong. But that's not what the founders meant when they set the constitutional standard for impeachment, which is high crimes and misdemeanors," I insisted. "I'm completely opposed to the efforts to impeach a president who hasn't committed high crimes and misdemeanors."

This kept happening. The Republicans saw this as a chance to get rid of not only Bill Clinton but me, too. They constantly pointed out that I was a leader on women's rights, had led the fight against Packwood, and yet was "silent" on the sins of a president who was part of my family. The media pundits bought into it and proclaimed that Matt Fong was my greatest nightmare, not only because of the impeachment but because he was a minority, and I was known for pulling so many votes from the minority communities who were my staunch supporters in the 1992 election. How could I attack him without alienating all minorities: Asian Americans, African Americans, Mexican Americans?

I remember one television debate, when Matt Fong kept saying, "Where do you stand on impeachment? Your silence is deafening."

Me, silent? Not really. They just didn't like my answer, which I said consistently.

"Listen, Matt. I agree that what President Clinton did was wrong," I said for the umpteenth time. "But it's not a high crime or misdemeanor, which was what the founders meant when they set the standard for impeachment. So let's talk about the issues that matter for the people of California."

It was frustrating. By early October the polls showed that my opponent had pulled ahead of me, so it was time for the art of tough. I refused to roll over and let the Republicans destroy me. We ran some tough TV ads about Matt Fong's positions on some real issues like abortion and gun control. We ended those commercials with a new slogan.

"Fong is wrong!"

It was the best we could do.

At the end of the day, I won by more than ten points: 53.1 percent to 43 percent, six points more than 1992, and I was on my way back to Washington for a second term. The media pundits were licking their wounds again, and the Republicans in Washington were morose.

The impeachment trial was a dark cloud still hanging over the nation in 1999 when I arrived in Washington for my swearing-in. Just one month earlier the House, under the "paragon of virtue" Newt Gingrich, was successful in impeaching the president and the trial was going forward as the first order of business. Under the Constitution, the House of Representatives determines whether a president should be impeached for "high crimes and misdemeanors." But the Senate conducts the trial and has the sole authority to remove him or her from office.

I was so upset, disgusted, and dismayed by the Republican playbook that I became very ill with the flu. I was so sick, I couldn't attend my own swearing-in party at a restaurant in Washington, D.C.'s Union Station on Capitol Hill. We had put so much effort into planning, and more than one hundred friends and colleagues had come all the way from California to attend. Stewart couldn't go either, because he had caught the flu from me, so our children, Nicole and Doug, had to keep the party going on their own until, finally, I couldn't stand it anymore. I got out of my sick bed, put my warm coat over my pajamas, got a ride to the party, and climbed up onto the stage.

"Thank you so much for coming," I croaked through my sore vocal cords. "And for all your support before, during, and after this tough election. But I'm sick and have to go back to bed or I'll give you all this debilitating flu, so enjoy, and have a great time without me." Ever the Jewish mother, I added: "And don't be like me, get a flu shot!"

With that, I went back to bed and the party went on in earnest. My kids came through again. But this flu wouldn't quit. The very next morning, I had to struggle out of our Capitol Hill flat to attend an important lecture to the Democratic caucus by Robert Byrd on the history of impeachment and why this Republican impeachment trial was illegal, since Bill Clinton hadn't met the impeachment bar. I tried to listen to what Robert was saying because I knew it was powerful and brilliant, but I couldn't focus. I became increasingly weak until it felt like I was going to pass out, so I ran out of the room. Luckily, a kindly staffer called for a wheelchair and they got me down to the Senate doctor's office, where I received intravenous fluids. I had become severely dehydrated; between that and the impeachment thing, I just got sicker than I'd ever been.

Unfortunately, CNN quickly reported that "Barbara Boxer broke her leg at the Democratic caucus this morning." It was the craziest thing. Someone had seen me in a wheelchair and assumed I had broken my leg and was on the way to the hospital. This inaccurate report caused much angst back home until I called Stewart and told him never mind, I had no broken leg and was actually starting to feel better—at least physically.

The real headline CNN should have run was: SENATOR SIDELINED DUE TO SHOCKING REPUBLICAN IMPEACHMENT HOAX.

To make matters more embarrassing, an AP reporter wrote that I was vying with Jim Inhofe, my so-called archnemesis on climate change, to see who used more tissues during the impeachment trial, since we both had the flu.

It didn't help that my Senate desk was right behind the House members who presented the case against the president. They were called House Managers, and all thirteen of them marched down the aisle of the Senate chamber every day with their chests puffed out. One of them sat in front of me during that endless trial, which lasted five weeks. His name was Jim Rogan, a Republican from California's twenty-seventh district, which included parts of Pasadena and Los Angeles County.

I should point out that it was a cramped space, but one day Rogan "accidentally" knocked over my water glass and I got a good soaking. Just what I needed. I sat there with damp clothes, thinking that, given the tension over that trial, it wasn't so accidental. (Ironically, it turned out to be Jim Rogan's last term in Congress. Many of his district's voters opposed the impeachment, and in 2000 he was defeated by Democrat Adam Schiff.)

Later, when George W. Bush nominated Rogan to be a federal judge in the U.S. District Court's Central District of California, despite the unanimous approval of Dianne Feinstein's judicial nominee review committee, the Democratically controlled Judiciary Committee declined to give Rogan's nomination a hearing because I put a hold on it. If he truly thought President Clinton committed a legitimate impeachable offense, a high crime and misdemeanor, then he didn't belong on the bench. That's my view, and despite heavy lobbying from Republicans and Democrats, I stuck to it and he didn't get the job.

Later, Republican Governor Arnold Schwarzenegger appointed Rogan to serve as a judge on the Superior Court of California in Orange County, where he's been ever since.

President Clinton had been impeached in the House on charges of perjury and obstruction of justice, but on February 12, 1999, the United States Senate acquitted him of perjury on a vote of 45 for conviction and 55 against. On the obstruction charge, 50 voted to convict and 50 opposed. That was well short of the 67 votes required to remove him.

It was over. But it had been as horrible, nasty, and brutal as it could be. Republicans thought they had snatched the brass ring. All their hostility over the Clinton victory poured out. You could see it on their faces, hear it on their talk radio stations. They acted like paragons of virtue.

Later, when I picked up whiffs of impeachment talk surrounding President Obama because of his executive orders—notwithstanding the fact that he has issued the fewest in recent times—I was nauseated at the thought that *any* president might be mistreated again in such a way.

By the time President Clinton finished his term, he had presided over the creation of twenty-three million jobs, the most in history. His presidency from 1993 to 2000 was, moreover, genuinely a time of prosperity. Here's what Louis Menand said about that in *The New Yorker* issue of March 30, 2015:

In 1993, the year Clinton became President, median household income in the United States was $48,884. Six years later, it was $56,080, and the federal government ran a $125.6 billion surplus. There was an even bigger surplus in 2000. The stock market began the nineteen-nineties with the Dow at 2,753. At the end of trading in 1999, the Dow was at 11,497. Middle-class Americans tend to feel that life is good when their 401(k)s are robust. Dozens of wars were under way around the world, but while Bill Clinton was President, the United States was involved in very few of them.

But ever since 2001 when George W. Bush became president, the federal government has been in the red.

Or, as the headline in humor magazine *The Onion* said of Bush's inauguration: "Our Long National Nightmare of Peace and Prosperity Is Finally Over."

As the senator from California, I was keenly aware of how important the movie business was, not only to the economy of Los Angeles but to the entire state. That's why I appeared in 1997 before the Senate Commerce Committee with Jack Valenti, the chairman and chief executive officer of the Motion Picture Association of America (MPAA), to oppose the government takeover of the TV rating system.

Jack had worked for fellow Texan Lyndon B. Johnson when he first went to the White House after JFK's assassination, but in 1964 had been persuaded by Lew Wasserman, the head of Universal Studios, and with Johnson's consent, to take charge of how Hollywood ran its business for the next thirty-eight years.

Among the most important things Jack had initiated were the rating systems. You know: G means the film is for kids of all ages; PG for films in which some material may be unsuitable for children; PG-13 for films with some material unsuitable for kids under thirteen; NC-17, no one under seventeen admitted. It's a good system, warning parents about inappropriate content for their children, and I've always thought it worked pretty well.

Valenti and I were at the Senate Commerce Committee hearing because there was concern at that time about sex and violence in TV and films. It was a huge movement and very easy to inflate to an alarming level of fear. I felt it was an overreaction to a serious issue and truly believed that there was a chance that an era of McCarthy-style government censorship might make a comeback.

"These movies are poisoning the minds of our children," both the Republicans and Democrats on the committee were saying.

This kind of response was not the first time the government was concerned. It was similar to the response to the widely discredited book *Seduction of the Innocent*, published back in 1954, which claimed that comic books created juvenile delinquency and worse. Because of the publicity generated by these wild assertions, Estes Kefauver had held hearings of his Senate Subcommittee on Juvenile Delinquency, which resulted in the comic book publishers establishing the Comics Code Authority (CCA) to self-regulate their content.

Which is what Hollywood had been doing now for years. But Jack and I were on the defensive. Even though the industry was rating films, there was a movement to take it further. It was hard to sit there and be attacked by such a unanimous wave of righteous alarm, so I thought our only chance was to go on the offense.

I tried to make a few simple yet obvious points when it was my turn to speak.

"Ratings are highly subjective and therefore the government taking on this responsibility is fraught with peril.

"Let's talk about *Schindler's List*," I said. "This film was a moving true story which has been shown recently on NBC network TV about Oskar Schindler, a German businessman who saved many Jews from the Nazi death camps. This film has won seven Oscars, including best film and best director for Steven Spielberg and been hailed as one of the greatest motion pictures ever made," I told the committee, "but Congressman Tom Coburn says that TV has been taken 'to an all-time low, with full-frontal nudity, violence and profanity.'

"I respectfully disagree," I went on, trying to be as unemotional and calm as I could on this very sensitive issue for me. "I believe *Schindler's List* is an amazing story of courage, bravery, and heart, as well as evil, and that every kid of high school age or older should be encouraged to see this film.

"My point is that Tom Coburn and I have very different, highly subjective opinions, and both are completely legitimate. But if the government took over the rating system, who would actually decide? The committee? Our staff? And what would a bunch of bureaucrats think as they prepared the rating? Isn't there a danger of the government becoming like Big Brother?"

Jack and I made our case and were politely excused. The MPAA ratings continued without any further hearings, so I guess we won by default.

But that's not the end of this story.

Republican Senator John McCain was the chairman of the Senate Commerce Committee and was presiding at the hearing. Later that same day I went up to John on the floor of the Senate while we were both there for some roll call vote.

"Thanks so much for allowing me to testify, John," I said to him. "The rating system is so important to my state."

His response was surprising at first, then increasingly shocking.

"I'm glad you reminded me, Barbara," he said, glaring at me. "You had no right to mention Congressman Coburn's name and put words in his mouth when he wasn't there to defend himself."

What?

"But I was quoting exactly what Coburn had said," I explained. "I was just trying to say how subjective and complicated it is to judge a film. He saw it his way and I saw it my way. There is no right and wrong."

That seemed to send John right into the stratosphere, and in just a few seconds he totally lost it, exploding at me right in the middle of the Senate floor.

"I'm banning you from ever appearing before my committee again... That's right, Barbara, I'm banning you. I myself was the victim of character assassination when they named me member of the 'Keating Five' during the savings and loan scandal."

"There's no comparison, John...."

But before I could finish, he stormed off without another word. I was left alone on the Senate floor, shocked. I didn't even know that a senator could be banned from a committee of the Senate.

I decided the only way to handle this craziness was to go up to the press gallery and tell everyone who cared to listen what an abuse of power that was.

As I was rushing through the chamber on my way to my mission, my friend and mentor Joe Biden must have seen my ashen face, because he rushed over.

"What happened?" he asked me.

"John McCain just blew his top about something I said at his Senate Commerce Committee hearing and banned me from ever appearing there again."

"What did you say?" Joe asked. I told him.

"Oh, that's just John being John," Joe said with a smile. "Don't worry, Barbara, he doesn't mean anything by it. He just gets mad like that sometimes."

"Too bad," I said. "I'm going up to the gallery to tell the press what happened. It's outrageous and I don't want him doing it to anyone else."

I was still determined and Joe saw that.

"No, no," Joe said. "Don't do that. You'll regret it. Not a good idea. *Wait!* I'll be right back."

With that, he rushed off to talk to John. I saw them huddling and, sure enough, in short order I had a written apology. Just a quick note that McCain dashed off, but it felt good. Of course I was as green as could be at the time. Years later, when I had gained seniority and was a chairman myself, I learned that no one can be banned from appearing before a committee. The chair can make it difficult, but your rights as a senator trump any personal vendetta.

Since then John McCain and I have had our ups and downs. Whenever I am in John McCain's sphere, or he is in mine, I never know whether he is going to give me a hug or the evil eye, be hostile or endearing, bark or smile. John McCain is complicated. No colleague comes close.

We were always on the opposite side of the aisle, but nevertheless agreed about a lot of things. I was proud of John's progressive stand on the immigration issue and leadership on climate change, at least during those pre-gridlock years.

I was also very proud when John McCain joined my California colleague Dianne Feinstein to defend her stand on opening up the truth on torture post–9/11. The perpetrators called torture by other names but the facts were the facts, and John and Dianne were brave to bring the truth forward.

On the other hand, John came to California to campaign against my re-election in 2010. He was in San Diego, where he called me "the most anti-defense" senator currently serving. Unfortunately for him, the same day he was there, the beloved veteran Senator Dan Inouye was in the same city campaigning for me, lauding my record for veterans. I hadn't planned it, but sometimes you catch a break.

After my victory and re-election, I went right up to John on the Senate floor.

"Weren't you a little over-the-top in your statements about me?"

"It's a campaign," he said, smiling. He and I were veterans of politics. After all, I had campaigned against him in his presidential race against Barack Obama, and as we say: "What goes around comes around."

John and I especially did not see eye to eye on the Iraq War. At the early stages of the conflict, John saw a very worried look on my face and took me aside to a quiet space near an entrance to the Senate floor. I was amazed that he could read me and touched that he would take the time out for a colleague on the other side. Then again, I've never learned how to put on a poker face.

The war was going very badly, which I had warned about when I voted against it. John was a fierce defender of the war and never strayed from that position, blaming tactics for its failures, rather than the decision to go to war itself. But seeing my angst, he asked what was bothering me, and whether he could do anything to help.

"It's the war, John," I said. "It's not ending as fast as predicted and we're seeing so many more deaths, and still no weapons of mass destruction have been found. It feels out of control."

"Barbara, stop worrying," he said with great confidence and a reassuring smile. "This war will be over in weeks, at the most a few months." He patted my shoulder and was off with his usual jauntiness.

That was roughly nine years before President Obama ended the war. All those years, John McCain was a hawk—and he still is. He never wavered on Iraq, not for a minute.

John and his allies in Congress, like Lindsey Graham and Kelly Ayotte, continued to call for military action again and again. Still, John and I could always talk about our differences without threatening to ban each other from our committees. Our last "debate" came over congressional legislation to go after ISIL. He wanted no strings on the executive; I did. No surprise there. Then he and I went at it over an ambassadorial nomination, after which he and I actually hugged when we met later in the hall. He wanted to slam the president on his ambassador picks and demonstrate his usual over-the-top anger at one of my constituents whom the president had nominated. I knew he was just letting off steam and we had the votes for her so I let it go, but not until after I said a few choice words against his argument on the Senate floor. It was a standoff.

I would sum up John's feelings toward me this way: he tolerates me. And he didn't when our paths first crossed. So that's progress, and one of the most unusual relationships I've had in politics.

Then I wrote this poem:

An Ode to McCain
You are unforgettable
But it's regrettable
That the only war where you walked away
Was the climate war
And our kids will pay
One thing I now feel
When you yell at me it's no big deal
It's not really in your heart
It's just the way you always start.

During the Clinton–Gore years, I had many contacts with both of them. Ocean protection, after-school programs, helping get their executive nominations through, such as cabinet and subcabinet members and judges. We worked particularly closely whenever there was a crying need in California, particularly regarding infrastructure development and emergency responses to earthquakes, floods, and fires.

I strongly supported Al's run for president in 2000, so I wasn't surprised when, the day after the 2000 elections, he gave me a call.

"Barbara," he said, "would you go down to Tallahassee, Florida? We thought we'd won the Florida popular vote, giving us the electoral votes we needed to win the presidency, but Katherine Harris, the Florida secretary of state, called it for Bush and we've demanded a recount."

It was a bizarre situation, which has gone down in history.

What was even more astonishing was that a precinct of key Jewish voters who had always voted Democratic for years and ordinarily would be assumed to have voted for Al Gore had apparently voted for Patrick Buchanan. What? That was and still is a totally and completely implausible scenario. And there were a huge number of votes uncounted due to the now infamous "hanging chads," pieces of paper that were supposed to be punched completely out of the ballot, but did not quite make it to their destination.

"Fine," I said to Al. Stewart and I would go there while the vote count was proceeding, to keep up the spirits of the grass roots.

It seemed very strange that after Election Day there would still be throngs of supporters standing in front of the county's elections office, organized and galvanized. But when we arrived, there they were: hundreds of people standing in front of the courthouse in Tallahassee—upset, nervous, clearly in need of empowerment and hope.

Enter the Speechifiers, and I was one. But as I started to speak, the shouting started from the back of the crowd.

"Go back to Brooklyn." "Get out of town, Babs." And worse things my defense mechanisms have allowed me to forget.

Mostly they were young men. Later we learned they were Republican staffers sent by Newt Gingrich and his friends to shout down the Democrats. Some were young Cuban Americans, who blamed the Democrats for the continuing dictatorship of Fidel Castro, and who saw Al Gore as their enemy.

I usually could handle rude detractors like this, but I was failing. Suddenly an idea occurred to me that I hoped could turn it around.

"So you guys know I am the senator from California, right?"

Grumble grumble. Boo boo.

"You know who else was from California? Your hero Ronald Reagan."

It got a little quieter.

"So whatever our differences, I served in the House when Ronald Reagan was president, and there was mutual respect for the offices we held."

All true. Although I had made no secret during the Reagan years of my disdain toward his "do nothing" attitude on AIDS, his attacks on the arts, his lack of interest in the environment, and his unprecedented nuclear arms buildup, Ronald Reagan, Speaker Tip O'Neill, and all of us were able to move past our deep differences. We didn't stand up and boo one another; we just kept working our side. I was telling the truth to these hecklers about respect for the office.

"When you hiss me and boo me," I went on, "you're really hissing and booing Ronald Reagan."

That was a bit of a stretch, but it worked. I went on to tell the crowd that all we wanted was a fair vote count. There were serious problems with ballots in certain counties, hanging chads, mix-ups of names, resulting in much confusion in many precincts.

"Thanks to the Florida Supreme Court," I concluded, "we'll get to the truth."

It became upbeat. We were convinced the vote would be recounted and go our way. Stew and I got on a plane back to Washington. When we landed, we learned that the U.S. Supreme Court had overruled the Florida court and had stopped the count in Florida. The court intervened, unlawfully in my opinion, and despite Gore winning the popular vote in the entire U.S.A., and though the recount in the crucial swing state of Florida never happened, they declared George W. Bush president.

One annoying footnote to the hijacking of the election in favor of George W. Bush was the presence of Ralph Nader, the Green Party candidate for the presidency in 2000. Even today I cringe when his name is mentioned. Sure, back in 1965 his book about automobile safety, *Unsafe at Any Speed*, was groundbreaking. And I remember the sleazy way General Motors tried to entrap him into a tryst with a prostitute in order to discredit him as he exposed the dangers of their cars. Incredible. And it totally backfired, since in 1966 Congress passed the historic National Traffic and Motor Vehicle Safety Act, mandating safety belts and stronger windshields. I give Nader enormous credit for that.

But after years of consumer activism Nader really went off the rails, running for president four times. And in 2000 he kept saying there was no difference between Gore and Bush. There'd be no difference if one or the other won, he proclaimed, since they had the same corporate, militaristic, anti-environmental politics. Either he was smoking something or he wins the prize for "Best Rationalizer" in the world. It gives me a kind of post-traumatic stress just to think about that.

About a year after the Gore loss, I talked about the stolen election with Barbara Mikulski. Anyone who knows Barbara well knows what a tough fighter she's always been. You have to be if you are the very first Democratic woman elected in your own right. You had to prove that women can take whatever blows are thrown. So I was touched and surprised to see her tear up. Al was one of Barbara's closest allies and she truly admired him.

"He would have been one great president," she told me one day after Al had given our Democratic caucus an extraordinary presentation on climate change. Her eyes welled up with tears but they never fell.

But Al Gore didn't want to dispute the court's insane decision. I would have used my senatorial prerogative to challenge the electoral vote in Florida, but he asked me not to, so I didn't.

I should have, though. It's still something I regret. It wouldn't have changed the outcome. I probably would have stood alone, but I still feel I failed to do the right thing in the face of a Supreme Court that had no shame. They picked the winner they wanted. It was a scandal and a disgrace.

After George W. Bush became president, the Clinton balanced budget and economic surplus were destroyed and a new deficit soared. The Bush administration stood by and did nothing to address climate change, education, women's rights, tax reform, or health care. And more than four thousand brave American soldiers lost their lives.

*   *   *

September 11, 2001, was the day that everyone's life changed.

It was a gorgeous Tuesday morning in the middle of my second term. I was at the Democratic leader's meeting room. We had charts in position in preparation for our meeting that showed how, after all the hard work by President Clinton and Congress, the Bush administration was plunging us back into deficits with tax breaks for the rich, while at the same time trying to undermine Medicare and Social Security with so-called privatization—meaning more profit for big business and no safety net for middle-class seniors.

Suddenly, at a little after nine a.m., I saw smoke billowing out of the Pentagon a few miles outside our windows. We thought there must be some kind of fire, but none of us knew how it happened or what was the cause. Then on a small TV in the corner of our meeting room in the Capitol, we saw constant replays of a plane flying into the World Trade Center in New York City. We thought the pilot must have had a heart attack. But then the second plane. It was surreal.

We were beginning to realize something big was going on when, about ten minutes later, a bunch of burly Capitol police ran in, grabbed Tom Daschle and Harry Reid, and ran out of the room. Tom was the Democratic leader and Harry his assistant, so they were the top priority. The rest of us looked at one another. We knew we were just chopped liver. That's how it is. In emergencies you save the leaders first so in the worst potential scenario the government still runs. The rest of us were told to get out of the building fast, since they expected a plane to hit the Capitol.

Jay Rockefeller grabbed me by the hand and, being at least a foot and a half taller, lifted me off the ground and down the Capitol steps. I remember calling my staff and telling them to "get out of the building and meet at my home" a few blocks from the Capitol, as he escorted me out of the building. My first thought was for Nicole and Zach. We had lived together in a duplex three blocks from the Capitol since Nicole's divorce. I ran home and found her there. She told me that Zach was at preschool, and Hillary was arranging to pick him up. When he arrived, we did our best to distract him from watching television so he wouldn't see the planes crashing into the World Trade Center over and over again.

Little did I know we would never again be able to walk up and down the Capitol steps at will. I always treated those steps as my *Rocky* moment before and after votes. Due to heightened security, things changed. I know it sounds like a small point, but the freedom to run up and down those steps in my high heels was a symbol of positive change to me.

That night, after we had learned the full extent of the three attacks, I called the one person I believed could answer the question: who did this to us?

Bill Clinton.

"Mr. President, who did this?"

"I'll tell you, Barbara," he said without missing a beat. "It has all the markings of Osama bin Laden."

That night, after we'd learned about the coordinated attacks on New York and Washington, D.C., Senator Mikulski, bless her big, passionate heart, suggested that all of us members of Congress who had assembled in front of the Capitol to hear our leaders speak should sing "God Bless America."

Which we did. *A capella, too.* It was an incredible, moving end to a terrible, awful day.

On September 14, 2001, I voted to approve George Bush's intention to pursue al Qaeda into Afghanistan. The only one who voted against that proposition in either the Senate or the House was Barbara Lee, the representative from California's ninth district, which included Oakland, Berkeley, Alameda, and Albany. Barbara, in my opinion, is a true pacifist. She'd won that seat after the retirement of my good friend Ron Dellums, and I think he would have voted against any armed intervention too, but I can't be sure because I never asked him.

I voted to go into Afghanistan and pursue Osama bin Laden because Bill Clinton had said bin Laden was behind everything that happened on 9/11 and I believed him wholeheartedly. I knew the Taliban had been hospitable to bin Laden and was glad that both the Clinton and Bush administrations had agreed not to recognize the Taliban as the official government of Afghanistan. They ruled the country with an iron fist, systematically punishing anyone who didn't believe in their radical fundamentalism.

Women were a particular target, forced to wear burqas, attacked for their desire for education—facts I learned from a wonderful group of Californians called the Feminist Majority. In a way, 9/11 helped to start an "accidental liberation" of Afghanistan because the U.S. invasion put the Taliban on the defensive and women began to get some rights restored.

During the early years of the Afghan war, there were many false alarms that terrorists were flying planes toward the Capitol. On one occasion, I was in a meeting with Rudy de Leon from the Boeing Corporation about the production of cargo planes in California, when the order came to evacuate immediately. I had known Rudy since my House days where he worked on the staff of the House Armed Services Committee, and always liked him. But I never knew what a guy he was until that moment.

When the evacuation order came, it was frightening. I told Rudy to run ahead of me. I was slow and in my high heels. No terrorist attack was going to make me take them off. I could hear my Jewish mother's voice in my ear supporting my decision:

"You could step on a nail and get gangrene while looking less than professional."

But Rudy held fast and said, "No!" He was going to see me down those stairs and all the way to my home.

"*GO*, Rudy!" I yelled at him. "You're twenty years my junior and have kids—*GO!*"

I tried to push him ahead of me but he stayed with me. Just as Jay Rockefeller had done on the morning of 9/11.

You remember things like that.

Unfortunately, President Bush made only half-hearted efforts to find Osama bin Laden in Afghanistan. The more bin Laden eluded him, the more he seemed to become frustrated and bored. So he listened to those hawks in his government who thought an easier target for a winnable war would be Iraq's

Saddam Hussein. I wish he had talked to his dad instead of his vice president, Dick Cheney, and the neo-cons, since George H. W. Bush knew that a war against Saddam Hussein would lead to utter chaos. That's why the first President Bush never went into Baghdad after the successful effort to expel Saddam from Kuwait in 1990.

But Bush listened to the neo-cons, who had persuaded themselves that Saddam Hussein was a perfect foil, a highly visible saber-rattling villain with a big sneer and a black mustache to go with it. Hussein had survived and restored his power after the first Gulf War and I'll bet that those urging W. on reminded him that Dad had left unfinished business.

Reporter and author Bob Woodward once asked W. if he had asked for his father's opinion on whether he should go to war in Iraq. Bush answered that his earthly father was "the wrong father to appeal to for advice...there is a higher father that I appealed to."

I was shocked by this. It worried me that President George W. Bush didn't ask his dad, who might have known a little more history than the neo-cons who surrounded his son. Divine intervention is always a plus, but a loving father's intervention wouldn't have hurt in this case.

Regardless, invading Iraq was a fateful decision that harmed tens of thousands of American families, not to mention hundreds of thousands of Iraqis. It turned the entire Middle East upside down; the flames are still burning from his incredible blunder to this day. There are now reports that Saddam's Baathist military is a strong component of ISIL, or ISIS or IS or Daesh—whatever that inhumane gang of monsters is called.

President Bush and his team—Vice President Dick Cheney, Secretary of Defense Donald Rumsfeld, Secretary of State Colin Powell, and National Security Advisor Condoleezza Rice—orchestrated a massive public relations campaign in the United Nations and in the media to persuade the world that Hussein had "weapons of mass destruction" including poison gas and nuclear warheads that he could use against our friends in the region. The Bush administration claimed that the case for weapons of mass destruction would be a "slam-dunk."

Ultimately it was Colin Powell, a military hero and man of integrity, who carried the day. He truly believed what the Bush team was telling him, and on February 5, 2003, told the United Nations there was "no doubt in my mind" that Saddam was working to obtain key components to produce nuclear weapons.

Secretary of State Powell's claim was the climactic moment of a well-organized publicity blitz. On September 7, 2002, Judith Miller of the *New York Times* reported that Bush administration officials told her, "In the last 14 months, Iraq has sought to buy thousands of specially designed aluminum tubes, which American officials believe were intended as components of centrifuges to enrich uranium." The truth was, however, that many government officials had already concluded that these aluminum tubes were unsuitable and not intended for uranium refinement.

On NBC's *Meet the Press*, Vice President Cheney cited the inaccurate *Times* article, which had probably been planted by the Bush team, as if it were an accurate news report from an objective outside source. He used it to accuse Saddam of developing nuclear weapons over the past fourteen months to add to his stockpile of other chemical and biological weapons of mass destruction.

ON CNN, Condoleezza Rice warned that "there will always be some uncertainty" in determining how close Iraq may be to obtaining a nuclear weapon but "we don't want the smoking gun to be a mushroom cloud."

Talk about inflammatory propaganda. It was enough to send every parent who remembered "duck and cover" from the Cold War of the 1950s to rush out and dig a bomb shelter in their backyard.

And finally, in his State of the Union speech on January 28, 2003, George W. Bush reported, "The British government has learned that Saddam Hussein recently sought significant quantities of uranium from Africa."

What? Where did this come from?

The famous "sixteen words" that Bush delivered in his State of the Union address were particularly upsetting to everyone who heard them. "The British government has learned..."? Well, let me tell you that it didn't take very long for many other sources to deny this allegation, labeling it as completely false. In fact, the infamous myth of African uranium "yellow cake," uranium oxide, was part of an egregious forged Niger document released by Italian military intelligence.

And the Bush administration knew it was a fake.

Here's the true story. The 2002 National Intelligence Estimate contained an opinion from the State Department that the Italian military intelligence report that first claimed the Niger yellow cake conspiracy was "highly questionable." The *Washington Post* reported that "Dozens of interviews with current and former intelligence officials and policymakers in the United States, Britain, France and Italy show that the Bush administration disregarded key information available at the time showing that the Iraq–Niger claim was highly questionable" in order to manipulate facts to take the U.S. to war.

In fact, the CIA had asked career diplomat Joseph C. Wilson to go to Niger and investigate the possibility that Saddam Hussein had bought enriched yellow cake uranium. He reported back that "it was highly doubtful that any such transaction had ever taken place," since Niger's Prime Minister Mayaki had declined to meet with Hussein.

Consequently, after he heard Bush's State of the Union Address, Wilson wrote an op-ed piece in the July 6 issue of the *New York Times* entitled "What I Didn't Find in Africa" that said unequivocally that he had "little choice but to conclude that some of the intelligence related to Iraq's nuclear weapons program was twisted to exaggerate the Iraqi threat."

But the story now takes an even darker turn: Shortly after this op-ed piece appeared in the *Times*, Robert Novak, a syndicated *Washington Post* columnist, wrote that he'd discovered through confidential sources that Wilson's wife, Valerie Plame, was an undercover operative for the CIA. Wilson was shocked and upset by this disclosure, which put his wife's life in danger and was obviously part of the Bush administration effort to punish him and discredit what he'd written.

He was right. In their 2006 book *Hubris*, Michael Isikoff and David Corn asserted that it was Deputy Secretary of State Richard Armitage who first revealed to Novak sometime before July 8, 2003, that Wilson's wife worked for the CIA.

There were no nuclear weapons in Iraq. I knew that was an utter falsehood because I'd been briefed as a member of the Foreign Relations Committee and saw, right in front of me, a clear disagreement among the intelligence agencies. So when Condoleezza Rice appeared on national television to announce to the world that every single intelligence agency in the U.S. government believed Saddam had nuclear capability, I couldn't believe it. I called George Tenet, then the head of the CIA, and he confirmed that all the intelligence agencies in America did not agree. But I was in a catch-22. I knew the agencies did not agree that Saddam had nuclear capability, but because our briefing in the Foreign Relations Committee was strictly confidential, I couldn't get clearance to say so. All I could do was protest, without the ability to back it up.

So I saw the lie unfold and I came to believe that Rice's focus on a nonexistent nuclear threat from Saddam was a way for her to distract attention from the chilling fact that as National Security Advisor, she had been warned two months before 9/11, by none other than CIA Director George Tenet, that supporters of Osama bin Laden were planning a massive attack on America.

There was another reason this was all happening: oil.

One of my colleagues, Democratic senator from Montana Max Baucus, told me that when he was being courted to vote yes on the Iraq war, he'd been invited up to the White House. Bush took him into an anteroom, where there were photos of oil wells in Iraq and notes about how much oil they produced. The president was most enthusiastic about defeating Iraq and Max got a full dose of the oft-repeated message that the oil in Iraq would pay for the war and then some. (What a sick joke that turned out to be. No Iraq oil helped pay for the war. Bush's war has cost the U.S. taxpayers more than two trillion dollars, and the end isn't in sight.)

So from what I knew behind the scenes and what I felt instinctively from my observations of the Bush administration, I was completely opposed to another war against Iraq. Consequently on October 11, 2002, I was one of twenty-three members of the Senate who voted against the authorization to go to war in Iraq. I was part of a coalition that included Robert Byrd, Carl Levin, Ted Kennedy, Russ Feingold, Paul Wellstone, and others.

Kennedy was the mastermind of our dissent and worked feverishly behind the scenes. He knew that as a conservative from West Virginia, Senator Byrd would be the best face for the opposition, because the rest of us were known to be liberal. Ted told me to ask Robert to hold organizing meetings in his office, reserve floor time, and call senators to get them to the floor to speak, which I did—always at Ted's instruction. By watching Ted work I learned that a truly good senator builds coalitions and steps back when it makes sense. Ted, the Lion of the Senate, didn't want to be the front man and wasn't concerned with credit. In fact, he didn't want his leadership role to be exposed.

Before the final vote, I strongly supported the Levin Resolution to build a "world coalition" before we went in. I believed that the "Levin Resolution offered us an alternative" to this war of choice and I called Senator Levin "independent, clear thinking" and felt he had the right approach.

Despite all of our efforts, however, we lost. The vote to authorize the president to use military force against Iraq was approved, 77 in favor and 23 against. Forty-eight Republicans voted yes, with one against; 29 Democrats voted yes, with 21 of us against, plus one independent, Senator Jeffords from Vermont.

In the House, meanwhile, 82 Democrats vote for the war and 126 against. Congresswoman Barbara Lee offered an amendment calling for more inspections for weapons in Iraq before we considered any resolution to go to war, but it was defeated 72 for, 355 against.

Fourteen days after the vote, Paul Wellstone, along with his wife, Sheila, and daughter, Marcia, died in a small airplane crash. A terrible tragedy. Paul had been the only senator facing re-election to vote against the war. Paul's passion for fairness and justice was such an important part of our senate debates. Stewart and I hosted a fund-raising reception at our home for him, which is something we didn't do that often. Robin Williams was the featured guest and he was as generous, kind, and funny as he could be on that occasion.

Paul's death cut deep for me. He was vibrant, with a compassion I found touching in a man. He wasn't afraid to show his feelings and he had the same sense of outrage and disbelief I often felt as we debated middle-class economic issues and the plight of so many children falling into poverty. I shared his intense anxiety about the war.

Thank God I voted against that war. The American people supported it very strongly at the start, but it turned out to be a disaster, and all of our allies who were behind us after 9/11 pretty much turned against us.

It was such a disheartening and difficult time for me because I had voted against a war that had popular support among the people of my state. I've never received more e-mails from Californians than I did about this issue. First they told me I was wrong to oppose the war. Very wrong. Later they encouraged me to end it and end it quickly. Their impatience matched mine. Meanwhile, I was vilified by many political commentators who said that my decision to vote against the Iraq War would be the end of me politically.

Joe Biden and John Kerry were really angry with me. They didn't want to have a big "no" vote because they had decided "yes." Well, their side won big, but those of us in opposition weren't going to be shy about calling for the war to end. They continued to have very vocal opponents in the Senate. Our small group never stopped trying to end that war together—soprano, alto, and bass. I never wavered in my opposition to the war in Iraq and neither did the rest of our "no" group. It got stronger and stronger as the American people began to open their eyes to the disaster the Iraq war was becoming.

I'm certain that historians will confirm that turning attention away from capturing bin Laden toward going after Saddam Hussein was one of the biggest blunders ever made. We lost the support of the world, more than 4,500 U.S. soldiers were killed, and more than 30,000 were injured, some of whom would never be the same. More than 500,000 Iraqis died, including armed combatants and civilians—the so-called "collateral damage." Meanwhile, the budget exploded and the region is still a powder keg.

*   *   *

The events of 9/11 changed my views on security. I began to understand, more than ever before, that a balance between freedom, privacy, and security has to be found. Especially when there are real and present threats against people all over the world.

Since I was known as one of the most liberal members of the Senate, many eyebrows were raised in 2002 when I teamed up with one of the most conservative members in the Senate at the time, Bob Smith of New Hampshire, to propose a new law about pilots having access to weapons on planes.

Bob was a darling of the NRA and I was, and still am, an anti-darling, to put it mildly. I've never seen an organization that is so incapable of moderating its opinions to the slightest degree, regardless of heinous events. Shootings in theaters, on college campuses, and high schools. Shootings of babies in elementary schools, at restaurants, at malls, shootings of police officers, shootings that never stop. And still the NRA totally refuses to embrace the simple idea of making sure those who buy weapons pass a background check. They just don't see any reason why guns shouldn't be sold to criminals, terrorists, people with mental disorders, or children—none of which would create any interference whatsoever with the second amendment. (Enough said about that. Nothing I write about sensible gun laws will ever change the NRA. I think our hope lies with their members, who have got to begin demanding sanity from those who run this tone-deaf organization.)

After 9/11, Senator Smith had written a "Guns in the Cockpit" law, and I contacted him with a few changes that I needed in order to co-sponsor. He accepted those, and the two of us became unlikely allies. That kind of coalition of opposites is usually very effective with powerful results in the Senate. And that proved to be true in this case too.

The reason we needed this law was very clear to me. Before 9/11, if hijackers took over a plane, the protocol was to cooperate with them fully, because no hijacker had ever used the plane as a weapon. After that horrifying act of terror, I realized the pilots should at least have a chance to restore their control of the plane, because if they didn't, the new protocol was that the plane would be shot down by the United States military. This meant that a pilot would first have the hijackers ready to take down the plane, then the military. I grew up in Brooklyn—that's two against one.

Not fair. Some of my liberal friends thought I was wrong about this, but I respectfully disagreed. You have to be tough to stand up to your base. Sometimes that's the toughest thing of all.

As of this writing, our program is still in place. I made sure flight attendants receive training, and as one said to me, "I don't need more training on how to make napkins look better on a tray, I need to know how to defend myself in the cabin." In 2002, the law was limited to passenger aircraft. Teaming up with another conservative, Jim Bunning of Kentucky, we expanded it to include cargo pilots.

The war in Iraq became my passion and obsession from the moment I voted against the October 11, 2002, resolution to authorize George W. Bush to use the U.S. armed forces "as he determines to be necessary and appropriate."

John McCain's glib assurance that "this war will be over in weeks, at the most a few months" was, needless to say, wildly overoptimistic. And when Bush declared "Mission Accomplished" a little over six months later on May 1, 2003, the insurgency against the U.S. troop invasion and the subsequent civil war between radical Sunni and Shia militants had in reality only just begun to poison both Iraq and the rest of our world.

Between 2003 and 2008 I focused every ounce of energy in my heart, mind, and soul to get us out of Iraq. When people ask me what my biggest regret is in the Senate, it's the fact that no matter how hard I tried to end that war, it went on and on.

People also ask me how it felt to be in a minority position on an issue. Well, I learned early in my career in my first office as a Marin County supervisor that when you hold a minority position on an issue of conscience, it's your duty to speak out, even when you're taunted; even when it looks hopeless. You must make a record; you must try to continue to change minds, if not in the legislative body itself, then in the constituency. Because when the opinions of your constituency change, everything else will follow.

When I look at how many speeches I made on the floor of the Senate, it surprises me. I spoke more about ending that combat mission than I did about anything else. When I read over those now forgotten old speeches, I can still feel the heat, the emotion, and the frustration of making them.

Every time I finished a speech, I thought about what I would say in the next one. I asked over and over what the war was going to cost in "blood and treasure." I asked, "What other nations would provide military support? What would the rebuilding of Iraq cost the U.S. taxpayers? How long would our troops stay there?" I worried that our troops would be a "target for terrorists," and that the war was a "diversion from the anti-terrorism mission." I railed against the Bush administration for calling those of us against the war "weak."

Two days before the so-called "shock and awe" invasion of Iraq on March 18, 2003, I asked Senator Byrd on the Senate floor if he had gotten even one answer to any of the questions that we had asked the administration. He said, "I have had no answers. The American people have a right to know what this war is going to cost in treasure and blood...but we get nothing."

On March 20, 2003, I said, "I prayed that the war would end soon and that casualties would be minimal." My prayers would not be answered.

On March 25, 2003, I began the saddest series of speeches I have ever had to give on the Senate floor. I started reading a list of those soldiers just from my state, California, who had been killed since the war began. Unfortunately, I had to make that grim journey to the Senate floor too many times over the next years as we lost so many soldiers from California.

I kept hammering away at the Bush administration. I read them a quote from spokesman Ari Fleischer, who said, "We are dealing with a country that can really finance its own construction and relatively soon." White House budget Director Mitch Daniels said, "Iraq would be an affordable endeavor." What?

I told my colleagues: "Secretary of State Rumsfeld said that the reconstruction funds from Iraq can come from frozen assets, oil revenues, substantial billions of dollars. How wrong he was. In fact, we had deficits that were totally out of control."

In 2004, I got an amendment through to make sure that injured troops wouldn't have to pay for their own meals when they were in veteran's hospitals being treated for wounds. I couldn't believe we had to do this, but we did.

When the death toll reached 999, Senator Reid, Senator Tom Harkin, and I called attention not only to the dead but to the wounded, who at that time numbered 6,919, of whom 57 percent were categorized as "severely injured." Despite that, the president proposed cutting the Veterans Administration budget by ninety million dollars.

This was almost too much. I addressed him directly in my remarks:

"President Bush, this is going to be an issue. It is one thing to send troops to war. It's another to be there with what they need when they come back."

On May 12, 2003, I chastised the president for his "mission accomplished" speech and lambasted Halliburton for war profiteering.

In 2005 I quoted Dr. Martin Luther King: "If we do not act, we shall surely be dragged down the long, dark and shameful corridors of time reserved for those who possess strength...without sight." Dr. King had said that about the Vietnam War, which was a catalyst for my entry into politics. And it was still true decades later, about the Iraq War.

I encouraged others to speak out by quoting another Dr. King pearl of wisdom: "Our lives begin to end when we become silent about things that matter."

I praised Senator Levin's amendment, which gained seventy-nine votes, asking that Iraqis take the lead in fighting the war. I took on Dick Cheney and reminded him that he'd said, "America will be treated as the liberators."

I spoke about the imaginary yellow cake fantasy, when the Bush administration claimed that Saddam Hussein had tried to purchase uranium powder, or yellow cake, from Niger so he could make nuclear "weapons of mass destruction."

I talked about going up to "that room" to "bear witness" to the disgusting torture photos from Abu Ghraib prison taken by the American soldiers who worked there. It was one of the most painful experiences I'd ever had as a senator. Trent Lott, a Republican leader from Mississippi, was there too, and was very kind to me. He must have watched me sink down in my chair with shock on my face as I saw those photos. He came up to me and asked me if I was all right. I wasn't. He walked me out of the room, for which I was very grateful. The fact that American soldiers did these things was beyond my imagination. What a war like this can do to an individual!

I brought up the issue of our soldiers facing three and four deployments. I even teamed up with Joe Lieberman, a staunch supporter of the war, on the issue of mental health, citing 170,000 vets of Afghanistan and Iraq who had been diagnosed with mental disorders. Lieberman broke my Democratic heart time and time again when he supported the war, but we set aside our bitter disagreements and worked very well together on this issue.

I offered an amendment to pay for enhanced mental health services for our vets by canceling future tax cuts to millionaires and billionaires. Needless to say, I lost. By this time the cost of the war was 251 billion dollars. The cost of the future tax cuts was about the same. I said to the president, "This makes me sick. We are waving a white flag of surrender over our children, over our seniors, over our fiscal responsibility, and over our homeland security." Still the war went on, with more dead, more wounded, and more soldiers with mental health problems.

In 2006 I wrote an amendment forcing Rumsfeld to appoint members of the Mental Health Commission, which he was supposed to have done. I also worked with Senators Dan Inouye and Ted Stevens to open up a new Comprehensive Combat Casualty Care Center in San Diego, so that west coast wounded warriors would no longer have to travel far distances to get help for their severe injuries. I consider that successful amendment a proud accomplishment.

Many of my colleagues who were against the war were also making eloquent speeches, but still the war raged on. Our anti-war group was pushing hard for an exit strategy.

This led to our being accused of being the "cut and run" crowd in the eyes of the Iraqi war hawks. "An exit strategy is not cut and run," I said, "it is smart and strategic." I went on: "In the light of all our military has done, and they have paid the price in blood and lost limbs and pain and suffering and death, what are the Iraq leaders saying? They have proposed amnesty to those who have killed American soldiers."

I continued to vent my barely controlled anger.

"Let's be clear about what happens when the president says we can make this work, when he claims we just have to stay in Iraq as long as it takes. Well, President Bush, you're asking for us to turn a blind eye and to give you a blank check. And every citizen in this country is going to pay for it. What kind of leadership is that? Do you think I like standing here having this kind of debate? No, I do not. But I haven't seen anything like this since the Vietnam war, folks. I lived through those years. That was the reason I got into politics: so we would not make this mistake again."

I quoted journalist Peter Bergen on how Bush's war had caused both a catastrophic insurgency against us and ignited a terrible civil war. Bergen wrote, "What we have done in Iraq is what bin Laden could not have hoped for in his wildest dreams...it ignited Sunni and Shia fundamentalist fervor."

I talked about the case of Joe Wilson and his wife, Valerie Plame. Wilson told the truth about there being no weapons of mass destruction, so to punish him, Cheney and his friends leaked the big news that Valerie was a CIA undercover agent to reporters. And that sent a message...To me it was the vice president of the United States and his henchmen acting like an illegal mob operation. The message was: you fool with us and we're going after one of your own. They put Joe Wilson's wife in mortal danger because he had told the truth. They sent the message that you screw with us, there will be a heavy price to pay.

What they did to Valerie is what they really wanted to do to all of us who opposed the war. They tried to intimidate us. But it didn't work. The opposition to the war actually grew.

We were outraged when Rumsfeld treated Iraq-bound troops as an annoyance when they complained that they were being sent into combat with insufficient protection and aging equipment (they called it obsolete "hillbilly armor"). Rumsfeld said, "You go to war with the army you have, not the army you might want." I asked rhetorically on the Senate floor why Rumsfeld hadn't said, "Young man, you had the guts to ask the question and I am going to make every attempt to make sure we do everything we can to make you as safe as you can be."

I called for Rumsfeld's firing. I said he sat "and did nothing as things got worse." I blamed him for Abu Ghraib Prison and the fact that our country has never been held in lower esteem. I urged the president, who I knew was a loyal person, to be "loyal to the troops, loyal to the families, loyal to the American people and replace Rumsfeld."

Rumsfeld resigned on November 7, 2006. My criticism was the least of it. It was the American people, even those within his own party, who ultimately forced him out of office.

In March 2005, I joined a group of senators and members of the House for a quick visit to Iraq.

Patty Murray and Harry Reid were on the trip, as well as Dick Durbin, Bob Bennett, and a couple of other Republicans, including Lamar Alexander. The official word was the war was going well.

Just fine. On target.

Sure. This was the war that was supposed to end in "sixty or ninety days." So for me, the fact that it was still going on, but the official word was everything was "going well," led me to believe that, in fact, the war was not going fine, well, or good. Not at all.

I was a bit apprehensive about going, but my friend Patty Murray said, "If I can do it, you can do it." Patty was and is a very close colleague.

We stopped in Kuwait, where Stewart and all the other spouses had to stay behind.

"No family members to Iraq," they told us.

From the minute we got on the helicopter, we had to wear helmets. Then the big rotary blades lifted us off the ground and began to swerve violently from side to side to avoid any potential heat-seeking missiles fired from the ground as we flew low across the countryside out of Kuwait and into the war zone. Luckily, none were actually fired.

We landed safe and sound in Iraq, but were told to keep our heads way down, jump out, and run as fast as we could to a group of vehicles waiting for us.

General David Petraeus himself was sitting in my car.

"Senators! So good to see you," he said. "Things are going great and I want to show you the impressive training we're doing for these Iraqis."

He was all smiles. General Petraeus has a strong smile.

We drove straight to some training ground and got out.

"Look at these maneuvers we're teaching them today," Petraeus explained. "We're showing them how to protect a motorcade."

The Iraqi trainees were indeed involved in re-creating a mock attack on an official convoy, learning how to protect dignitaries. We watched them leap into action as the staged attack began. It was very impressive. But I couldn't be a nice quiet guest, so I started to ask questions.

"General Petraeus," I began, "how many troops have we already trained?"

"Tens and tens of thousands and they are terrific."

"So does that mean we can start bringing our troops home?" I asked.

"Well, that's something we're working toward."

"You've spent billions on this," I went on. I couldn't stop.

"Yeah," he said right back at me, "and it is going really well."

"That's wonderful."

The result of the argument was a draw, but I'm sure the general was sensitive to the drift...and prepared for it. He knew that would be my mantra when I got to talk about it at home.

After that we went to the American embassy, which had been set up in one of Saddam's former palaces, and had some meetings there. There was more of the same carefully prepared public relations spiel from the official welcomers. But I could tell from the look on some of those State Department personnel that they were scared as hell. So was I, even though we were in the Green Zone, the safest place to be, or so they told us.

Then we went to the Iraqi Parliament, but surrounded by Blackwater hired mercenaries, which I found pretty ironic. We have all these deployed and redeployed troops but still have to hire private guards from Blackwater? Despite all the security, moreover, we were told to duck and run from our armored cars into the Parliament building.

We were originally scheduled to have a meeting with the leaders of the Parliament, but they refused to meet together. Hmmm…interesting. We had to have separate meetings—first a meeting with the Shiites, then a meeting with the Sunnis, then with the Kurds—and I just fell in love with the Kurds. They said, "We don't know why those two groups keep fighting each other. We want everyone to come together."

I've always been a big fan of the Kurds. I want our government to help them more. One of their leaders said to me, "The Shiite and the Sunni, they call us the Jews. We Kurds are as Muslim as they are, but they don't like the way we practice."

Oh, boy, I thought. Even here in Iraq you can't get away from the smallest of the smallest minority religion being used as an insulting comparison in a political conflict that has nothing to do with them. But that is a whole other conversation.

We were supposed to have some kind of press conference, but first Patty and I wanted to use the ladies' room.

"You can't go into the ladies' room without me," a female Blackwater guard said.

So Patty and I followed her to the door of the bathroom.

"Hold it," our escort commanded.

Good thing this wasn't an emergency, I thought.

"Wait here."

She went toward a long line of stalls very slowly, crouching low, and kicked open each and every door, slamming it back against the next one. Patty and I looked at each other with a meaning that was clear to both of us.

What on earth are we doing in a place where you need someone to practically break down the bathroom door before you can even wash your hands?

Patty and I used the ladies' room and on the way out I whispered to her,

"Let's make that press conference very fast and get out of here." If the heavily guarded Parliament building wasn't safe, what was? How good could it be going—despite General Petraeus's reassuring smiles.

After the polite, softball press conference, a young reporter came up to me. He was practically shaking.

"This is a horrible situation here. The true story here is a nightmare. Tell everyone you can."

I told him I would. So when I went home after this visit, I was more for ending the war than before, and that is saying something. I escalated my efforts and my words on the Senate floor.

The direct attack of my speeches escalated. General Petraeus kept saying how these Iraqi soldiers are so great. I said, "Why do we have to put our own people through this if they are so great? They keep killing each other because of religion. We can't want democracy and freedom more than they want it for themselves.

"We went into Afghanistan to get the terrorists with the vote of every single senator," I went on. "Then we made a detour. The adventure in Iraq has weakened the war on terror... Iraq, Iraq, and more Iraq 24/7... no timelines, no hope, no vision, no plan. The only thing we know from this president is that as long as he is in power we'll be in Iraq."

In March of 2007, I rose to support a Reid amendment that would change the mission in Iraq away from combat, toward training Iraqi troops and counterterrorism. I called that amendment a "breath of fresh air in a situation where you can't even breathe, you are so suffocated from tragedy. From the deaths, from the wounds from the explosions every single day." And I said, "If you love the troops as we all do, why put them in the middle of a civil war where they can't tell who is shooting at them?"

That vote was forty-eight in favor to fifty opposed. It failed, but we had grown from twenty-three to forty-eight votes against the war.

On September 11, 2007, the sixth anniversary of bin Laden's attack, we had a hearing of the Senate Foreign Relations Committee during which I confronted General Petraeus.

"Back in November 2003," I reminded him, "you told the *Boston Globe* that 'We want to be seen as an army of liberation and not an army of occupation...there is a half-life on our role here, you wear out your welcome at some point. It doesn't matter how helpful you are. We aren't here to stay.'

"Please, General," I went on, "don't do what you did in 2004, when you painted a rosy scenario. Consider that others could be right. Listen to the Iraqi people. Seventy-nine percent of them oppose the presence of U.S. forces and 70 percent believe that the surge has made the security situation worse. Listen to them, to the American people, to the majority of Congress.

"Take off your rosy glasses..." I implored.

He didn't.

The same month, I quoted Ronald Reagan, who once said: "History teaches us that war begins when governments believe that the price tag of aggression is cheap," and then of course I compared that to Dick Cheney, who said, "They are in the last throes, if you will, of the insurgency." Sure. Like they said the war would end in a week!

It felt like nobody in high positions in the Bush administration cared enough about our soldiers.

"What would it be like if every person in the Cabinet lost a child?" I asked. "How much longer would this war last, but who's paying the price now? Our military families."

Whenever I mentioned death and injuries from the war, the Bush administration tried to change the subject, but I kept pressing. Hard.

The right wing chastised me severely for telling that to Condi Rice at a hearing. I was trying to find common ground with her and pointed out that she had no immediate family members in the war, and neither did I, since my kids were too old and my grandkids were too young. I got skewered for being "anti–single woman."

Me? Anti–single woman? Talk about below the belt.

As usual, Rush Limbaugh took the prize. He said, referring to my comment: "Here you have a rich white chick, with a huge big mouth, trying to lynch an African-American woman...hitting right below the ovaries."

Coming to my defense on the *McLaughlin Group* on January 14, 2007, was *Newsweek's* Eleanor Clift. She said, "Her [Boxer's] point is that a very small segment of society is bearing the burden of this war...And our elite, the people who send these people to war have...no personal investment...It is entirely appropriate what she said."

As the debate in the country raged about my statement, Gloria Steinem added her voice for me. "Senator Boxer was trying to draw a parallel between herself and Secretary Rice."

But the right wing wouldn't let go. They were very well organized.

Calls of outrage poured into the Capitol from those who detested my opposition to the war, among other things. I tried to explain my attempt to find this common ground, but it didn't matter. The clamor went on and on. I never backed down, nor did the other side. There were continuing calls for my resignation. Resign? Were they kidding? They didn't understand that I was never afraid of them. The more they came at me, the more I spoke out.

The far right skewered me again, when I asked an Army Corps general to call me "Senator" rather than "ma'am" at an official Senate hearing about flood control. I guess it is a crime in their eyes to speak in favor of protocol when they don't like you. They never stopped hissing and booing at me. But I expected it. It never bothered me. Never did. Never will. And by the way, the Army Corps general and I got along just fine after that.

Eventually our soldiers started to speak out more and more against the war. I pointed out one soldier who said, "It's a war between Iraqis, and we are just interfering and letting our soldiers die."

I begged the president to change. I asked him to "read a Red Cross report and an Iraq study group report." Then I asked the senators, "Doesn't he read these articles?"

I quoted Thomas Friedman, who said, "Our troops are protecting everyone and yet they are everyone's target." On October 2, 2007, my amendment failed; it would have ensured that Americans with serious felony convictions would no longer be able to serve in the military. I'm happy to say it finally passed in 2012. Americans with sex crimes on their record can no longer enlist. The least we can do is protect our soldiers from within.

It is my firm belief that if Senator John McCain had become president in 2008 we would still be surging and dying there in a never-ending conflict. Of course our challenges in Iraq continue because, as Colin Powell said, "Once you break it, you own it." But our combat mission is over.

Looking back at these years of frustration, there are clear lessons that I hope we have learned from the blunders in Iraq:

1. War should never be a first resort; only a last resort.
2. Don't get involved in a war of choice with faulty information.
3. Don't go it alone unless there is truly no other option.
4. Never put our troops in the middle of a religious or civil war.
5. Don't want something more for another nation than it wants for itself.
6. Don't get our soldiers killed for oil.
7. Don't tell lies.

Chapter Eight

Unforgettable Colleagues, a Lonely Dissent, and the Best Election Ever

Our group of senators was far from the only ones who fought passionately against the war in Iraq. In addition to our team in the Senate, over on the House side my dear friend and fellow Californian Nancy Pelosi, the highest-ranking female politician in American history and the only woman ever to serve as Speaker of the House, worked tirelessly with her team to stop the war from the moment George W. Bush sought authorization in 2002 to use the armed forces of the United States against Saddam Hussein.

"Tirelessly" is the word. Nancy is the most energetic human being on earth. Now, I know I'm considered extremely energetic. At one point my staff told me, "We have to hide your vitamin pills because we can't keep up with you." But Nancy is truly unbelievable. I don't know how she does it. I say this with tremendous admiration and love for her. And she is very tough, so tough.

Nancy and I come from different backgrounds. Nancy Patricia D'Alesandro is a Catholic girl from Baltimore, where her father, Thomas D'Alesandro, Jr. was the Democratic congressman from 1939 to 1947 and subsequently mayor of Baltimore from 1947 to 1959. Her brother, Thomas D'Alesandro III, was the mayor too, from 1967 to 1971. She and her husband, Paul Pelosi, moved to San Francisco in 1969, where Paul's brother Ronald was a member of the San Francisco Board of Supervisors. Nancy had grown up within the Democratic Party, first in Baltimore and then in California. She was born with Democratic politics in her blood and earned her stripes working through the system. I came at it in a totally different way.

Nancy always knew that party politics was her way to fight for change, so she came from within. I kind of stayed away from the party and was more of an outsider. The first office I ran for, the Marin County Board of Supervisors, was actually nonpartisan. You just ran as a human, without a D. or an R. next to your name.

Our paths first crossed when Phillip Burton died in 1983. Phil was succeeded in office by his wife, Sala. But she became ill with cancer, then picked Nancy to be her successor, and died just a month after being sworn in for her second term. I stayed out of the tough primary that Nancy won narrowly against San Francisco Supervisor Harry Britt that year, because he was a friend of mine and had helped me get elected, so it was a little uncomfortable between us at first. But Nancy and I were thrown together, working on important local issues, and both realized very quickly how much we liked each other.

Nancy took office in June of 1987, by which time I'd been in the House for four years. She now represented most of San Francisco and I represented a slice of the city and points north. It didn't take long to realize how great it was to have such a fierce partner. Everyone who knows Nancy says that she adds a lot to your life: heart, warmth, determination, loyalty, and a never-give-up attitude. It's invigorating to be around her because she brings such force and urgency to the work at hand.

But, yes, we not only came from totally different family experiences, but were brought up in different religions. She's Catholic and I'm Jewish. But what I learned at a very young age is that there is a huge amount in common between Italian families and Jewish families: very warm and very close relationships, a lot of love, and a lot of guilt. My best friend through high school was Juliette Cucco, an Italian Catholic. We were like sisters. She took me with her to confession, and I took her with me to bar mitzvahs. So as I came to know Nancy, I had that wonderfully familiar feeling. It was comfortable for both of us. We also faced absurd discrimination from within the House of Representatives and that brought us even closer. We had no idea when our friendship began in earnest that both of us would wind up making history in our careers.

There are photos of Nancy and me that I treasure which go back to our House days. We were constantly thrown together from 1987 until I ran for Senate as "the two women" who represented San Francisco, and wondered why our male predecessors were never introduced that way. We fought together against systemic prejudice against women in the House. We teamed up on AIDS and funding for rebuilding our infrastructure after the Loma Prieta earthquake in 1989. And we worked to rescue the Presidio army base as it was closing, since we didn't want to see it taken apart by private development.

So we became close. Our relationship was made as we traveled across the country together on those endless flights. Our husbands liked each other and our children became really good friends. She has five: Christine, Jackie, Nancy, Paul, and Alexandra. Christine and my daughter, Nicole, became very dear friends and they remain so today. Now their children are good friends—little six-year-olds. It's very sweet. Christine spent many happy times at the home I shared with Nicole and her family in D.C. and seeing Bella, Christine's daughter, with Sawyer, Nicole's son, makes Nancy and me glow because the friendships in our family now cover three generations.

I want to say this loud and clear: I believe Nancy's achievement in becoming the Speaker of the House in 2007 and her other leadership roles are not as appreciated or celebrated as they should be. Yes, there's been some recognition, like scholar Norman Ornstein at the American Enterprise Institute saying that the 111th Congress Nancy led was "one of the most productive Congresses in history." But as I write, I believe she's still not given enough credit for what it took for her to keep getting elected and sustaining the confidence of all those guys in the House of Representatives.

I served ten years in the House. I know firsthand what a male-dominated institution it was. It was when she got elected and still is now. For Nancy to win the confidence and support, not only of the relatively small number of women at that time but also the overwhelming support of the men in the House, is an amazing tribute to her intelligence, hard work, and personal skills.

Nancy is fearless and has said many times that "fear" is not a word in her vocabulary. She keeps everything in perspective.

"If they can't take my children away, then I can handle it," and "Politics is not for the faint of heart" are two of Nancy's truisms.

When I marvel at Nancy's ability to have won the trust of so many in the House, I remember that she was born into a family where she was the only girl out of six children. I am sure that she had to work to prove her tough side and I am sure she added a great perspective to their lives. Nancy had to learn to be relevant.

We shared the representation of San Francisco, and when I left the House, she began to rise up the ladder of influence and responsibility. I was proud of everything she did along the way. She never, ever was afraid to speak the truth to power.

In 2007, when Nancy was Speaker of the House, she responded to President Bush's statement that the Congress was "ineffective" and "the American people deserve better" by firing back at the president in strong terms: she called the president "a total failure, losing all credibility with the American people on the war, on the economy, on energy, you name the subject" and said that Congress had been "sweeping up after his mess over and over and over again."

Talk about tough.

There are few leaders as strong and courageous as Nancy. You can't intimidate her or in any way back her down. I so admire that, since the result of her actions included being scorned and vilified by the far right for her leadership in the House for decades. Too bad for them, when it comes to Nancy Pelosi.

We've had such fun together. I remember one time we decided to dress as the Andrews Sisters for a charity. I had arrived at the studio early for the publicity photo, when there was a knock on the door. I opened it and there she was. A vision of the forties.

I never laughed so hard with Nancy until one night in 1987, when Reagan was president, when we found ourselves at a White House Christmas party. This was right around the time that Congressman Barney Frank had confided to us and other colleagues that he was gay. It sounds easy now. It was far from easy then.

I remember Barney telling me that he and his partner, Herb, were going to the White House together. Again, sounds easy now. I told Barney I was excited for him and Herb and looked forward to seeing them at the party.

Barney, Herb, Nancy, and I stood near the dance floor. Then all four of us started to dance together when suddenly our two colleagues danced off without us.

So there we stood, Nancy and I. We looked at each other as we stood on the dance floor and laughed, thinking the same thing: It was one thing to strongly support our friends, but it was another to be dancing with each other. We didn't.

Now Barney is very kind to us in his memoir about this incident. He writes that he remembers us "graciously" walking away. I don't remember us being gracious, but we were cheerful about it, and that experience stuck with us. We both are pleased and relieved that in many places in our nation, the truth is being lived at last, when it comes to the LGBT community. The battle is not over, but it is moving in the right direction.

Another very important and amusing thing about my personal and political relationship with Nancy Pelosi over the years: Nancy and I actually look nothing alike. So who knows why, but we're often taken for each other. Yes, often.

It started when Nancy became whip in 2002, a very important leadership role in the House, and a photo went out with her holding a whip. I didn't realize how many people saw the photo until I found myself on a plane heading back to the Bay Area one day, and several fellow passengers came up to me with big smiles.

"We are so proud of you."

Okay. Great. I was pleased they liked my work in the Senate. Then, finally, after the tenth person came up and added: "Love the way you are holding that whip," I realized it was a case of mistaken identity, and was forced to correct the record.

"Oh, that's Nancy. I'm Barbara, your senator."

The constituents were so embarrassed that I was sorry I corrected them. They were deflated and so was I.

This comedy of errors continued when Nancy took the lead against human rights abuses in China. She opposed normal trade relations with them and I supported normal trade relations. I was often complimented for standing strong for human rights and sometimes yelled at for opposing normal relations with China. Once, when I was called out by a businessman, I told him, "I think you are confusing me with Nancy Pelosi. I *am* for normal trade relations."

"No, you're not!" And then he walked away, with me mumbling, "No, I'm not Nancy? Or no, I'm not for normal trade relations with China?"

I kind of gave up after that and just smiled when people said, "Hi, Nancy."

Another major event happened immediately before the awful period of our fight against the war in Iraq. Hillary Clinton was elected to the Senate in 2000.

I'm not sure how early in her husband's presidency she'd begun thinking about running, since she never said a word to me about it. But I do remember very clearly that I went to Camp David in 1999, while Nicole and Hillary's brother, Tony, were still married. I wanted to let Bill and Hillary know that I was hugely in favor of her running for the Senate from New York State, since Daniel Moynihan had decided to retire and the seat was open.

I couldn't grab Hillary, who was busy taking care of everyone's needs, so I decided to talk to the president alone. I went to his office at Camp David, where we had met many times during the period we were family. I laid it out from my perspective, saying that I knew New York was a really difficult place to run for office due to the harsh newspaper and TV coverage and their unrelenting punditry that always seemed abusive to me, but that New York had shown it was open to electing superstars like Robert Kennedy.

"Hillary should run," I told President Clinton. "She's so talented, such a good speaker."

He took it all in, not revealing his thoughts on the subject.

Stew and I had always marveled about who was the better speaker, Bill or Hillary, since they both had so many political skills. When Hillary ultimately decided to run, she became the first First Lady ever to pursue public office. They bought a home in Chappaqua, New York, just north of New York City, in September of 1999. Some of my male colleagues were surprised and couldn't understand how or why she'd run, not so much out of malice but concern. I felt their concern was misplaced and a bit condescending.

Chris Dodd, for one, came up to me looking very worried.

"What does she need it for?" he said in the sweetest way. "The New York press is ruthless."

"Don't you think women are tough enough to take the heat?" I responded. I really was incredulous, since the women who served with me at the time had gone through the same hellish campaigns as our male colleagues, and we made it. "Hillary has already gone through the hazing stage at every level, and she has proven to be up to the task."

In any case, Hillary built the support network she needed, was a great candidate, and won the Democratic primary. Her Republican opponent in the general election was Rick Lazio, a Republican congressman. Throughout the campaign, she was accused of being a "carpetbagger," since she'd never lived in New York State before, but she shrugged it off, visiting every county, taking a "listening tour" in small group settings.

In September, Lazio made a big mistake during a televised TV debate with Hillary by marching over to her podium, brandishing a piece of paper that he called the "New York Freedom from Soft Money Pledge" and demanded she sign it. Hillary refused. His demeanor and invasion of her personal space were startling, chauvinistic, and bullying. It offended me, along with a lot of other women, and was widely regarded as a decisive moment that led to Hillary winning on November 7, 2000, with 55 percent of the vote to his 43 percent.

We were all very excited when Hillary joined us. She didn't come in there and hog the spotlight or try to take over. Oh, no, she was low key and deferential to Chuck Schumer, the senior senator from New York, and to the other women in the Senate, to everyone. She joined the Environment and Public Works Committee, where Moynihan had made his name as a strong environmentalist. I had been there since 1993 and loved what she did on that committee, particularly focusing on children's environmental health. She became such a workhorse, on several other committees as well, but what really molded and determined her success as a senator was 9/11, a tragedy that changed the world, and she was in the very middle of it all.

It was just eight months after she had come to the Senate, where she had been absorbing the ways of the Senate, from speeches on the floor to the writing and passage of legislation in committees, adding her voice cautiously and learning the ropes. Then suddenly she was front and center with Chuck Schumer, responding to a vicious terrorist attack, thousands of deaths, and a new, fearful atmosphere for New York City in particular. By that time, Hillary had won the respect of her colleagues. Schumer and Clinton made a formidable team as the Senate passed a number of Hillary's bills, including the extension of unemployment benefits for 9/11 victims, new funds for emergency preparedness, and expedited benefit payments for first responders.

Hillary was there. She went down to the huge smoking crater at the World Trade Center in lower Manhattan. She called attention to the hazardous quality of the air around ground zero, despite strong assurances from the Bush administration that the atmosphere was safe and nobody was at risk. She demanded quality medical care for those who spent so much time in the middle of the debris, tirelessly finding remains. She was focused and she didn't let up. She doubled down when the TV cameras were off.

She and Chuck worked together to get billions of dollars of needed funds to restore the physical and mental well-being of the city they represented.

Along with every single United States senator, Hillary supported the 2001 invasion of Afghanistan, saying it was a chance to combat terrorism while improving the lives of Afghan women who were so abused under the Taliban. She didn't join me in opposing the invasion of Iraq, but gradually shifted her stance, and by 2005 said that Bush's pledge to stay indefinitely, "until the job is done," was misguided. And she voted against Bush's tax cuts for the rich, as well as the confirmation of John G. Roberts as Chief Justice and Samuel Alito to the U.S. Supreme Court.

The divorce between Nicole and Hillary's brother, Tony, happened around the time Hillary took office. It was a hard time for everyone involved. But, as I mentioned, we managed to keep working together politically, and when it came to family affairs, we focused our attention on Zach, Nicole and Tony's son—my grandson and Hillary's nephew. Whatever was best for him, we agreed.

My memories of George W. Bush's administration are pretty much shrouded in despair, punctuated with a few distinct moments of hope.

The first hopeful moment came with the 2004 presidential election and what I thought would be a sure win for our Democratic candidate John Kerry. The economy was stagnant and Bush's "mission accomplished" speech on May 1, 2003, rang hollow.

I was on the ballot myself for my third Senate term. My opponent was former California Secretary of State Bill Jones, who proved to be my weakest opponent so far.

It was a good year for me to be running. A presidential election brings out the vote, and although I'd taken a very unpopular position against the Iraq War in 2002, it was beginning to be seen as a position of conscience by a senator who didn't worry about being on the popular side of such a big moral issue. Public opinion was catching up with me.

Bill Jones's big issue was that I was "anti-military" and I was prepared for the charge when he made it during our TV debate.

I looked at him and told him to lay off.

"Listen, Bill," I said, "protecting our soldiers from wars of choice that are based on false pretense is not anti-military, it's pro-military." And besides, I added: "You never served in the military and my husband did. Stewart was in the Army Reserves for six years so I know what it feels like to be constantly worried about your husband being activated."

Bill Jones never went there again and I defeated him 57 percent to 37 percent, in a race with the most votes ever cast for a United States senator—just under 7 million—a record I held for eight years. That record stood until Dianne Feinstein overtook me in 2012, garnering 7.3 million votes in that Obama re-election year. Nice for both of us.

But election night 2004 was by no means all good news. Four years after hanging chads, the no-recount recount, and the Supreme Court stealing the election for George W. Bush, we were all very worried and sensitive to potential election irregularities this time around.

Sure enough, the morning after the election, Bush and Kerry were tied neck and neck. It was clear that the result in Ohio would decide the winner. Bush had established a lead of around 130,000 votes, but the Democrats pointed to provisional ballots, initially reported to number as high as 200,000, that had yet to be counted. The electoral vote in Ohio would determine who won that race.

And, wouldn't you know, there was clear evidence of systematic flaws during the voting process in Ohio. Having felt that we were robbed in 2000, I was nervous, my stomach churning, as I watched the Ohio vote come in. Suddenly pictures appeared on the screen showing impossibly long lines snaking around the blocks in a predominantly African American neighborhood in Cleveland, Ohio.

Hours went by, until that afternoon Ohio Secretary of State Ken Blackwell announced that it was statistically impossible for the Democrats to make up enough valid votes in the provisional ballots to win. At the time provisional ballots were reported as numbering 140,000 (and later estimated to be only 135,000).

Faced with this announcement, John Kerry conceded defeat.

But wait a minute, I said to myself. It was raining all that day in Cleveland. What happened to those voters? How many didn't vote because the line moved so slowly that the polls eventually closed? And what about voters who just couldn't get soaked for five or ten hours without shelter, for health reasons? And if you were elderly or had a child with you or had a short window to vote because of work, could you have waited hours and hours? Decidedly no. Voting is a privilege for sure, but it is also a right—a right that Americans not only died for abroad in wars, but also here at home.

The next days were unsettling for me. I hadn't objected to the Electoral College vote after Bush "beat" Gore. Any senator or House member could make an objection to the electoral count in a particular state, but Al Gore had asked us not to dwell on the court decision. He made a remarkable speech about bringing the country together for which he won great praise, and I complied, I never objected. But the price was too high. The terrible damage Bush's presidency was doing to the country was in full force in 2004, and I couldn't agree so meekly this time around. It went against the art of tough.

Therefore, at the official counting of the electoral votes on January 6, I joined Stephanie Tubbs Jones, the African-American congresswoman who represented most of Cleveland, Ohio, in a motion contesting Ohio's electoral votes.

Stephanie was a former judge from Ohio who became a congresswoman following the retirement of Louis Stokes, a fine member with whom I had served in the House. She was sharp and straightforward and I admired her from afar.

I had read some of her comments in the press, saying, "How can we tell millions of Americans to simply get over it and move on?"

When we met, Stephanie, who'd been re-elected to Congress four times, told me that she had personally witnessed voter after voter giving up, not being able to vote, and she was sick about it. I pressed her really hard. I knew the scorn that would come my way from all sides, so I wanted to be on solid ground. Stephanie said she would be very proud to stand with me in the well of the House and object to the certification of the Electoral College vote.

So we did object, Stephanie from the House, me from the Senate. We stood alone. Nobody else who could do anything about it really cared, not even one other senator. People basically looked at us askance, as if to say, "You are on a fool's errand." Years later, though, a few people who could have done something about it finally said we did the right thing.

Kerry himself said later that is was impossible to really know whether the Ohio vote reflected the voters' will. Howard Dean, chairman of the Democratic National Committee, expressed his concerns, citing "substantial voter suppression and unreliable machines." He used words like "unethical" and "manipulation."

And did I mention the voting machine controversy? The voting machines used in the 2004 Ohio presidential elections were manufactured by Diebold Election Systems. The chairman of the board and CEO of Diebold was a generous contributor to Bush's re-election campaign, had visited the president's Texas ranch, and pledged to help "Ohio deliver its electoral votes to the President."

The touch-screen voting method of the Diebold machines, by the way, created no paper trail. You voted and that was it. No way to have a recount. An open invitation to corruption.

We had already decertified all Diebold Election Systems touch-screen voting machines in California because of security flaws. Studies indicated all kinds of problems in these machines compared to other voting machines.

Nevertheless, Stephanie and I were laughed at, hooted at, even scoffed at.

The comments of my Republican colleagues were colorful. Senator Mike DeWine of Ohio couldn't wait to spew his venom at me, senatorial courtesy aside. Here he was about to win a big victory, as not one senator would stand with me, but he felt compelled to address me personally:

"Because I am limited under the rules to five minutes, I will not have the time to respond to the wild, incoherent and completely unsubstantiated charges that have been made..."

He quoted from an editorial that said I was "driving myself further toward the political fringe and that long grass is already tickling my knees."

Of course he ignored the newspaper editorials that confirmed the voting irregularities. Apparently he had absolutely no sympathy for his own Ohio colleague Representative Tubbs Jones, who deserved at least some respect, not to mention his own constituents who were unable to vote due to impossibly long lines and the rain.

Here's an interesting postscript to Mike DeWine. He did lose his re-election race for the Senate two years after his righteous outburst about the integrity of the Ohio voting system. He was replaced by an extremely effective progressive named Sherrod Brown.

Ultimately, we were only able to delay the inevitable electoral vote count for four hours. I said, "We cannot keep turning our eyes away from a flawed system." I knew there were undisputed reports of a shortage of voting machines with no alternative equipment, discriminatory challenges at polling places, and obstruction of voting. There were some reports that some students at Kenyon College had to wait in line for ten hours, the last votes being cast at four a.m. In Columbus, in a black neighborhood, it was substantiated that people waited for four hours in the rain. Many left without voting.

Long lines suppressed the vote. The *Washington Post* reported that six of the seven wards with the fewest voting machines were Kerry wards, while twenty-seven of thirty wards with enough voting machines were the wards that voted for Bush.

And me? After the grass tickled my knees from the political fringe?

I won another election to the Senate by more than one million votes, while Ohio became the Florida of 2004, and I believe another presidential election result remained under a cloud called George W. Bush.

Four years later, on August 20, 2008, we lost Stephanie Tubbs Jones. She died in her car from a cerebral hemorrhage, way too young at fifty-eight. It was not only a loss to her family but to the cause of equal justice and fair voting and all the issues she believed in.

I really miss her. Stephanie and I were thrown together by our shared sense of outrage and injustice. She saw the suppression with her own eyes; the civil rights movement was in my DNA. She was a great partner. We made our voices heard and I am proud of that.

*   *   *

Too many people like Stephanie have been lost in my time. Paul Wellstone, Ted Kennedy, John Chafee, all of whom woke up every day with one thought: whom can I help? These were my kind of senators.

The lines in Ohio were a sample of what was to come in the presidential election of 2012. We saw them in Florida and Virginia. Why is it always in Democratic areas? It made me have that same wave of unease and dread when I saw those lines. Had it been a close election, who knows what could have happened?

Are we now at a time and place in which Democratic candidates have to win with large margins just to be sure the election won't be stolen? It has become clear in state after state, with the help of the court that overturned part of the Voting Rights Act, that voting is becoming harder and harder. Lines around the block, ridiculous voter ID laws, smaller windows for early voting... these are just some of the obstacles.

In January of 2013, I wrote a simple bill, co-sponsored by Senator Bill Nelson of Florida, which is called the LINE Act. That stands for "Lines Interfere with National Elections." It's simple. If you had to wait more than a half hour in line while waiting to vote, then your county needs to write a remedial plan for the next election approved by the Justice Department. Remedies could include more voting machines, more early voting, and more voting precincts. This is not rocket science.

Chuck Schumer of the Rules Committee called a hearing on the bill and the testimony by Nelson and me went very well. Clear questions and clear answers. I thought we would get that simple bill through.

Chuck told me that the ranking Republican on the committee, Senator Pat Roberts, with whom I have a cordial relationship, thought the bill was good and contained common sense. But then he said he simply couldn't support it. This is so sad. What's happening to Republicans? It must be that when more people vote, Democrats win. End of story.

It's so simple. Don't fear the voters, work for them and their rights, and then they'll vote for you.

But the Republicans don't get it. There has been a red state epidemic of voter suppression laws. They are asking voters to bring the kinds of identification that are very difficult for low-income voters, students, or senior citizens to obtain, like a driver's license or a photo ID that sometimes requires a long trip to the county seat to acquire. Passports are fine, but you don't need a degree in voter suppression to know who has those.

The voting rights battle is another example of the need for constant vigilance. It has been such a long and arduous road from women's suffrage to the African American vote. Who would have thought that in this century we would still be facing this new form of voter suppression?

But I see hope. The media is very aware of this problem and it is being exposed. Also, if we can't pass the bills we need to stop it, people will find a way to vote regardless. They will get angry that something is being taken away from them and they'll be determined to preserve it. We are already seeing organizations gearing up to be of assistance, driving people to the courthouse, helping them obtain the ID they need, and advocating for them.

When Americans see elderly voters of all races on television telling their stories about being blocked from the voting booth after a lifetime of voting, it begins to make a difference in public opinion. When they see college students being challenged at the polls as they try to vote for the first time, they'll be angry. They see that all this talk about "voter fraud" is basically just that—talk. It's a disgrace that Congress and the Supreme Court are not advocating for this basic right.

We need a change in Congress and the courts so that those institutions passionately back the right to vote for all of us. Voting in America is nothing less than the centerpiece of our nation. It makes our democracy the envy of the world. But that change requires more, not fewer, people voting, doesn't it?

In 2004, my old friend and colleague Dick Durbin, the senior senator from Illinois, took me aside to tell me about this great candidate running for the Democratic Senate primary in Illinois in 2004.

"He's only forty-three years old, a very smart and charismatic African

American, Columbia University, Harvard Law School, worked as a community organizer and taught constitutional law at the University of Chicago Law School."

"What about his political experience?" I asked. "How did he get to be running for senator?"

"He's represented the thirteenth district in the Illinois Senate for three terms, lost an election for the U.S. House of Representatives in 2000, but looks strong to win the Democratic Party primary in March. I think he's on his way to Washington, D.C., for sure."

"Sounds impressive," I agreed. "What's his name?"

"Barack Hussein Obama."

"Wow...well," I said, in one of my great prognostications, "he may be great, but who is going to vote for a guy whose name will remind them of *Osama* bin Laden or Saddam *Hussein,* for that matter. He'll never win that Senate race."

"No, listen, Barbara, the guy has something special. No kidding. There's only one man my wife would leave me for...Barack Obama. You'll see... just wait," he said.

I did wait and see. Dick was right. I was wrong. In March of 2004, Barack won an unexpected landslide to become the Democratic candidate for senator, which made him an overnight rising star in the national Democratic Party.

A few months later, I was in Chicago, raising money for my own 2004 Senate campaign at a private party in someone's home, when this very tall, beautiful woman walked into the room. Her entrance definitely started a buzz.

"Who's that?" I asked the hostess.

"Michelle Obama," she told me. "Barack's wife."

I thought how nice it was for her to stop by while her husband was running himself.

The first time I saw Barack in action was when he delivered the keynote address at the Democratic National Convention in July 2004. Stewart and I never missed a convention. I'll never forget the terrific speech he made.

"We're not a red country or a blue country, we're a red, white, and blue country," he said. "There's not a liberal America and a conservative America—there's the *United States* of America."

Nine million people were watching this on TV and I'm sure they were all as impressed as I was.

"In no other country on Earth is my story even possible," he proclaimed. "A skinny kid with a funny name who believes that America has a place for him too. The audacity of hope is God's greatest gift to Americans, allowing me to feel optimistic that the lives of average Americans can be improved with the right governmental policies."

Right after the speech political commentator Chris Matthews said, "I just saw the first black president." And he was right, too.

In November, Obama was elected to the Senate with 70 percent of the vote. When he arrived in Washington, he was on two of my committees—Environment and Public Works, and Foreign Relations—so I was able to watch him make a difference in every debate he engaged in. He made you see the issues just a little bit differently and he challenged your assumptions. I remember working with him, but more than that, I remember watching him. He was so effective as a speaker, whether the issue was lead in children's toys or the war in Iraq. I remember he tried to bridge both sides, find common ground, all the time. And he was very good at that. I also found Barack to be kind of an old soul. Even though he was so much younger than me, we could talk about shows and plays and songs from my generation. He just had a wonderful way about him. We had an easy relationship.

Then everything turned upside down. Not our camaraderie, but his forward momentum and its impact.

One day late in 2006, Barack approached me on the floor of the Senate where we were having a series of votes and asked if I could step outside the chamber for a moment. So we went into the senator's lobby, a private hall with couches and chairs, and sat down, one of us on a couch, the other on a chair.

"Barbara," he said, "I'm thinking about running for president next year. What do you think about that?"

I was shocked. It was very sweet and respectful the way he did it, but I was shocked. I didn't expect it.

"Really?" I managed to say, in a kind of choked-up whisper.

"Really. This coming election."

I knew that Hillary Clinton was already the prohibitive favorite.

"You know Hillary is running and she's going to win. She's a wonderful candidate. She's organized... Have you thought that maybe this isn't the best time for you to do this? It's early, you're young." My voice trailed off.

"Yes, of course I know I'll be considered a long shot," Barack said. "But my instincts are telling me something else. I have a feeling about this."

I was about to try to talk him out of it, but then I thought of the times in my own career when everyone said I didn't have a chance.

"Barack, you have to follow your heart. If you feel this is your time, then go for it. You gotta do what you gotta do, because you'll always regret it if you don't."

But then I added *again*: "Hillary's going to win, so you better be prepared. You'll never beat Hillary."

That was my attempt to give him a dose of reality. But he didn't let it go.

"You never know."

And then he smiled that fabulous smile and ducked back into the Senate chamber.

Two things about that conversation:

1. I was wrong (again) about his chances.
2. He was right to go for his dreams, just as Hillary was right to go for hers.

I don't know if he talked to a lot of other people, asking for their opinions. I don't know if he came to me because he thought I'd be for Hillary and wanted to see my reaction. But I do know his running created an impossible situation for me. A few months later, when the campaign started up full steam ahead, I told the press it was like choosing between a sister and a son. I respected and cared so much for both of them. It was an impossible choice.

My solution was to not campaign for either one of them, which was not well received by Hillary's supporters. Luckily, I wasn't running for re-election myself in 2007, so I was able to maintain a low profile. At least for a while. Then I got in trouble with Bill and Hillary. Well, really just Bill.

Barack announced he was a candidate in the primary campaign for the Democratic presidential nomination on February 10, 2007. Nine days later, he appeared at a major fund-raiser for me in San Francisco. It was highly unusual for a presidential candidate in a tough primary fight to make such an appearance at the start of his or her own campaign, but Barack had promised this to me, as we both knew how crucial it was for me to begin fund-raising in earnest for my 2010 election. Yes, my next campaign was three years away, but that's the way it works. You have to start fund-raising early.

Barack's staff tried to get him out of it, but he insisted. He'd given his word. I'm glad he came, because our event was fantastic, a huge success on all levels. My friends and supporters in San Francisco loved him.

His appearance, however, set off alarm bells in the Clinton camp, since I'd told everyone I wasn't going to campaign for either side. I tried to explain that this was just a follow-through commitment he'd made to me before the primary campaign began, but I'm pretty sure they didn't believe me. And from that moment on and for a long time afterward, President Clinton didn't speak to me. Oh, maybe a "hi" and "bye" when it was unavoidable, but that was it. The big chill.

For example, 2010 turned out to be a terrible year to be running as a Democrat. President Clinton went all over the country for everyone else— but not for me.

I understood why Bill did that. He felt I had failed to support his wife in 2007, when she was in what turned out to be a tough and ultimately losing campaign for the nomination. Well, I have a husband. Stewart still remembers every single individual who didn't help me in my 1972 election to the Marin Board of Supervisors. Spouses get hurt. Husbands take it hard. So I understood President Clinton's cold shoulder.

After 2010 the ice broke. I was so relieved. I was never angry at Bill. Loyalty is loyalty to him. He's tough and I respect it and never took it personally. That's being tough too.

In contrast, Barack called me on my cell phone and left me a voice message after he learned I would stay out of the race. He told me that he understood how tough that was for me, and that he appreciated it. I never deleted that message and have it still.

Barack won the primary in 2008, in any case, so then I was free to help our standard-bearer. I worked hard to bring the Hillary camp into the Obama camp, saying shortly after the primary vote that "we women should be proud, not angry. The glass ceiling has been shattered. Hillary said it herself. It's been shattered by her and it's been shattered by Barack."

And when Wolf Blitzer asked me on CNN, "How can you bring those Hillary supporters around to actually support Barack Obama?" I shot back, "As much as people in the media like to report bad news, I think when everyone takes a hard, cold look at these two candidates, McCain and Obama, and sees what they represent and believe in, women particularly will flock to Obama's side, not only because of his life story and the fact that he was raised by a single mom and a grandma, or that he's married to a working woman who has to balance all the demands of a busy career and being a mother, but because of the voting records of the two men on women's issues—the freedom to choose, equal wages for equal hours, fighting sexual abuse and domestic violence."

Meanwhile, I issued what would be the first of many statements pointing out the dangers of having Sarah Palin running for vice president.

"The vice president is a heartbeat away from becoming president, so to choose someone with not one hour's worth of experience on national issues is a dangerous choice... If John McCain thought that choosing Sarah Palin would attract Hillary Clinton voters, he is badly mistaken. The only similarity between her and Hillary Clinton is that they're both women. On the issues, they couldn't be further apart. If he wanted to choose a woman, he should have chosen Senators Olympia Snowe or Kay Bailey Hutchison."

In October, the Obama campaign asked me to go around the country to help them turn out the women's vote, the Jewish vote, the progressive vote. I said yes, yes, and yes, and went to Ohio, where I represented Barack at a debate with McCain surrogate Governor Linda Lingle of Hawaii at a Jewish center in Cincinnati. I also went to Florida with our dear friends the Bergmans and the Goldbergs, where we did our part to get out the Jewish vote for Barack. Gary Goldberg had written the iconic TV series *Brooklyn Bridge* and regaled the seniors with stories from the old days. They loved it. I also went to Minnesota and wound up back in California where my campaigns had started.

I went to the Democratic headquarters in Marin where they were working on getting out the vote. One of my pitches from that appearance was this:

"About Sarah Palin: I'd rather have a vice president who thinks, not winks."

I'm sure this quip had nothing to do with it, but California went for Barack Obama 61 percent to 37 percent. He defeated John McCain 52.9 percent to 45.7 percent in the popular vote and 365 to 173 in the Electoral College. What had seemed impossible had happened, to the great joy of millions of Americans, including me: we had our first African-American president.

Not only that, in mid-November 2008, President-elect Obama and Hillary Clinton discussed the possibility of her serving as his secretary of state. Hillary did ask me what I thought about that, and I told her I thought it was great.

"I hate to lose you from the Senate, but secretary of state is a *huge* honor and responsibility and the president needs someone high-profile as he deals with so many economic problems at home."

Confirmation hearings before the Senate Foreign Relations Committee began on January 13, 2009. Two days later, the committee voted 16 to 1 to approve Clinton, and on January 22, 2009, the Senate voted overwhelmingly to approve her appointment.

President Lincoln, who was the first to put together his "team of rivals," would have been proud. And I was so proud of Hillary. She was strong to have seen her dream die and yet help her rival's dream come true.

The inauguration of Barack Obama as the forty-fourth President of the United States was on a blustery cold Tuesday, January 20, 2009. It set a record attendance for any event held in Washington, D.C. It was seen on television and the Internet all over the world. My fellow California senator, Dianne Feinstein, chair of the Joint Congressional Committee on Inaugural Ceremonies, acted as the day's master of ceremonies, the first woman to preside over a U.S. presidential inauguration. The San Francisco Boys Chorus and San Francisco Girls Chorus performed and Aretha Franklin sang "My Country, 'Tis of Thee."

I still have to pinch myself that all this really happened. A miracle!

As usual, I had a dose of reality. With a house full of guests who'd all come to celebrate, my basement pipes froze and water shot throughout the basement, making it a nightmare with torn-out carpet and loud fans throughout. But we put it into perspective and didn't let it "dampen" our joy.

By then, Nicole had married Kevin Keegan, Zach's Little League baseball coach, and they had moved to a wonderful Capitol Hill historic Victorian with room for Stew and me in the basement. Nicole's family now included a brother for Zach, Sawyer, born in 2009. Two more grandchildren also added to our joy: Zain and Reyna, born to Doug and Amy in 2007 and 2009. The timing of this happiness couldn't have been better, given what was to come.

Elections are tough. The only one I've ever lost was my first in 1972 for Marin County supervisor, and it was to a very nice guy. Most of my other opponents in the ensuing forty years weren't as nice, and in all candor, I wasn't always so nice either.

When you've been battle-hardened by tough opponents, you learn that simply telling the voters your stand on the issues may not be enough to win. Not even explaining your deeply held views and having enough funds to do it in a captivating way may be enough. That's because your most unsavory and unscrupulous opponents will often distort your story and your positions and even the essence of your being. Eventually you see yourself depicted in the media, negative advertising, and public debates in a way that you can't recognize any longer as truly you.

No opponent did that better to me than Carly Fiorina, my last opponent in 2010.

Fiorina was then a fifty-five-year-old former business executive. She had been the chief executive officer of Hewlett-Packard from 1999 to 2005 and an executive at AT&T before that. While she was chief executive at HP, the company lost half of its value. In 2005, Fiorina was forced to resign as chief executive officer and chair of HP following "differences [with the board of directors] about how to execute HP's strategy." Not only that, my staff found out that she'd been ranked frequently as one of the worst tech CEOs of all time.

For example, Professor Jeffrey Sonnenfeld at Yale University Business School described her as "the worst tech CEO because of her ruthless attack on the essence of this great company," noting that "she destroyed half the wealth of her investors and yet still earned almost $100 million in total payments for this destructive reign of terror." NBC, CBS, and *USA Today* said pretty much the same thing about her.

The *Los Angeles Times* wrote that Fiorina had conservative positions, opposed abortion, and voted for Proposition 8, which defined marriage as a union between one man and one woman, thereby prohibiting same-sex marriage.

In one of her attack ads on TV, Carly called my concern about global warming "worrying about the weather" and claimed the scientific research on the subject was "inconclusive...I think we should have the courage to examine the science on an ongoing basis." She accepted large contributions from the coal industry as well as from Koch Industries, the multinational oil, chemical, and energy company well known for its $400 million (and counting) in fines for environmental violations and hundreds of millions spent on conservative politicians and institutions. She also opposed the carbon pollution legislation I supported, and thought any efforts to control greenhouse gases would cost three million jobs and be "massively destructive."

By October 22, it became public that Fiorina had contributed $6.5 million to her own race. I guess she thought that her run for the Senate, despite not having one minute of experience in any elected office, would offer her a diversion from thinking about her record in the private sector, where she was repeatedly fired. And it appeared that she saw no impediment to her ambitions. Well, it's a free country! Good luck.

When Bill Jones had gone on the attack back in 2004, I pointed out that in contrast to him, my husband had served in the National Guard and could have been called up for active duty for a period of six years. I talked about how anxious my family was every time there was an international crisis and therefore we totally understood the anguish felt by families of National Guardsmen who were being called up in unprecedented numbers. That particular opponent never brought up that line of attack again.

About three weeks before the election of 2012, however, a right-wing blog supporting Carly Fiorina called my Senate office to say that I had no proof that my husband actually served in the military.

"We want to see proof," they demanded, "or we're going to write that Boxer made it all up."

What?

My campaign staff took over the request.

"This is easy," they told me. "Just find the discharge papers."

Really? Let's see…the discharge papers were more than forty years old. We searched everywhere. Meanwhile, the bloggers kept calling and threatening to run the story. When we couldn't find anything in our usual files for that kind of old paperwork, we decided to call the Army. Surely they would have copies of the honorable discharge papers. But they had no way of tracing them quickly because when Stewart was in the military they didn't store any records by Social Security number, but rather his ten-digit military identification number, which of course we didn't have.

We asked them how long it would take them to find his papers without that number. They said, "Oh, just a few months." We only had a few days!

"Deadline's up. We're going with the story that your husband never served in the military," the blog people threatened again.

"You can't do that. He really did serve," we protested. "One more day…"

Scouring our home, I found a store-bought card that I'd sent Stewart on the occasion of his military discharge. It was dated 1961, frayed around the edges. In it I had written one of my quickie rhymes:

Those manly days are over
Those days of strength and brawn
And now you know the answer,
To son, "Why were you born?"

You served your country to the end
Never wandered, never roamed
You stayed at Dix, your honor high
and made it your new home
Now six months are over
You'll miss those lovely men.
But I've got special news for you,
I've signed you up again!

Would this be proof? Knowing what was at stake, I doubted it. If the Fiorina campaign could say that I made up a part of my life story, they would probably say I made up that card with the silly poem too.

Here I was arguing in the press about jobs, the economy, war and peace, women's rights, and education and behind the scenes, in between prepping for appearances and press conferences, I'm rummaging through every part of my house looking for a forty-year-old document. Part of me was laughing but another part was crying.

Then I discovered that love really can conquer all.

In a last-ditch effort to find the ID number, I searched the laundry room. I readily admit I am not a great housekeeper. It's definitely not my strong point and one reason is that I'm a saver. I may have a case of what psychologists call a "hoarding disorder." But in this case it was a blessing.

I stood next to my washer and dryer, surrounded by shelves of old detergents and fabric softeners, when I noticed that in one of my little cubbyholes, packed in with unopened packages of sponges, was an old box.

I took it down, opened it, and there was a packet of letters, which I took out to read with trembling hands. They were love letters written on crinkly onionskin paper from Stewart, dated 1961, and each with a return address from Fort Dix, New Jersey, including his ten-digit military ID number.

And that saved us from this made-up garbage. The army sent us the discharge papers and the public never learned about this ridiculous diversion. This incident shows how you never know going into a campaign what will hit you and when, especially when you run against someone like Carly Fiorina.

The main lesson of a high-profile race is that you can't hide your record *or your character*. To learn all you had to know about Carly Fiorina, all you had to do is meet with even a couple of the wonderful people she'd stepped on as she went up the ladder of corporate America. You can't outsource thousands of jobs and bring pain to so many so callously without paying a price yourself. We met with some of those people, and they were willing to tell the truth about the way she treated them.

In any case, something else occurred that suddenly revealed the true Carly Fiorina. It was even more bizarre than the video they produced showing my face as one huge, swollen, hot air balloon floating from Washington, D.C., to California, where I'd been an elected public servant since 1976, all the while mumbling nonsense, looking like a freak, and finally exploding with a big pop from all the overinflated hot air.

I had to hide that one from my grandkids.

But what I'm referring to as unexpected and bizarre is something else, a totally absurd and ultimately very damaging event that Fiorina didn't plan. But, as I said, your character comes out in a campaign, try as you might to control things.

Dana Milbank told the story in the *Washington Post*. Carly Fiorina got a rather unfriendly welcome to the big leagues yesterday. She made the rookie mistake of assuming the video camera and microphone she was wearing while having her makeup done for an appearance on KXTV in Sacramento were not turned on. So a video with sound was created for everyone to watch as she scrolled through her BlackBerry, yawned and said of her opponent Barbara Boxer, "God, what is that hair?" She laughed and touched her own hair, adding, "Sooo yesterday."

The *Huffington Post* ran the story with a blazing headline GOP SENATE CANDIDATE MOCKS BARBARA BOXER'S HAIR, and also ran the complete video with Fiorina's entire open mike moment. Other print and broadcast media covered it in similar fashion all over country. It went viral.

So it wasn't my ideas, my politics, my philosophy, the recession, women's rights, the environment—no, her focus was on my hairstyle, which she dubbed "so yesterday." Well, the campaign took a big turn—not to my hair, fortunately, which does have a life of its own—but to her character.

Our campaign strategy shifted to ads with a few of the thirty thousand former employees explaining their suffering as she shipped their jobs overseas while rewarding herself with millions. The picture that emerged of Fiorina from those sad testimonies, plus her own self-inflicted hair comments, was of someone self-absorbed, nasty, and greedy.

With only one week until Election Day, however, the Fox News/Rasmussen and Reuters polls reported there was less than three percentage points between Fiorina and me. So we decided to bring in the big guns, and make a "full-court press," as my husband, Stewart, the former basketball star, would say.

First President Obama came to Los Angeles with me just eleven days before the election.

"In two events at the University of Southern California," reported RTTNews, "Obama lauded Boxer, calling her one of his 'all-time favorite senators...Barbara is somebody who's got more fight in her than anybody I know. And she's always fighting for the right reason.' Obama credited Boxer's support for the Democratic legislative achievements of the past two years, from enacting a middle class tax cut, creating jobs and rebuilding roads in the stimulus bill, to standing up to insurance companies and fighting for the health of her state with healthcare reform.

"Boxer," RTT went on, "an 18-year incumbent, finds herself this year in an unexpectedly close race with former Hewlett Packard CEO Carly Fiorina in a state where a GOP victory could upset Democrats' control of the Senate."

At USC that day, I added,

"While my opponent was laying off thirty thousand workers, she was taking a hundred million dollars in pay and perks for herself, including twenty-one million dollars on the day that she was fired. Imagine that. The average Californian would have to work two hundred years full time to make what my opponent took on the day she got fired.

"Now Carly Fiorina says she wants to go to the U.S. Senate from California," I added, "and do for the country what she did for HP. And that's exactly what we're worried about, isn't it?"

After that, Barack came up to San Francisco for a reception at the Fairmont Hotel and dinner at the home of Ann and Gordon Getty.

First Lady Michelle Obama was also an enormous help, raising more than $150,000 for California Vote 2010, a joint committee for me and the Democratic National Committee.

"It's because of folks like Barbara that we accomplished health care and financial reform in such a short time," she said. "We believe in some simple truths: if you're sick, you should be able to see a doctor . . . and you should be able to earn a living wage."

Never one to stay in the background, I couldn't help but add: "This race is between someone who wants jobs in China and someone who wants them in Chino." Okay. Not so brilliant, but it sounded good in the moment.

What Barack and Michelle Obama did for me at the very end of the campaign really made a difference, I'm sure, adding to the momentum of Carly's "caught on the air" attack on my hair. I don't know anyone who hasn't had a bad hair day. I figured if every Californian who ever had a bad hair day voted for me, I would win big. And I did.

I beat her by ten percentage points, 52.2 percent to 42.2 percent. I had

5,218,441 votes and she had 4,217,366. And that's how I was re-elected to the Senate for the fourth time.

Big sigh of relief.

Back to work.

One of my favorite poems relates to my 2010 Senate win over Carly Fiorina:

As I struggled to keep my state blue
Amid jobs that were falling and few
That Carly would care
To focus on hair
It's clear that she hasn't a clue.

It's a fact that my hair
Is sometimes a mess
But I think that voters would clearly confess
If a senator's hair's always perfect and right
She'd probably have little time left for the fight.

While she feathered her nest
And had the best hair
The voters said no by a one million share.
They stuck with the lady who didn't have fashion
But worked for them hard
With all of her passion.

Chapter Nine

The Crash, Leaders,
Sexual Harassment 2.0,
and the Sudden Partisanship
of the Environment

In late September 2008, I was spending a weekend at home, when my phone rang.

"Barbara! It's Harry Reid."

It was unusual for Harry to call me on the weekend, but then he went on.

"I'm on the line with about thirty Democratic senators—everyone I could reach," he said. "We have a crisis on our hands. Treasury Secretary Hank Paulson asked for this emergency call and Chairman of the Federal Reserve Ben Bernanke is also on the line."

It was less than two months before the presidential election, at the climax of the campaign between Barack Obama and John McCain. Hank Paulson sounded like he was nearly hysterical. He told us in a quick, tense narrative that our economy was "on the brink of failure" and the housing crisis had caused all the problems.

"The banks have been issuing new kinds of derivative securities backed by mortgages," he said, "and some of these mortgages turned out to be pretty shaky. Not only that," he went on, "the new securities don't have just one mortgage behind them, but slices and dices of a whole bunch of mortgages." He talked about "credit default swaps" and "collateralized debt obligations" and a few other terms that were new for most of us on the call. I don't remember all the questions the senators asked, but I could tell everyone was in shock. Someone wondered aloud, "How could we be sitting on a devastating economic earthquake when just a few weeks ago President Bush said the economy was on solid ground?"

I asked whether taxpayers would ever be repaid by Wall Street and the big banks. "Is this a total giveaway?" I said. Bernanke said we would hold papers, become partners with all these firms, and yes, taxpayers would be made whole when we "get out of this mess." I was skeptical. He was right, as it turns out.

We pressed for the bottom line. Paulson wanted close to one trillion dollars in taxpayer money to bail out the banks, and as far as we could tell, he wasn't suggesting any regulatory reform nor one idea of holding anyone accountable.

Those of us on the call knew we had to act, but we also agreed not to give a blank check to an administration that caused all these problems in the first place by turning a blind eye to Wall Street and the greed and excesses they exhibited. On that call it was clear that we Democrats would insist on better oversight and regulation if we were going to bail out the banks. You could hear it in our voices—tense verging on angry.

On October 3, 2008, one month before the presidential election, we passed the bailout bill. We molded it from its original incarnation to be far more balanced—we included greater FDIC protections for bank depositors which, as I said on the Senate floor, was "crucial to deterring an epidemic of bank closures—something that was at the heart of the Great Depression."

Supporting this bill was not pleasant for me. That's an understatement. My gut told me we had to pass it to save the economy from total collapse, unfreeze credit, and restore confidence. But my heart kept reminding me that those reckless, selfish Wall Street players should just sink.

The problem was if we didn't act everyone would sink.

It didn't help that in my mind was a constant replay of the secretary of the treasury, Hank Paulson, standing just two feet in front of me at an urgent meeting answering questions from nervous senators. I raised my hand. "Mr. Secretary, can you explain in simple terms what a credit default swap is?" He looked down, placed both his hands at the sides of his head and said quietly, but emphatically, "Not now!" Not a confidence builder.

We cut $300 billion from the package and then added $16 billion in incentives for renewable energy business and billions more for tax relief for businesses and individuals, since, as I pointed out, we'd "lost 84,000 jobs in August alone."

The guts of the bill loaned $115 billion to banks by having the government purchase their preferred stock. We attached needed oversight and included help for homeowners facing foreclosure by requiring the treasury to both guarantee their loans and assist them in adjusting mortgage terms through a new program. We simply had to do whatever we could to stop the foreclosures and the crash in the housing market.

An oversight committee was set up to review transfers, purchases, and sale of mortgages. We needed to make sure that the terms of mortgages were fair and the lender was capable. The committee was comprised of Federal Reserve Chairman Ben Bernanke and leaders of the SEC and other agencies.

We allowed the treasury to negotiate a government equity stake in the companies that received assistance. We added limits on executive compensation of rescued firms who could no longer deduct as an expense any executive compensation above half a million dollars, a common practice.

Most if not all economists believed the bill was necessary because a record $140 billion had already been pulled out of money market accounts by worried investors moving funds to U.S. treasuries. That started the credit freeze, and without the ability to raise capital, many firms were in danger of going bankrupt, as had Lehman Brothers. The credit freeze was a disaster for most businesses and for state governments as well.

California's governor, Arnold Schwarzenegger, weighed in heavily, as well as then State Treasurer Bill Lockyer, to say that without a bill California was sinking. They called me in a panic, telling me that they couldn't even borrow overnight funds to keep the state government going.

The entire $700 billion was never spent on the bank bailout; $350 billion was lent out in 2008, and when Obama became president, he used the remainder of the funds toward his economic stimulus package. At the end of the day the financial crisis was averted, but as I said at the time in a speech on the Senate floor, "We must never forget why it was caused."

I blamed deregulation and the tearing down of the firewalls that had separated various financial institution activities that used to protect mortgage lenders and savers. The destruction of those regulations allowed many opportunistic bankers to become gamblers with depositors' money. My legislation to ban future bailouts of Wall Street firms passed as the very first amendment. I was proud of that, because I believed that if "too big to fail" became the common belief, then the gambling by these large financial banks would never end.

"I hope this package will do what is needed to restore trust in the short term," I went on, "but in the long term we need regulatory reform and change that will bring us job-producing investments in America, not in foreign lands." And then came my refrain for all those years: "Remember, ten billion a month is going to Iraq. We need those dollars here at home."

After the bailout bill, it was time to turn to the stimulus package.

About two weeks after Obama was inaugurated, I went to the Senate floor to talk about how a thousand people showed up in Florida for thirty-five firefighter jobs.

"I want to help the middle class and the working poor, the backbone of America," I said, "because without that, we have nothing. We're in a deepening economic crisis in my home state of California where the unemployment rate is 9.3 percent. We all know California is trendsetting, but this is one trend I hope the rest of America will not follow. But, by God, if we do nothing, if we don't embrace the bipartisan package, which I know is not perfect—but if we do nothing, in my view that would be a hostile act. Not a passive act, because to do nothing endorses the status quo and the status quo includes 2,589,000 good-paying jobs America lost just in 2008."

When the Republicans tried to stop the bill, we overcame their filibuster with the necessary sixty votes and got the job done. The spending package, called the "stimulus," passed by a hair and was signed by President Obama on February 17, 2009. We needed it desperately to put people to work, because that month more than 200,000 jobs were lost. It was a time of high anxiety as we debated. Jobs were bleeding away and we desperately needed a tourniquet.

Looking back on the bank bailout and the $800 billion stimulus bill, I realize what a delicate and frightening time we lived through. But we stepped up and we avoided Armageddon. The great recession lost us more than eight million jobs and it was an arduous climb back. I give a lot of credit to President Obama and I think history will bear me out. We finally got those jobs back; it started with the bailout bill and continued with the successful stimulus package known as the American Recovery and Reinvestment Act of 2009. Most Republicans vilified both of these bills, but they were wrong.

On July 21, 2010, President Obama signed the Dodd–Frank Wall Street Reform and Consumer Protection Act and there were finally some reforms on the books. One of best was the creation of the Consumer Financial Protection Bureau. This was the idea of Elizabeth Warren, a professor at Harvard Law School. Consequently the Republicans vowed to block her nomination to head the agency, so President Obama appointed Richard Cordray instead.

Being mindlessly rejected in this kind of political warfare was shocking to Elizabeth, and to a lot of us, but this turned out to be a blessing in disguise. I called her and urged her to run for the Senate in Massachusetts against the incumbent, Republican Scott Brown.

"Don't get mad, get even," I said.

A hackneyed phrase, but perfect for the occasion. Elizabeth ran, she won, and she's continued to be a fierce defender of the middle class. I love the passion she's brought to the Senate.

But the economic crisis was only part of the three-legged big mess Bush left us. The other elephants in the room were the two wars he put on the credit card: the first in Afghanistan, the second in Iraq.

On February 27, 2009, just one month after his inauguration, President

Obama announced that "by August 31, 2010, our combat mission in Iraq will end." Consequently, by August 19, 2010, the last combat brigade exited Iraq. What remained were troops to train Iraqi forces and a counterterrorism mission. I could breathe easier, even though I knew from the start that the war's supporters had unleashed a nightmare of sectarian civil war and terror on the region that is still playing out.

Leaders in the Congress have such a critical role. While their first responsibility is to their membership, if they're in the same party as the president, they also have an obligation to work well with the White House. This isn't always easy and sometimes it's near impossible.

Since I went to Congress in 1982, I've been led by, among others, two Toms (Foley and Daschle), two Richards (Gephardt and Durbin), and one Harry. Other Democratic leaders I have served with include Jim Wright and George Mitchell.

Harry Reid in particular is perhaps the least understood and most underappreciated leader with whom I've ever worked.

Harry Mason Reid was born in Searchlight, Nevada, on December 2, 1939, which makes him about a year older than I am. A year wiser, too, but also part of the same post-Depression, pre-war generation that came of age before the baby boomers.

To say that Harry was born poor is an understatement. He grew up in a house with no toilet, telephone, or even running water. In order to attend high school, he had to move in with relatives forty miles away. Harry told me many times about a high school coach who helped him in his athletic pursuits as a football player and a boxer.

Eventually Harry graduated not only from high school, but from Utah State and George Washington University Law School, while he worked for the U.S. Capitol Police. After his education, he returned to Nevada, became city attorney for Henderson, and was elected as an assemblyman. He served as lieutenant governor and then was the chairman of the Nevada Gaming Commission from 1977 to 1981.

Reid notified the FBI when he was targeted with a bribe by a criminal element in the state. He set up a sting operation with law enforcement and the criminal activity came to an end. The story goes that Harry was wired, and became so enraged when the actual bribe became a reality in front of him that he screamed an expletive at the criminal and actually tried to physically assault him. After the mobster served six months in prison, Harry's wife, Landra, discovered a bomb attached to one of their cars. Harry has always suspected it was connected to the bribery incident.

This tendency to use his fists started even earlier in his life. Harry met Landra Gould when he was a junior in high school and she was a sophomore. The first time he went to pick her up for a date, Landra's father, a Jewish immigrant, vehemently opposed his daughter dating a man with no discernible religion who came from a truck-stop town with nothing but brothels and gambling. But Reid was so determined to go out with Landra that he and her father got into a scuffle about it. He actually punched his future father-in-law in the face, grabbed Landra, and they ran out together.

"It wasn't the greatest beginning," Harry said. But her parents realized that it could be something serious, even though the last few years of courting were a difficult time.

Harry and Landra eloped during college, and finally her parents came around to accepting him.

"They said, 'We did everything we could to stop the two of you... now we're going to do everything we can to make your lives a success.'"

Harry and Landra decided to convert to Mormonism, but always kept a mezuzah on the door of their home, Harry told CNN in March of 2015, and until Landra's parents died, they celebrated major Jewish holidays, like Passover, as a family.

The Reids have five children, one daughter and four sons. As they raised their kids and as Harry rose through the political ranks in Nevada and in the U.S. Senate, the two have rarely been apart.

In fact, while many lawmakers like to socialize and hobnob with other powerful people, that's the last thing that Harry ever wanted to do. He always preferred to stay home and have a quiet night with Landra. Stew and I love to be with them in those rare moments when we can entice them out to dinner, and even once to stay with us in our California desert home—where I actually cooked, to Harry's disbelief.

Harry arrived in the House the same year I did, 1983, then left for the Senate in 1987.

Harry then succeeded Tom Daschle as the Senate minority leader in 2005; he became majority leader after the 2006 election. He's one of only three senators—along with Alben W. Barkley and Mike Mansfield—to have served at least eight years as majority leader. After the bruising loss of the Senate majority in 2014, Harry became minority leader again.

Unless you have served in the Senate as part of a party caucus, it is almost impossible to understand what a majority leader or a minority leader does. It's like learning about how a bill becomes a law. It seems simple, but it isn't. I often thought about writing a book entitled *How a Bill REALLY Becomes a Law* but that might discourage all but a brave few from running for Congress, and we're already having a hard enough time recruiting enthusiastic candidates.

In the simplest of terms, the majority leader in the Senate must hold his or her caucus together. That is a challenge few can master. Lyndon Johnson did it magnificently, but he had the luxury of a huge majority—more than sixty Democrats.

Regardless of the number, to keep that crowd of senators together is no small feat. During the long years of the Iraq war, Harry had to deal with both hawks and doves. During the recession, there was the tax cut crowd versus the stimulus crowd. During the environmental debates, there was the oil state crowd versus the coastal state crowd. During the gun debates, there was the gun control crowd versus the NRA crowd. During the healthcare debate, there was the public option versus the no public option crowd.

Harry had to deal with ideological splits in his own caucus—from the deep blue senators like me, to the purple state senators, to the red state senators. And not one was shy or humble.

Harry knows how to listen, and listen well. A man of so few words, he's uninterested in small talk (unless he has a spare moment). When you call him or he calls you and the business is done, he will usually say something like "got it," and before you can say thanks, he's gone, and you smile at the phone because you know that when Harry says "got it," it's taken care of.

He's very interested in the stories of his colleagues, because he knows how his own story shaped him. A good majority leader needs to understand what makes each of us tick, where our lines in the sand are, so that when he needs us to move on an issue and he is counting votes, he knows what is even possible. A few years ago, Harry started a tradition in the caucus lunch in which every couple of weeks a senator would tell his or her life story. I always found it fascinating because it opens up a colleague in a way that is unique and important, when you know what has touched our hearts and souls, and how and where we got our value system.

Harry Reid's sensitivity and empathy gave him valuable insight into his fellow senators' passions, so he knew who to call on in a crunch. Early one snowy evening in late 2009, I got a call from Harry and Chuck Schumer. They were trying to negotiate the last issue on President Obama's Patient Protection and Affordable Care Act, commonly called the Affordable Care Act (ACA) or Obamacare, which was stuck in the Senate, held up by a Republican filibuster.

Not one Republican was going to vote for the bill, even though it had many similarities to a 2007 Republican bill and was patterned after Republican Mitt Romney's state healthcare plan when he was governor of Massachusetts. No matter how it was revised, the Republicans were going to vote against it, in accordance with their policy of opposing anything President Obama did. So we needed every single Democrat, all sixty, in order to invoke cloture and end a Republican filibuster.

Cloture is a Senate rule allowing a cutoff of debate in order to force a vote. In the 1939 movie *Mr. Smith Goes to Washington*, the hero, played by James Stewart, launches a twenty-four-hour, nonstop speech on the floor of the Senate to prevent a vote on a "corrupt appropriations bill." His exhaustion pays off when the scandal is unmasked. He clearly mastered the art of the filibuster, but in more recent times, a cloture petition would have been filed, and it would have forced a vote to end debate if sixty senators so determined.

But we'd reached a stumbling block, the last holdout before we had sixty votes for cloture, and that was Ben Nelson of Nebraska. Ben had been the governor of Nebraska from 1991 to 1999, and was now its Democratic senator. But as one of the most conservative Democrats in the Senate, one who frequently voted against his party, Ben had a major problem with the ACA. Since so many Americans were going to receive subsidy payments for their health insurance, it would mean federal funds going toward insurance that covered abortion, and he was solidly anti-choice.

Harry knew my position and he knew Ben's. He and Chuck knew how upset I would be to see those middle-class American women being denied affordable access to a legal procedure simply because they weren't wealthy. They also knew Ben was not going to relent. If we didn't figure this out, the fifty-year drive for near–universal health coverage would be lost.

Harry had not one vote to spare. If Ben and I couldn't reach agreement, the bill would die. Pro-choice senators would not vote unless we fixed this to their way of thinking, and anti-choice senators were just as adamant on the other side.

It started out seeming quite hopeless. Harry and Chuck were sitting in Harry's Capitol office looking grim and anxious. They were great negotiators, yet they couldn't seal the deal. Chuck said he would be the go-between, passing proposals between me and Ben, because they'd established a trust even though no agreement had been reached. If Chuck believed anything I came up with could be sold to Ben, he would present it. Kind of like a mediator, a role in which he excels.

I appreciated this plan, because I wanted to focus all my energy, and the energy of my chief of staff, Laura Schiller, on coming up with idea after idea rather than taking time out to sell each one to Ben.

Every time we came up with a good idea, Chuck literally ran over with it through the underground tunnel to Ben's office in the Hart Building, about fifteen minutes away. His staff was working there, coming up with their own ideas. Hours and hours passed. Patty Murray and I talked on the phone and her staff was also very helpful.

The problem centered around Ben's firm belief that the federal government should not in any way pay for insurance that covers abortion. To me, of course, the whole thing seemed so wrong. Abortion is a legal procedure, so if we don't worry about vasectomies being covered by government-subsidized insurance, or Viagra, for that matter, why discriminate against women in this way? But I realized that I couldn't focus on disagreements. I had to solve the problem or millions of uninsured Americans would never get health insurance—and why? Because of abortion. That story was not one I wanted out there in any way, shape, or form. We simply couldn't let health care die because of an ideological dispute among Democratic senators!

Finally, we hit on an idea that could work for everyone. "Why don't we make sure that the amount of the premium that covers abortion is paid by the individual and not by the government subsidy?" I suggested. "In this way, women would get coverage, with the government only paying for the non-abortion part of her premium, and she can simply pay for the abortion portion out of her own pocket."

The amount was relatively small, so my first idea was for the woman to write a separate check for the abortion coverage. We called some of my outside advisors from Planned Parenthood and NARAL Pro-Choice America to get their thoughts. They hated it, so eventually we figured out a way to do two transactions electronically—one for the government payment and the other for the individual's payment for the abortion coverage.

Chuck went over and presented this latest proposal to Ben. Lo and behold, after thirteen hours straight of negotiation, Ben agreed to support the bill! Ben came down to Harry's office, and we shook hands and actually hugged, both of us knowing that if we failed to reach agreement, the bill would have been deader than dead. I finally left the Capitol in the wee small hours of the morning, a blanket of white snow covering the streets and my Prius. I wiped the soft white stuff off the windshield and drove the six blocks to my D.C.

home. I couldn't wait to tell my family the inside story of the healthcare bill. But as it should have been, everyone was fast asleep by the time I arrived.

On December 23, 2009, the Senate had a cloture vote to end the filibuster with a vote of sixty to thirty-nine. Every one of the sixty was a Democrat. Let me be clear, nobody liked our abortion compromise—not the pro-choice side and not the anti-choice side. But people could live with it and the bill was saved. In the caucus lunch before that vote, both Ben and I sold the deal to our colleagues. It worked and the bill passed.

On March 23, 2010, Barack Obama signed the most significant reform of the United States healthcare system since the passage of Medicare and Medicaid in 1965.

Now I see the uninsured rate in California going down by more than 40 percent. I thank God that we came to that agreement. Looking back, I know that as one of the Senate's most vocal pro-choice leaders, I had to be the one to cut the deal. The point is that Harry knows whom to call on in a crunch. He knew if I could go with this compromise, other pro-choice senators would no doubt follow, and if Ben could accept it, other anti-choice senators would follow. He was right.

People in California ask me from time to time, why is Harry the leader? He's not great on TV. He doesn't seem strong. He's not charismatic or eloquent.

Harry once went on Jon Stewart's *Daily Show*. He looked drawn and tired and he answered in a monotone. Harry's not a show-biz guy. The pundits keep writing about how Harry uses unintended words and speaks so softly you have to read his lips. But let me say this: When it comes to standing up to the far right for what is right, he is right there—in the room, on the floor—when others try to slip out of it by dodging or ducking or running scared.

He doesn't care about bad press, or reviews, or threats to destroy or defeat him. Once a colleague came up from the Republican side and said, "I hear you need more bodyguards since the healthcare act," with a big smile on his face.

Around the Senate, it was a known fact, particularly during the Obamacare battle, that Harry received death threats. The right wing was hysterical about Obamacare, constantly saying the president's plan featured "death panels"—groups of bureaucrats deciding whether you would get care and be saved, or be denied care and die. Utter insanity. News outlets like Fox News fanned these claims, and because Harry was leading the charge on passing Obamacare, he became a huge target of some decidedly unstable individuals.

Harry responded to the cavalier comment of his colleague and shot back: "Yes, we are getting more death threats, and you think that's funny?"

Harry is collegial with everyone, but the glib remark by that Republican was out of line, so Harry made his point with just a few short words.

Barack Obama has had the roughest presidency since FDR. The 2008 recession, the housing crisis, two awful wars, the new threat of ISIL, huge deficits, Ebola, an inherited immigration crisis, an inherited healthcare crisis, a mean-spirited, impossible Republican congress, a country divided on race and guns...and this is just a partial list.

History will show that he handled all of this with calmness and determination that allowed our nation to land and stand on its feet.

I shudder to think about what would have happened if the Republican ticket had won with McCain as president and Palin a heartbeat away.

I also feel that the president hasn't received enough credit for Obamacare. Millions more Americans now have the security of knowing they're no longer one paycheck away from disaster from an unexpected illness, that they'll no longer be punished with no insurance if they have diabetes or their child has asthma, and that they won't find out in the dead of night that they've capped out on their annual health insurance limit. Thanks to Obamacare, there are no more limits or prejudices of any sort allowed.

Unfortunately, the rollout of Obamacare didn't go smoothly. That's a nice way to put it: it was a disaster. That's one of the reasons why we Democrats took such a beating at the polls in the 2014 election cycle. But those technical problems were solved, and health care is on its way to becoming far less of a problem for the American people than it was. Healthcare costs are going down and hospital errors are going down too. I'm so glad I provided a necessary vote to ensure one less recurring crisis for American families. It's an issue that will never disappear, because of the ideological fervor of Obamacare critics, but as more and more people benefit, it's clear that the worst is over.

If I have one criticism of President Obama, it's that, with the notable exceptions, of course, of Joe Biden, Hillary Clinton, and John Kerry, the people he's chosen to be around him are too taciturn. I understand that the president himself has a "no drama" approach. I admire that in so many ways, but I have always believed that those of us in office should surround ourselves with those who have a different style.

Picking Hillary Clinton as secretary of state was a very smart move. Her star power made it possible for our president to stick close to home and deal with the economic pressures of the moment. "No Drama Obama" describes our president, but I would have loved to see someone like the former governor of Vermont, Howard Dean, as head of Health and Human Services or Surgeon General. And maybe former governor of Michigan Jennifer Granholm as labor secretary. Her passion about middle-class jobs would have made a strong contribution in the debate over income inequality.

President Obama is smart, deliberative, and has the toughest, most time-consuming job on earth. I know critics say he doesn't spend enough time with members of Congress, but I defend him mightily on this point. Not that I think spending more time wouldn't have helped. Barack has an incredibly wise, empathic, winning personality. So, sure, the more he can meet face-to-face with both sides of the aisle, the better. But with so much on his shoulders every day, he has little time to waste. It's crucial for him to make time and keep it real with his family and close friends—those who want nothing from him, who root for him without fail, *and* who will tell him if he's off track. I am sure many would disagree that keeping time for your family and friends is more important than meeting with members of Congress. But I believe, given the unprecedented crises President Obama has faced from day one, it was necessary.

Okay, I know it sounds contradictory. On the one hand, I think members of Congress needed more schmoozing, the kind Bill Clinton did as he talked to you. It was like no one else was in the room. And when his hand was on your shoulder, you felt you were part of history. On the other hand, instead of schmoozing, I applaud President Obama for thinking, planning, strategizing—addressing how to clean up the gigantic, outrageous mess he was handed by George W. Bush. Add to all of that raising two young daughters in the challenging preteen and teen years. How well I remember what that's like.

I should add that the president *did* in fact try to reach out time and time again to Republican leaders in the Senate, though with little success because, with few exceptions, they never wanted to in any way be part of his team. He probably felt that he didn't have to do that with Democrats and that we would understand. Some did and some didn't. But the bottom line is, President Obama is not a schmoozer. I'm not a schmoozer either. I get it. Yes, I interact constantly with colleagues, but after hours, I want to be with my family.

His historic significance is not only tied into what he's accomplished but who he is, and the pressures of that. How difficult it must be to know that some political colleagues can't get past the color of your skin. I have watched those colleagues oppose the president with disrespect, calling him a socialist, a foreigner, a traitor. It's sickening. I don't know why else they would say those things.

I remember what President Obama said when George Zimmerman was acquitted of shooting Trayvon Martin in Florida:

"When Trayvon Martin was first shot, I said that this could have been my son. Another way of saying that is, Trayvon Martin could have been me thirty-five years ago."

By saying that, the president explained to the American people that as an African-American man, he faces challenges that other presidents before him have not.

As I think is clear by now, I know something about discrimination as a woman in politics. When I started out, people couldn't accept the fact that I was a woman, hinting that there was something wrong with me for wanting to be in office, abandon my children, and anyway, how much could I know about finance? Racism isn't the same as sexism, but being a Jewish girl from Brooklyn has inspired plenty of prejudice against me, too. And it's never stopped, really. I wish I had a dollar for every time I was called "brash" or "pushy" or "overemotional." "Overemotional," believe it or not, is what some colleagues called me when I decided to read the names of the war dead on the Senate floor.

It's infuriating. Someday all those prejudices will die of their own stupid weight and Barack Obama will go down as the Jackie Robinson of the presidency. One of my favorite pictures of President Obama is proudly displayed in Harry Reid's office, just as you walk in. It's a picture of Barack bending down so that a little African American boy can touch the president's hair. The message is so clear to this little boy. He too, with hair like this president, can be anything he wants to be.

Someday the prejudice will all seem ridiculous, just as having to walk to the back of the bus because you look different is ridiculous. Someday, politicians like Iowa Congressman Steve King, who talk about Hispanic workers with "thighs like cantaloupes," will be kicked out of office in a heartbeat. And someday, anyone running for office who tries to tell a woman what decisions to make about her own body will be a nonstarter.

Barack Obama and Hillary Clinton, by their very strong personalities and talents, challenge these prejudices. They're together in history as rivals, friends, and colleagues. I've been privileged to work with both of them in ways that make me proud not only of them but of our work together. About this rivalry, I wrote words to "Three Coins in a Fountain." In part, they read:

Two stars in the Senate.
One became the President.
One would hire the other.
I hope she follows where he went.

* * *

The Senate treatment of Anita Hill played such a huge part in my election to the Senate in 1992 and the Bob Packwood case in 1995 confirmed how important it was to have strong women in Congress.

In 2011, there was another egregious case of the sexual abuse of power in the Senate. I had become chairman of the Ethics Committee in 2007. (Bob Dole was indeed prescient when he asked sarcastically during the Packwood affair: "Why don't we turn [the policing of the Senate] over to the senator from California?")

The story begins on June 11, 2009, when Douglas Hampton, the chief of staff for Senator John Ensign of Nebraska, had sent a letter to Megyn Kelly, a Fox News reporter, in which he said that his boss was having an affair with Hampton's wife, Cynthia. He wrote, "The actions of Senator Ensign have ruined our lives and careers and left my family in shambles. I need justice, help and restitution for what Senator Ensign has done to me and my family."

Fox didn't do anything with this story at first, but somehow it was leaked to the *New York Times*, who, on June 16, published a report by David Herszenhorn.

Senator John Ensign, Republican of Nevada, admitted he had an extra-marital affair with a member of his campaign staff...Mr. Ensign led the Republicans' campaign efforts in 2008 and had been contemplating a run for president in 2012. An aide said the consensual affair took place between December 2007 and August 2008 and that the woman worked for both Mr. Ensign's campaign operation, Ensign for Senate, as well as a conservative political action committee, Battle Born PAC, from December 2006 to May 2008. Mr. Ensign is honorary chairman of the PAC. The woman's husband was a member of Mr. Ensign's official Senate staff. Mr. Ensign, 51, is married and has three children. During college at Colorado State University, he became a born-again Christian and he and his wife, Darlene, were active in the Promise Keepers, an evangelical group.

Democratic majority leader Harry Reid, who is Nevada's senior senator, issued a statement expressing concern for his fellow Nevadan.

"This is a very personal matter," a spokesman, Jon Summers, said in a statement. "Senator Reid's thoughts are with Senator Ensign and his family as they go through this difficult time."

What a shock. I knew John Ensign. I had worked with him on several bills, one near and dear to my heart: an after-school programs for kids. Together we achieved the first ever federal funding for after-school programs, which for many years since has given one million children a year a chance to be safe and to continue learning in those dangerous hours after school, when some have no parents at home.

John had been very helpful in getting Republican votes on that bill and he did it by explaining that he had a very tough life until his mom remarried. If there been after-school care, he would have stayed out of trouble, he told us.

John was a doctor of veterinarian medicine who'd represented Nevada's first congressional district based in Las Vegas for two terms in the House of Representatives in 1994 and 1996 before becoming the second senator from Nevada in 2000. He and Harry actually had a pretty good relationship, and worked frequently together on Nevada issues. John was ambitious and was planning a June 1 trip to Iowa, which some interpreted as a foray into a 2012 presidential run.

But then the story broke, and the awful truth about his behavior was revealed. It's painful to recollect how this soap opera gradually emerged as a clear case of an egregious abuse of power by a senator over a distraught and passive female victim. It chilled the bones of all of us on the Ethics Committee. We had to take action, and fast.

In May of 2010, we sent investigators to Las Vegas, where they spent several days interviewing every witness they could find who had knowledge of Ensign's dealings with the Hamptons. Apparently the affair had gone on longer than what we had originally estimated, from 2006 to 2008, and the details were sordid. Ensign saw Cynthia repeatedly, saying he wanted to marry her, giving her money for clothing, hotel rooms, and to pay for her therapy. After Douglas Hampton discovered the affair, John refused to give it up. Both Douglas Hampton and his wife were 100 percent reliant on the senator for their livelihoods, which essentially trapped them in a bizarre triangle.

In February 2011, we appointed a special counsel to lead the investigation. Just hours later Ensign said that his re-election campaign was increasing its fund-raising efforts. I guess he didn't want to lose his Senate seat, and felt the need for a bigger media effort to offset the scandal. But in April, three weeks before we were scheduled to deliver our findings to the Senate, Ensign announced that he would resign his seat, effective May 3, 2011, stating that he "will not continue to subject my family, my constituents, or the Senate to any further rounds of investigation, depositions, drawn out proceedings, or especially public hearings."

In any case, after investigating for twenty-two months, on May 12, 2011, as chairman of the Senate Ethics Committee, I told the Senate upon release of my committee's report that the evidence was "substantial enough to warrant the consideration of expulsion" had Ensign not resigned in early May. We referred our findings to the Justice Department and the Federal Election Commission, since the Ethics Committee had no more jurisdiction in the matter.

The Ensign case disturbed me for many reasons. John was a fellow senator whom I had liked and trusted. How could he have done such awful things and gotten into such terrible trouble? It was such a twisted story of lust, power, and recklessness. And of course my sadness and compassion reached to his victims.

The whole story is in the public record because the Ethics Committee felt the people needed to know why Ensign resigned. None of the three Republicans or three Democrats on the committee wanted to hush it up in any way. In all the years I was either chair or vice chair of the committee, we've had total bipartisanship, of which I am extremely proud.

My Republican counterpart on the Ethics Committee was Senator Johnny Isakson of Georgia. Our politics are night and day, but when it comes to the Ethics Committee we work very closely together and share the same sense of what is ethical and what is not. Our work is clear: to ensure that senators understand the critical importance of the basic rule of a senator's behavior: *Do not bring shame upon the Senate.*

Meanwhile, a woman is beaten in America every nine seconds, even today. So having women in powerful positions, including as our president, is important. And protecting women is something I've tried to do every day of my political life. As more and more women are elected it's grown from a lonely effort to a coalition. As more and more young men are elected, we have received help from those Senator Mikulski calls "Sir Galahads."

This battle takes many forms. For example, the battle over a woman's right to choose is about respect for women. It's also about freedom of religion. That's right. If your religion prohibits abortion, then, if you wish to follow that religion, you absolutely should. If your religion, or lack of it, doesn't prohibit abortions, then make your decision in accordance with your beliefs. The point is, everyone should be free to follow what they believe, with their God, or their family, or their doctors. Choice means respect for an individual's beliefs.

But somehow, this battle has intensified every year, and I think it is so unfortunate. We should find common ground and ensure that women can plan their pregnancies and then allow Americans to follow their own consciences. I don't understand how the Republican Party can talk about preventing the government from becoming Big Brother, while it also wants to put senators in the most private moments of their constituents' lives. But the beat will go on and on, until voters speak more clearly on the issue.

I saw life before *Roe v. Wade*, and it was deadly for women. Many lost their fertility as well as their lives. It's difficult for younger women to imagine that women and doctors in America could again be treated as criminals when abortions are performed. And who will pay the ultimate price? Women.

Democratic and some Republican women have been able to fend off the worst of these assaults on women's rights in the Senate. There were bills from the Republican House to criminalize doctors and even put grandmothers in jail if they wanted to help their granddaughters. They tried to interfere with a woman even if she sought to end a pregnancy because it might paralyze her or make her permanently infertile if the pregnancy was carried to term. There have even been Republican bills opposing birth control.

Dozens and dozens of bills have been passed by the Republican House, but women in our Senate coalition like Patty Murray, Dianne Feinstein, Maria Cantwell, and others have stopped them. Male colleagues like Frank Lautenberg and Bob Kerrey were champions for women's rights, adding their voices to ours. They stood up to Senator Rick Santorum, for example, who acted like he knew more about giving birth than women do. Santorum would often appear on the Senate floor with diagrams of a woman giving birth. I'm not kidding. He would lecture us about what childbirth is like. This didn't go down well with the women of the Senate.

Santorum and I went at it tooth and nail repeatedly. Once he asked if he could have a small child in the Senate gallery to hear him lecture women on giving birth. His point was that this child could have been aborted but wasn't. The child wasn't old enough to sit in the gallery according to long-standing Senate rules, so I objected. I also didn't think it was such a hot idea for a five-year-old to hear Santorum intoning about "killing" and "murdering." Nor did I think it appropriate for the little one to look at those charts of women's private parts that Rick continually used to make his points.

Santorum had a fit and told the child's mother to tell me she was "praying for me." No problem. After battling with Rick, I was happy to take all the prayers I could get. One of my biggest prayers was for Santorum to lose his seat, and he did—to Bob Casey, who is pro-life but far from radical.

Santorum continually took my words out of context, telling crowds that I believe a baby is born when the baby is taken home from the hospital. Really! Since I gave birth to two premature children and kept them in the hospital for weeks, I know very well when a baby is born.

Anyway, when did he ever give birth? Rick and I did manage to work together on a couple other issues—the Syria Accountability Act and an environmental bill or two. That is amazing, considering our insane debates on choice, but such is the art of tough. You have to get over it.

The right can have a mind-boggling tin ear sometimes. For example, have you heard of "legitimate rape"?

The longtime anti-abortion activist Todd Akin was a congressman from Missouri from 2001 to 2013, and then the Republican party nominee for Senate in 2012. When a reporter from KTVI St. Louis television asked him whether women who've been raped and become pregnant should have the option of abortion he said:

"Well, you know...from what I understand from doctors...if it's a legitimate rape, the female body has ways to try to shut that whole thing down."

My colleague Claire McCaskill from Missouri, who was defending her seat against Akin, was all over it.

"No, Todd," she told him. "Rape is rape." And a woman who is raped can't just tell her body not to get pregnant!

Claire demolished him and held on to her seat in a very difficult state for Democrats.

One of my favorite responses to Akin came from Karen Hughes, former advisor to George W. Bush, of all people, who wrote in *Politico*, "And if another Republican man says anything about rape other than it is a horrific, violent crime, I want to personally cut out his tongue. The college-age daughters of many of my friends voted for Obama because they were completely turned off by Neanderthal comments like the suggestion of 'legitimate rape.'"

But Rick Santorum doesn't care what Karen Hughes, or anyone else, for that matter, says. Here's another quote from him:

"Rape victims who become pregnant should make the best of a bad situation," he proclaimed. "Women in such a position should not get an abortion but instead welcome their 'horrible gift from God.' I think the right approach is to accept what God has given to you."

Can you believe it? That is the kind of outrageous, out-of-the-mainstream thinking that I have fought against my entire career. I also realized early on that having more pro-choice men take on these anti-woman diatribes is very important. Sometimes the men feel we women want to handle it alone, but of course we really want their help.

Richard Blumenthal, the Democratic senior senator from Connecticut, is so strong on this issue and a welcome male voice in our fight for women's health.

On another front, Congress became sharply divided in 2013 over the reauthorization of the original bipartisan 1994 Violence Against Women Act (VAWA) authored by Joe Biden and Orrin Hatch. We fought hard to include the LGBT community and Indian tribes. Harry Reid was on our side, and I give an enormous amount of credit to Patty Murray and Amy Klobuchar for laying out the strategy for enactment. There was a move to leave those communities out, but once Chairman Pat Leahy saw how determined the women were, he joined with us, and our collective toughness won the day.

Although women in Congress united, even across party lines, when it came to VAWA, it was a different story, particularly with respect to sexual assault in the military. Of course women can't agree on everything, but here was a case where I wish we had.

This had been an ongoing problem for several years. There was the notorious Tailhook scandal of 1991, the Aberdeen scandal in 1996, and the 2003 Air Force Academy sexual assaults. Not only that, but in 2007 the *New York Times* reported that a significant number of women soldiers who served in Afghanistan and Iraq had screened positive for sexual trauma.

A 2012 Pentagon survey revealed that about 26,000 women and men reported cases of unwanted sexual contact, but just 3,374 of these were officially reported, and only 302 were prosecuted. And another investigation reported that only one in five females and one in fifteen men in the U.S. Air Force would actually report being assaulted if they had been.

The problem was that the issue stayed within the system itself. It never left the chain of command, leaving the military hierarchy in charge of investigating, charging, and prosecuting the case, even when the crime was committed by a senior officer whom the commander knew. Talk about a blatant conflict of interest! The victim would be blamed, harassed, and even driven out of the military, if not out of her mind. It was like the foxes guarding the henhouse, the victim being punished while the assailant usually got off with a rap on the knuckles, if that. Therefore the victims—both men and women—feared retaliation or the end to their careers if they reported their complaints. And this military culture had been going on for decades.

A 2013 Rand Corporation report states that the cost of sexual assaults in the military in 2012 alone was $3.6 billion. These criminal acts are despicable and costly for all of us.

It seemed simple to me. All you had to do was look at the small number of cases of sexual assault that were being reported in the military: 10 percent. In the civilian world it's still too low at 50 percent. Victims told us one by one that they would not report their assailant to their commander. Clearly, change was needed so these heinous crimes are reported and then acted upon fairly.

In 2013, Kirsten Gillibrand, the junior Democratic senator from New York who'd won a special election when Hillary Clinton left the Senate to become secretary of state, was leading us in the right direction with her proposal to leave these cases to be prosecuted within the military, but putting them in the hands of legal professionals outside the chain of command. This would inject fairness, objectivity, and skill into a process that is severely broken. Kirsten, a member of the Armed Services Committee, was passionate and effective, and we became very close friends during this time.

Kirsten proposed legislation co-sponsored by Republican senators Rand Paul and Ted Cruz to enact her ideas, but the bill failed to gain enough votes to break a filibuster in March 2014. We had twenty female senators serving at that time. We knew we had a fight on our hands, and we knew if *all* the women were on the same page we could win. Unfortunately, that was not to be.

Senator Claire McCaskill led the charge against Kirsten's proposal. I didn't for one minute doubt that she believed she was doing the right thing, but that doesn't change the fact that we needed five more votes to end the filibuster and Claire led three of the twenty women senators to defect. Claire had her reasons. She had been a prosecutor and had reservations about such a dramatic reform. She didn't like making commanders step to the sidelines. She was confident in her views. But I've been around long enough to know that there's a moment in time when real change is possible, and that was it. Unfortunately, Claire's opposition gave some of our male friends on both sides of the aisle something to hide behind and it deeply hurt our cause. We got fifty-five votes but needed sixty.

Change is hard. Very hard. You ruffle feathers, shake it up, and those who have the power hate change. There is so much resistance to real change, and yes, Claire gave the "status quo-ers" an out. After all, this issue was about protecting women and she had much credibility in that space. We did, however, get some very unusual supporters in addition to Ted Cruz and Rand Paul, like Chuck Grassley of Iowa. Kirsten and Claire, moreover, made other changes, such as making sure a woman who is attacked gets an advocate, and I had an amendment that became law to end asking irrelevant questions of a rape victim at a pretrial hearing. But we couldn't get the prize: real change for victims.

One footnote of this story: after this battle, Kirsten and Claire teamed up to fight against rape on college campuses. They know the art of tough, which is that even after an emotional disagreement, we must come together for the good of the country.

Another footnote to this story is that on January 10, 2013, when the Senate Armed Services Committee held hearings to confirm President Obama's nomination of Deputy Undersecretary of Defense Dr. Jo Ann Rooney to the higher position of Assistant Secretary of Defense, Senator Gillibrand asked her what she thought about taking prosecutions of sexual assault outside the chain of command.

She was totally against it.

"I believe the impact would be decisions based on evidence rather than in the interest of preserving good order and discipline," she said.

What? Unit cohesion should trump following the evidence and getting the perpetrator? Clearly she had no idea what justice is supposed to be about. So I objected. I said no to her promotion.

The media had a field day.

Per the Associated Press in *USA Today*, "Senator Barbara Boxer, Democrat from California, said she was shocked by what Rooney wrote, saying, 'It sickened me.'"

They also reported that Senator Kirsten Gillibrand, Democrat from New York, was furious.

"'The United States legal system is based on evidence, justice and due process. Why isn't this good enough for our service members who risk everything to protect those freedoms?' Gillibrand said, adding, 'Jo Ann Rooney's testimony should send chills down the spine of any member of the armed services seeking justice.'"

We fell under heavy pressure to promote Rooney. Kirsten ultimately lifted her objection, but I would not. I was lobbied up and down and inside out by the Obama administration and also by some of my Democratic colleagues on the Armed Services Committee. But how could I in good conscience support someone who didn't understand what was real justice for sexual assault victims? I told them, including my dear colleague Carl Levin of Michigan, who was then the chairman of the Armed Services Committee—whom I had dubbed "my rabbi," that's how much I respected him—that I simply would not cave on this matter.

I'd never approve a nominee for Assistant Secretary of Defense who believed that unit cohesion trumped the evidence of a heinous crime. Rooney stayed where she was.

I had a dream that Republicans and I were on the same team, leading the charge for a healthy and clean environment. I dreamed that then President Nixon signed the Clean Air Act in 1974; and George Herbert Walker Bush signed the Clean Air Act Amendments in 1990 and Gerald Ford signed the Safe Drinking Water Act in 1974. And I thought my dream included Senator John McCain leading the fight to put a price on carbon in order to fight climate change.

But wait. That was no dream. That was history. I was there and saw it all happening. It made me appreciate that saving the environment was an American value, not a partisan gotcha. So what a rude awakening it was for me to see this issue, one of the driving forces of my career, becoming such a lightning rod once again, and provoking some interesting right-wing blog postings, one of which called me "pathetic." Another, Hotair.com, called my pro-environment speeches "mortifying."

The attacks against me escalated during January of 2014, when I began to express my extreme concern about the controversial Keystone XL, a proposed pipeline that would bring a huge quantity of tar sands oil, the dirtiest sludge on the planet, from Canada to Port Arthur, Texas. I was head of the Senate Environment and Public Works Committee, and I worried about how this tar sands oil would affect human health. There was research that showed increased cancer rates among people who lived near the oilfields in Canada, and Canadian doctors testified to this.

"Children and families in the U.S. have a right to know now—before any decision to approve the Keystone tar sands pipeline—how it would affect their health," I told reporters on Capitol Hill. I knew from the tar sands already being shipped into our country from Canada, without the pipeline, that "misery follows the tar sands." I knew this because community leaders from Port Arthur, Texas, where the tar sand is refined, told me about a huge increase in asthma cases and breathing problems.

I also talked with community leaders in the Midwest, where pet coke, which is the waste product from refined tar sands oil, is stored. More than once it blew around a Little League park, causing kids to run off the field, some covered in black dust. All this misery from a small amount of imported tar sands oil, while the Keystone XL, which would vastly increase imports of tar sands oil, hasn't been built yet. I joined the coalition of environmental groups to stop that pipeline.

Politicians don't usually live near refineries. Politicians don't generally live where oil is being excavated or along a pipeline that can burst. Years ago communities in Michigan and Arkansas experienced bad spills from the existing pipeline carrying tar sands. It turns out they still haven't cleaned up the spills after months and years, because they're so difficult to clean up.

I stood with nurses and public health doctors from our country who are concerned about the health impacts of the tar sands. If the pipeline is built there will be a 45 percent increase in tar sands imports. Because far more carbon is released, it will undo a lot of the progress we have made in our fuel economy efforts, not to mention add to the woes of climate change. On November 3, 2015, the Obama administration announced its decision not to approve the pipeline. My sigh of relief could be heard for miles.

Years ago, I compared climate deniers to tobacco deniers. But I didn't realize at the time how real that comparison is. Big Oil is using the same techniques that Big Tobacco used in their shameless and ultimately unsuccessful effort to convince people that smoking cigarettes was not really harmful to their health. Anyone with a heartbeat and a pulse knows what a dangerous campaign of lies that was.

The Union of Concerned Sciences in January of 2007 released an amazing report about this. And they included some damning quotes. This one, for instance, from the tobacco company Brown and Williamson:

"Doubt is our product since it is the best means of competing with the body of fact that exists in the minds of the general public. It is also a means of establishing a controversy."

Doubt? Controversy? Sounds familiar, doesn't it? That's exactly the plan of today's polluters—the big oil, coal, and other industries who deny climate change. Make climate change controversial. Sow seeds of doubt, even though there is overwhelming evidence that of course climate change is here, now, a scientific reality.

Shame on the elected officials who were on that team and are now on the climate denial team. "I am not a scientist!" is their rallying cry, the latest lame excuse meant to plant doubt in the minds of the American public.

From the time the Republicans took over the House in 2011, I was forced to spend far too much time burying their anti-environmental amendments— almost one hundred of them within just two years—that would weaken toxic waste laws, clean air laws, safe drinking water laws, the Endangered Species Act, and virtually every other strong, protective environmental law.

They've tried to derail our landmark laws through the back door. I fear that's their continuing plan, since they can't possibly come straight at these laws. Clean air and water are just too popular among voters for any politician who wants to get re-elected to oppose them openly. So the big-polluter–controlled Republicans try to starve the Environmental Protection Agency, weaken enforcement, and roll back American leadership on the environment around the world in every way possible. The word they substitute for "rollback" is "reform." The word they use to undermine the word "protection" is "regulation." These Republicans title their anti-environmental bills in such a way that you would never know what they're really about.

For example, the Clean Air Strong Economies Bill, S-2833, introduced in 2014 by John Thune, the Republican senior senator from South Dakota, actually freezes the EPA from improving air-quality standards until an impossible list of conditions is met. The net effect is the exact opposite of clean air.

In 2013 there was S-1006, the Preserve the Waters of the United States Act, from John Barrasso, the junior senator from Wyoming, another Republican. This one actually prohibits the EPA from protecting waters covered under the Clean Water Act. It's hard to read this doubletalk without laughing! It's truly a page out of George Orwell's novel *1984*, where government, Big Brother, tells people, "War is peace. Freedom is slavery" as a way to brainwash the people.

And my favorite—S-485, The Clear Skies Act of 2003 by Senator Jim Inhofe, senior Republican senator from Oklahoma, which permits increased air pollution by millions of tons over the EPA's scientists' recommendations and also delays enforcement of smog and soot pollution standards.

Makes you sleep better at night, right? Let me be clear here: In all my years in public life, not one person, Democrat or Republican, has ever come up to me and said: "Barbara, the air is too clean and the water is too safe."

What used to be a bipartisan consensus issue has become a divisive partisan one. The Republican Party that used to stand for environmental protection now stands with the powerful polluter lobby, doing everything it can to please them, and to ward off harsh primary challenges for polluter-backed candidates. They're on a mission to derail an American value that their party once championed. The travesty of Flint, Michigan's drinking water is the poster child of Republican policy. It's revolting!

The seeds of my motivation to be a leader on environmental protection in the United States Senate were planted the day I set foot in California for the first time in 1962. The beauty of California took my breath away. Coming from Brooklyn, which had its verdant spots—but not in my neighborhood—we used to joke that only in Brooklyn could one large, strong, and resilient tree have inspired a successful novel and movie called *A Tree Grows in Brooklyn*. (Just to be clear, however: Brooklyn was a wonderful place to grow up and is now "way cool.")

Almost every book I've read about California history begins with a description of our unique environment—from the coast of the Pacific Ocean, to the ridge lines, to the mysterious fog that cools us down; from our bays, to our deserts, the redwood groves, the wetlands, the green and brown mountains, the lakes and rivers, the national and state parks, the snows in the northeast, to the amazing and productive farmlands and fisheries. What a state!

I never want to see that beauty destroyed. I know it is an ongoing battle. The good news is that in California respecting our environment is still a much shared value. In Washington, D.C., much less so.

One of the harshest battles I have ever had to endure involved protecting us all from harmful chemicals.

This is a story of deception, manipulation, special interest influence, and the revolving door.

It started two months after I lost the chairman's gavel of the Environment and Public Works Committee, in January 2015, when my Republican colleague, David Vitter, sporting a 5 percent lifetime positive record on the environment, teamed up with my Democratic colleague Tom Udall to introduce the Frank Lautenberg Chemical Safety for the 21st Century Act.

That bill, which would reform TOSCA (the Toxic Substances Control Act), was based on a bill that had been introduced by Vitter and Lautenberg just three weeks before Frank died in June 2013.

That bill had stunned me, because it had completely contradicted Frank's incredibly fabulous record on the environment, which had included four previous bills, starting in 2005, on the same subject, that I had enthusiastically co-sponsored.

Frank's usual health and environmental allies, including groups fighting for children's health and against cancer, told me that the Vitter–Lautenberg bill was a disaster, worse than current law, and that was saying a lot because the current law was weaker than the palest tea.

I used my power and influence when I had the gavel to keep the Vitter–Lautenberg bill from moving forward, but now that I had lost the chairmanship and Senator Jim Inhofe had taken my place, the equation changed and the chemical companies saw an opening—and did they take it!

News articles appeared telling the world that the American Chemical Council had actually written the Vitter–Udall bill, but it didn't seem to matter to colleagues who were being pressured to sign on and put this unpleasant battle to rest at last.

Well, the bill with a beautiful name, Frank's name, was a shuck-and-jive. It claimed to protect our families from toxics but it actually made it impossible to ban a chemical at the federal level while preempting state action. That won it the wrath of attorneys general in eight states with strong and protective chemical laws. But still, the momentum was with the chemical companies.

Four hundred fifty health organizations vigorously opposed it: the American Nurses Association, Safer Chemicals, the Asbestos Disease Awareness Fund, children's cancer groups, Physicians for Social Responsibility, to name a few. Still, I couldn't stop this bill from gaining co-sponsors.

The chemical companies had spent, according to the *New York Times*, four million dollars rewarding their supporters in the 2014 election, and clearly they wanted a return on their investment. They pushed. Senator Lautenberg's former staffer pushed, and Frank's widow, Bonnie, pushed and pushed.

I found myself in hand-to-hand combat with so many on this bill, and I could tell that many colleagues in my own party were really annoyed with me. I could see it in their eyes. Some told me they couldn't resist the bill because it was named after our beloved Frank. Bonnie was begging them over and over. Finally, one colleague who was known for her directness said: "I am telling you for your own good, you are now the most unpopular colleague in the Democratic caucus."

I admired her for telling me the truth, but I said: "What is this, high school? I will not back down. This is a health issue. Kids are getting cancer from these chemicals."

I proved her point with my comments. I was annoying. I got it, but I had no choice. I knew too much about this bill.

Inhofe called a hearing on the bill on March 18, 2015. It was a chance to point out its dangerous flaws. Senator Sheldon Whitehouse called out a defect he named "the death zone," a long period of time during which no jurisdiction could stop a dangerous chemical.

The only good news part of this story has to do with a few of my colleagues and my brilliant staff director, Bettina Poirier, and her team.

After the hearing, Senators Sheldon Whitehouse, Jeff Merkley, and Cory Booker offered to help make the bill better. I was glad, because my relationship with Vitter was not conducive to negotiation, so I blessed their effort. They did a good job in improving various aspects of the bill, and I was grateful. But the bill still had many problems and the "good guy" organizations were still strongly opposed. I was ready to make the bill better still and had one bit of leverage.

You have probably heard that one senator can hold up a bill and force days of delay. I did just that. In an effort to get me to back off and allow the bill to move forward, I was finally invited to negotiate for more positive changes.

We worked overtime and won big improvements to the preemption clause with a more workable state waiver. We put in faster timelines for the EPA to assess a chemical. We preserved tort law. We made persistent biocumulative toxic chemicals that build up in your body, like asbestos, a priority. We won inclusion of a provision to give assistance to localities in which there are childhood cancer clusters as well as making it a priority to assist when chemicals get into drinking water.

Finally, the bill was no longer dangerous. It still wasn't what it should be: the strongest protection for our families with a specific provision for the states to do even more. But it was no longer dangerous. Whew!

Now for the sad personal story that shook me to my core and was an experience I have never had in my forty years of elected life.

When Bonnie Lautenberg called to ask me to stop opposing the Vitter–Udall bill, named after her husband, I told her straight from the heart that in good conscience I could in no way support that bill and neither should she. I tried to tell her the problems with it and the groups that opposed it. She didn't want to hear any of it and kept telling me to back off.

I told her Frank deserved a real legacy. I promised her I would work to make the bill better and worthy of him.

I asked her to trust me; I would work night and day.

She would not relent. I could sense her extreme frustration with me.

Recently, she told reporters that I had actually lobbied against the original Vitter–Lautenberg bill on the way to Frank's funeral. I have no words to express my sadness at this.

Stew and I well remember that flight from Washington, D.C., to New York. We sat in the front of the plane reminiscing with colleagues about Frank's amazing accomplishments and remembering his long list of jokes, too risqué to repeat here, which he told over and over, enjoying them each time as much as we did.

I lobbied no one. I did answer questions about the bill if someone asked me if they should co-sponsor it. I said:

"Be careful. Vitter has a horrible environmental record. Let's make the bill better."

I have given so much thought to this entire sad and discouraging episode. How did this happen?

I have only one theory, besides the power of the American Chemistry Council.

It turns out that Frank's staff member who advised him and then Bonnie on this bill, who actually sat next to her at the March 2015 hearing, went to work for a lobbying firm that put out a notice on the web on May 7, 2014, months before the hearing on the bill.

They wrote that this staffer's "new practice includes advising companies on legislative proposals to overhaul the Toxic Control Substances Act."

So when this former staffer sat next to Bonnie at that March hearing, he was no objective advisor pushing for the best bill, but he was actually being paid by a company that boasts a long list of chemical companies as clients.

So if anyone ever asks you what is wrong with Washington, tell them the true story of how a bill *really* becomes a law.

There is an overriding, depressing story on the changing nature of being an environmentalist lawmaker: Republicans with whom I served and who were actually leaders on climate change have turned away with a vengeance. I still can't understand it. The only explanation is that they have grown to fear the consequences of getting some powerful and rich corporations and people angry. If I am right on this, then we are in serious, serious trouble, because huge money in politics is not going away, unless there is a change in the Supreme Court or a huge majority of Democrats in Congress—both houses. In the meantime, we do nothing on such a burning issue.

Here's where we are on the climate change debate. We have colleagues listening to 2 percent of scientists who claim there's no such thing, instead of paying close attention to the 98 percent of scientists who have proven that there is. If we don't add another dimension to this fight in the face of the overwhelming facts, I fear for our grandchildren. This new dimension must be overwhelming public support to match the overwhelming scientific consensus that climate change is a catastrophic global problem.

People are going to have to move the issue far up on their list when they consider whom they're going to support for office. It will take massive organization to overwhelm the big money being thrown at candidates in both parties to systematically deny, downplay, or rationalize not taking action.

I've sat through many a hearing of the Committee on the Environment and Public Works where scientists were attacked by Republicans who were led by "Mr. Climate Change Is a Hoax," senator, chairman of the committee, and my friend, Jim Inhofe.

I'm sure you are wondering how Jim could be my friend, but he is. He and I know that we come from different planets when it comes to climate change, and we embrace the debate. But on other issues that come before the committee, such as rebuilding our infrastructure, we work very well together, and most important, never undermine each other or use tricky parliamentary maneuvers to prevent an open discussion.

Nevertheless, Jim stands by his astonishing analysis of what he calls the hoax of climate change. Even more astonishing are Republican leaders in Congress, Boehner and McConnell, who, when confronted by the hottest August, September, and October 2014 in history, witnessing extreme weather, out-of-control wildfires, historic droughts, and contaminated drinking water in America's heartland, all simply said the same silly thing:

"I am not a scientist."

How true that is. So why in heaven's name don't they listen to the scientists who tell us how devastating it will be if we don't change to a clean energy economy? How arrogant can they be when so many more American families will feel the pain if they do nothing about climate change?

I guess, according to them, if you are not a scientist, you don't listen to the scientists. Got that? In particular, you don't listen to the 98 percent of scientists who agree that climate change is happening even faster than originally predicted and is already a major disaster.

That is beyond crazy.

I can assure McConnell and Boehner that if either of them went to the doctor and were told they had large cancerous tumors and they saw the X-rays of those tumors and the results of the biopsies that showed them malignant, they wouldn't walk out of there saying, "I don't know, I'm not a doctor." Yes, they might seek a second opinion, but if there was a 98 percent certainty of the diagnosis, they would take care of the problem and call anyone who would try to stop them from doing so a dangerous lunatic. And they would be right.

When I took the chairman's gavel of the U.S. Senate's Committee on the Environment and Public Works in 2007, it was so different. I initiated an attempt to place a price on carbon, which is the smartest way to move toward clean energy. We were doing it in California and our clean energy sector is booming with really good jobs and lower prices for consumers, who are benefiting from solar and wind power.

During my first hearing on climate change, many Republicans—including Olympia Snowe, John McCain, and Judd Gregg—either testified or put statements into the record about the need to address climate change as a scientific fact. I must have had an inkling of the trouble ahead, because I put all their testimony into a book that my Environmental and Public Works Committee printed up and put a binder around just for posterity, and also as a way to remind everyone that there once had been bipartisan agreement about the clean air crisis on our committee. Most of those Republicans who testified so eloquently are either gone from the Senate or have backed away from their views.

I led a committee trip to Greenland. You know how people say they felt the earth move? Well, we saw the glacial ice move pretty steadily as it melted, moving toward the ocean on the way to rising sea levels. Everyone was amazed. I thought I'd won over my Republican colleagues who were on that trip. But they backed away too. What they saw with their own eyes was subjugated to their campaign coffers and fears over their next election.

Does that sound harsh? It is.

Even after we had a hearing in which a brilliant call to action on climate change was made by none other than five Republicans leaders from both the Reagan and Bush administrations, the partisan divide remained. I think our witnesses were as shocked as we were. Nobody could break through the wall of resistance built brick by brick by the big, old polluting industries.

My hopes for more bipartisanship lie with Maine Independent Angus King and his Republican colleague Susan Collins. Angus has been eloquent on the threat of climate change to the lobster fisheries in Maine and Susan is working with Connecticut senator Chris Murphy to go after certain super pollutants, such as black carbon and methane, that are very potent sources of carbon. Susan is my biggest hope for greater enlightenment from the Republican Party at this point. Maybe her action will give some courage to others. I certainly hope so. And if she leads on this, history will notice.

It has been lonely to take on a lot of these battles.

Standing alone, all by yourself, isn't a lot of fun, but there is no choice once you decide what is right. You must go forward. At least that is how it is for me.

I was one of fourteen votes against the Defense of Marriage Act in 1996, which tried to make it impossible for same-sex couples to marry. I was one of thirty-three votes in favor of my own amendment to stop "Don't ask, don't tell" from being put in place in 1993, forcing those who were homosexual to live lives of lies in the military. In 1999 I was one of eight votes against repealing the Glass–Steagall Act, which regulated bank investments and which many feel would have prevented the worst of the Great Recession. I was one of twenty-three against the Iraq war brought to us by Bush and Cheney in 2002. I stood entirely alone in the Senate to protest the Ohio electoral vote after the 2004 election. And more recently I stood with a minority of the Senate supporting the Iran nuclear deal, in which Iran gives up its path to a nuclear weapon in exchange for relief. So far, so good on that one.

These are just a few examples, but I can tell you this: you don't forget those lonely moments and you develop a bond with those who stand with you.

There is one time where and I was one of thirty "no" votes, however, that I've grown to regret. That was my vote against Ben Bernanke as Federal Reserve Bank chairman in January 2010. I was just so frustrated with the blind eye the Fed had toward the mortgage gambling that I felt I needed to vote no. I believe I was wrong on that one and told him so after he proved he would move mountains to help our country get out of the worst recession since the Great Depression, while Republicans did as little as possible on this issue in Congress. But as I look back to those times that I stood with just a few, it makes me proud because I wasn't afraid.

I was tough.

Chapter Ten

The End and a Beginning

——— · ———

My favorite part of the Constitution is the preamble. When I get the chance to visit classrooms, I always start the conversation about our nation by having the students read it out loud and then we discuss what they think it means.

"We the People of the United States, in Order to form a more perfect Union, establish Justice, insure domestic Tranquility, provide for the common defense, promote the general Welfare, and secure the Blessings of Liberty to ourselves and our Posterity, do ordain and establish this Constitution for the United States of America."

Only fifty-two words, but to me it says it all. It's elegant and clear. It's guided me ever since I got to Congress. It's what I have fought for ever since. When I watched the amazing documentary about the Roosevelts by Ken Burns, I was really pleased to learn that FDR felt that the preamble was in many ways his guiding light too.

I love the words "a more perfect union." Our founders didn't say we had *already formed* a perfect union, but that we should strive to do so. They knew that nobody's perfect and nothing is perfect and our union, our nation, will never reach perfection. But perfection is what we should strive for. Gouverneur Morris, who wrote that preamble in 1787 when he was a thirty-five-year-old delegate from Pennsylvania to the Constitutional Convention, was a statesman and politician who believed in one nation, not a collection of states. He was totally opposed to slavery. He was the champion of an executive branch, but wanted to be sure it could never become a monarchy. So Morris was a leader who won a few and lost a few. Some of his concerns are still being resolved today.

Fortunately, many men and women who have led our nation since the Constitution was written understood what Morris meant in those fifty-two words. They have done everything in their power during their flash of time in the arena to make it "more perfect." They have tried to represent the people of our nation and they have struggled for America's soul. Sometimes they have done so against enormous obstacles and, as I know from personal experience, very tough odds. They have fought for justice, peace, and individual rights, for a society that's fair and strong from within and without.

All of them, like Gouverneur Morris, have won some and lost some.

It's important for every one of us in America to understand the difference one person can make in the White House, the Senate, or the House of Representatives. I've tried to show that in this memoir. It's easy to become disenchanted, because just as our nation isn't perfect, neither are our leaders. They all make mistakes, as have I. But the ultimate test is whom these elected leaders fight for every day: themselves or their constituency; the everyday people of our nation or the wealthy, big business, and connected special interests. The fact is, so much of what we take for granted is present in our lives because good people have won office for the right reasons.

How do you think we got free public education, Medicare, and Social Security? How did we build roads, highways, and bridges? Where do you think the minimum wage comes from? And child labor laws? How did we get student loans? National parks and wilderness areas? Or emergency help after a natural disaster? Clean water? Clean air? Vaccines against polio and measles? AIDS treatments? Safety standards for automobiles? Healthcare reform?

All of these crucial aspects of our lives and much more were achieved by individuals who believed in the political philosophy that Abraham Lincoln described at the end of his first inaugural address. Speaking on March 4, 1861, just after seven southern states had actually seceded from the Union, he used conciliatory tones in an effort to maintain peace and preserve the Union. He described secession as anarchy and explained, "We are not enemies, but friends. We must not be enemies. Though passion may have strained it must not break our bonds of affection. The mystic chords of memory, stretching from every battlefield and patriot grave to every living heart and hearthstone all over this broad land, will yet swell the chorus of the Union, when again touched, as surely they will be, by the better angels of our nature." *The better angels of our nature.*

I love that sentiment, but even Lincoln with all his eloquence, strength, and toughness could not stop the Civil War. Instead, he had to win it. And when he did, he exhibited "the better angels of our nature" when the country came back together and slavery was ended because of his extraordinary leadership.

Lincoln represents a level of spiritual devotion to the perfection of our union matched only by President Franklin Delano Roosevelt during the deep, dark days of the Depression and World War II. But I also greatly admire brave congressmen and senators like Sam Ervin, the Democrat from North Carolina, whose leadership of the Senate investigation committees brought down both Senator Joseph McCarthy in 1954 and Richard Nixon in 1972. It was Ervin who led the Senate Select Committee to Investigate Campaign Practices, also known as the Watergate Committee, and his fearless work brought about the end of a nightmare. Those were dark times and we needed what Ervin gave us in everyday common sense and courage, all wrapped up in his country humor and cracker-barrel authenticity.

Another politician who stepped up at a time when destiny called was Congresswoman Barbara Jordan, an African American who was the first woman to represent Texas in the House. Lyndon Johnson helped her get on the House Judiciary Committee and in 1974 Congresswoman Jordan made an influential televised speech supporting the impeachment of Richard Nixon. She also gave memorable keynote speeches at the Democratic National Conventions in both 1976 and 1992. I remember watching her with the greatest admiration and respect. I can still close my eyes and hear her strong, distinctive, and unforgettable voice.

During the 1976 election that pitted Gerald Ford against Democrat Jimmy Carter, Barbara Jordan said something that I carry in my heart every day: "Let each person do his or her part. If one citizen is unwilling to participate, all of us are going to suffer. For the American idea...is realized in each one of us." Then in 1992, as Democrat William Jefferson Clinton was nominated for president, she said, "Some people say that it makes no difference who is elected president of the United States. You must say to those cynics: You are perpetuating a fraud. It *does* make a difference who is president." She pointed out Supreme Court appointments and "principles, programs and policies which help us help ourselves."

Barbara Jordan was a trailblazer who died from complications of leukemia at the young age of fifty-nine, only four years after that speech. I see America very much the way she did, and her words inspired me throughout my years in office.

Another national legislator I learned much from and admired greatly was Ted Kennedy, the "Lion of the Senate," who served for forty-seven years and wrote more than three hundred bills that were enacted into law. Kennedy's first major priority from 1962 until his death in 2009 was health care for all, which he called "the cause of my life." He worked very well with Democrats and Republicans alike, reaching compromises on such issues as immigration, AIDS, education, and children's health.

None of these men and women had it easy. They had to be tough as nails to fight the battles against those who represented only the wealthy few or who thought they would advance their careers by dividing us through prejudice and hatred, people like Joe McCarthy and Newt Gingrich. But despite those who try to turn us away from "the better angels," the union can be made more perfect. And as we look over time this *has* happened, although we have a long, long way to go. Battles are constantly being fought, on such fronts as civil rights for African Americans, Latinos, women, and the LGBT community. But it's my firm belief that if everyone stays involved in the process, if everyone pays attention and votes, we'll keep moving in the right direction.

To quote Barbara Jordan again: "If one citizen is unwilling to participate, all of us are going to suffer. For the American idea...is realized in each one of us." How can we become a nation "of, by and for the people," if we don't? The sad truth is that so many Americans don't realize how important it is to vote. They fail to realize how their vote can elect members of Congress and the Senate who have a profound impact on their personal lives. I'm so frustrated when people tell me it doesn't make a difference, it won't count. I keep trying to connect the dots, to explain how we achieved Medicare and child labor laws and all those efforts to change things and make a more perfect union—by voting.

Only 57.5 percent of eligible voters turned up at the ballot box for the national election between Barack Obama and Mitt Romney. That means 126 million voters exercised their privilege and responsibility to participate in our democracy and 93 million didn't. Ninety-three million didn't vote at all. It breaks my heart.

Not only that, fewer than 25 percent of eligible voters ordinarily turn up at the ballot booth for so-called "off-year elections," that is, when there's not a presidential race at the top of the ballot. But that's crazy: it's *never* an off year when we're voting for local, state, and federal officials who can and will make a big difference in our lives.

How can we achieve a more perfect union if all of our citizens don't step up and understand that whom they elect is important?

I'm one of those politicians who has run for office with the notion that the founders were right to focus our efforts on perfecting our union. I have devoted my heart and mind for more than forty years to fighting for the issues of our time that I believed were critical to the well-being of my state and nation: for ending war and promoting peace, for health care, for individual rights, for education and the environment, for consumer rights, for dignity and opportunity for all of our citizens.

So why, you might ask, did I announce on January 8, 2015, my decision not to seek re-election in 2016, and thereby retire from the Senate? People have, and here's my answer.

First, let me say this. It's not because I'm too old. It's no secret that I was born on November 11, 1940, so do the math. But I feel as young as I've ever felt, and my retirement has nothing to do with my chronological age.

The chief reason is that, whereas I want to keep up the battle for America's soul, I feel that I can be more effective by being in different settings, outside the Senate, where I can speak and act with little constraint other than my own sensibilities. And I would not have left had there not developed over these many years a deep bench of progressives in California. Just as you will find in baseball, we have terrific hitters and pitchers waiting their turn, ready to get into the line-up.

When I first ran for the Senate, politics in my state was really purple, not blue, with a Republican senator, Pete Wilson, who then became governor, and many other Republican congressmen, particularly in southern California. That is no longer the case. Today I can leave the Senate confident of being replaced by someone just as strong, liberal, and progressive. A fighter. Maybe even a woman.

Second, there are now enough people in my Senate Democratic caucus who want to and will carry forward the issues to which I've given my heart: the environment, the survival of the middle class, infrastructure building, equality for all, the right to choose for women, and zero tolerance for violence against women, children, and seniors. All those things, plus a peaceful world where war is the last resort, not the first.

Also, retiring from the Senate means not having that huge weight on my shoulders of having to fund-raise for two full years out of the six-year term. All that time, stress, and the constant pressure of raising the money for myself: it's awful for me. I would now have had to raise thirty to forty *million dollars* were I to run again. Not having to do that gives me two years to devote to my work in the Senate for Californians and to the never-ending battle for the soul of our nation. What a relief not having to raise that money for myself again!

I'll have time to escalate my work with my political action committee, PAC for a Change. Raising funds for others is so much easier for me. Since I started the PAC, we've helped elect more than a hundred strong Democratic candidates and will continue to expand our impact and influence. I want to go toe-to-toe with Karl Rove and other right-wing players who have every right to influence election outcomes. We can't sit back, decry the outrageous rules surrounding campaign finance, and complain about it. Until the Congress changes, or the Supreme Court, or until we can pass an amendment to the Constitution, we have to play by the rules of the game that essentially allowed unlimited money in campaigns and very little disclosure.

Even though this unlimited special interest money goes primarily to the right wing, we can't give up. We must fight and I intend to. We can't afford to cede the money chase to the Republicans. We have to make the case for reform and ending the current terrible system in which big money rules, while at the same time raising everything we can from everyone who stands for a fair and just government.

My PAC for a Change has been in existence for fifteen years now. My son, Doug, helped me get it started with forty thousand names and now it's many thousands. That allows me to stay in touch with everybody, help my colleagues win their races, and push for issues I really care about.

In fact, I have a list of new initiatives that I call my "legacy issues," the big problems I want to work on for the rest of my career in public life and beyond.

Among the first is Adapt America. My idea is to pass new legislation that will authorize the issuance of bonds to help us fund projects to deal with fallout of climate change. Like the old War Bonds during World War II. In those days you could buy one for $18.75 and in ten years get back $25.00. Eighty-five million Americans bought 185 billion dollars' worth of these War Bonds, which is the equivalent of *three trillion, seven hundred thousand* dollars today.

The idea for these Adapt America climate change bonds is to set up a blue ribbon commission to determine what projects should be undertaken, like major flood control programs for places like Louisiana, desalination, recycling and other water supply projects for the west, crop adaptation to keep our farmers working, and new measures to protect our children from the microbes and toxins we're seeing in lakes because of the heat. All of these projects will create jobs and help our people.

Another important legacy issue is going after tobacco companies, who are now hooking young smokers on e-cigarettes. Studies are showing us that 13 percent of high school students in the U.S. smoke e-cigarettes—a huge increase from a couple of years ago. So much for e-cigarettes being an alternative for old smokers who need to quit. And did you know that the same tobacco companies who were finally forbidden to advertise to kids and teenagers with cute cartoon characters like Joe Camel are now buying up smaller e-cigarette companies and advertising e-cigarette flavors like bubble gum, cotton candy, and cherry? So much for them not advertising to little kids.

It's a great unknown story. But what is not unknown are the dangers of nicotine and the absolute lack of concern for the effect of these products on our children by the peddlers of nicotine delivery systems. More attention to this must be paid by the Congress and the Food and Drug Administration before we have another health crisis on our hands. Nicotine is addictive. It causes heart attacks and high blood pressure, and restricts blood flow to extremities. Other chemicals that we know of in e-cigarettes include benzene, formaldehyde, and cadmium. Believe it or not, the FDA will have to force e-cigarette manufacturers to list the ingredients of this lethal product on their packaging.

And their advertising is really scary. Makes it looks like this product is a gift from God.

Fortunately, I leave behind some senators dedicated to this issue, including Senator Richard Blumenthal, Senator Jeff Merkley, and my pal Senator Dick Durbin, who was so instrumental in working with then Senator Frank Lautenberg to ban smoking on airplanes.

Another issue that never seems to go away in our country is race. We have to confront the crisis between our police and our communities, which in my view has come about for these reasons:

1. **Not enough community policing**—which is the best way to bridge the divide, by creating continuous interaction on both sides. Community policing becomes personal. It allows familiarity and friendship that can help avoid problems before they lead to a breakdown. I instituted community policing when I was a county supervisor, and relationships really blossomed.

2. **The proliferation of weapons**, which can lead to the police actually being outgunned. Fear on both sides becomes so real that incidents become life-and-death situations when, with more gun control, they could have been defused.

3. **Not enough reflection of a community's makeup on the police force or in local government**. Ferguson, Missouri, was a classic template for this. When members of the police force live in and represent the communities in which they serve, things improve. Police officers are role models for our young people, and good officers really have an amazing influence. I have seen it and applauded it. We need to ensure that this is the goal. Then everyone will be much safer.

4. **Not enough information**. Every law enforcement agency needs to gather and make public information regarding injuries or deaths to both civilians and police officers. Senator Cory Booker and I have introduced legislation to make such information readily available so that the public has full disclosure on violence going in all directions.

These kinds of efforts require cooperation at the local level, but a strong federal attorney general can help a lot too, which is why there was such a fight over the confirmation of Loretta Lynch, a great pick to be attorney general. Some don't want an active attorney general, but we need one now more than ever. I am hopeful that with her background and experience, she will take on this issue.

Another legacy issue around race is voter suppression. Ever since Stephanie Tubbs Jones and I worked together and I stood up alone in the Senate to protest the electoral vote in Ohio in 2004, I have dedicated myself to the fight against suppressing the vote, however it reared its ugly head. When more people vote, progressives win. That is the fact and that is the truth. That's why Republicans do everything in their power to suppress voter turnout. We've seen it again and again. A few times they have been caught, as in the Obama–Romney race in 2012, when Michael Turzai, speaker of the Pennsylvania House of Representatives, boasted, "Voter ID is going to allow Governor Romney to win the state of Pennsylvania...Done!"

Wow. So this Pennsylvania politician felt that by jamming a law through his state legislature that would require a government-issued voter ID, he could guarantee that Mitt Romney would win. How could he say that? Because 750,000 Pennsylvania voters, mostly elderly African Americans who would vote for Barack Obama, wouldn't have a government-issued ID and there wasn't enough time to get one before the polls closed.

I understand that many voters have become disenchanted and don't believe that anything they do can make a difference. The most recent example of this has been in Ferguson, Missouri, where for many years the African American community faced worsening relationships with their city police force, and yet they didn't vote for a city council that had the power to change things. As we all know now, this disconnect resulted in months of deadly violence, civil unrest, and a non-representative government that is only now being painfully remedied. Our work needs to continue and I intend not only to continue my legislative advocacy on this but to visit communities that need encouragement to power through the obstacles. Senator Bill Nelson was very involved in my LINE Act and I trust he will continue this fight, since Florida has major issues.

Here's a legacy issue that may surprise you. It's hard to believe, but the leading cause of death, after heart disease and cancer, is medical errors. There are between 200,000 and 400,000 deaths a year from things like infections in a hospital setting from bedsores, inattention to hand washing, medication mix-ups, and more. This is a national disgrace and another issue that doesn't get enough attention. I've visited many hospitals to call attention to this issue, which was first brought to me by one of my constituents, Joe Kiani, who founded a patient protection group. Imagine the suffering that can be avoided if we attack this straightforward issue.

Provisions in Obamacare require progress on reducing errors and saving lives. These improvements are tied to hospital reimbursements. Already tens of thousands of lives are being saved.

Another legacy issue is finding cures for the diseases that cause such pain for our families. Senator Durbin is taking the lead on this. I believe the preservation of a fair and balanced estate tax can pay for such an initiative. Right now, if you leave less than ten million dollars per family, your survivors pay nothing when you die. But that's not good enough for Republicans. They want to do away with all estate taxes whatsoever, so no rich person will ever have to pay a dime.

You know if the money from a good and fair estate tax were earmarked for finding a cure for Alzheimer's, cancer, or ALS (Lou Gehrig's disease), most of us would say yes to that. Everyone would benefit, and the children of the very wealthy would still be keeping at least 60 percent of their parents' wealth. Really. Truly.

There's my legacy issue of making sure the middle class gets attention, not the shaft. Between the high costs of housing and education, it's a wonder people aren't marching every day on Capitol Hill. I think they must be too busy making ends meet. Where is the increase in the minimum wage? Where are the breaks for our college students, some of whom may still be paying off their loans when they're grandparents themselves?

And finally, crucial women's issues are a legacy issue close to my heart. Where is the guarantee of equal pay for equal work for our women and minorities? I can breathe easier knowing that Senator Elizabeth Warren will be front and center with all her passion and toughness, arm in arm with Bernie Sanders and Sherrod Brown on this, just like Kirsten Gillibrand is there for our women in the military and Patty Murray is there to organize our caucus around women's health, including a woman's right to choose.

And in California it is a great comfort to me that whoever takes my place will have the extraordinary guidance and friendship of Senator Dianne Feinstein, my partner in the Senate for all these amazing years.

I remember when I first arrived in the House of Representatives, my colleague George Miller from California sighed and said, "Thank God. Reinforcements." This work I have chosen in politics is not a one-woman or a one-man show, it's a collaboration. Yes, you need to be prepared to stand alone or almost alone once in a while. But usually it's about a common effort and that is very rewarding. And I leave some incredibly talented colleagues behind to be the champions on those issues that united us while I was there.

I have been looking over my papers recently as I get them ready for my archives. Memories of work that I want to be available for as long as people are interested. I realized that since I got to the House of Representative in 1983 and then on to the Senate ten years later, more than one thousand of my initiatives were moved forward by legislation, appropriation, or presidential executive order. In many ways that's one thousand stories unto themselves, but don't worry, I won't list them here. But my stories will be preserved.

People often ask me what I'm most proud of. It's hard to say. It's like picking which of all your children is the favorite. In a way, it's easier to remember my biggest disappointments. I wish I could have been more effective in ending the war in Iraq sooner. I wish I would have fought harder to support Anita Hill and the other women who wanted to testify against Justice Thomas; another big disappointment is that I fell six votes short of a sixty-vote threshold to address climate change through a cap-and-trade system. That breaks my heart too. My next disappointment was not doing more to object to the Florida vote count in 2000 and then in 2004 standing utterly alone after the Bush-Kerry race, not being able to get even one senator to stand with me against the Ohio electoral vote count.

But since people do ask me all the time, here are a few accomplishments I'm happy about.

- The first-ever funding of after-school programs, now covering one million children.
- One million acres of California wilderness preserved.
- The first-ever Comprehensive Combat Casualty Care Center in California for wounded warriors.
- Setting clean drinking water standards to protect pregnant women, children, and other vulnerable people.
- Protecting the privacy of personal information on driver's licenses.
- The dolphin-safe tuna label.
- Ensuring that our transportation programs remain in place for years to come, including a manifold expansion in interest-free loans to states for major transportation projects and prohibiting the rental of recalled vehicles.
- Establishing the first-ever subcommittee to oversee global women's issues.
- Protecting victims of rape in the military from irrelevant, harassing questioning that had already been barred in civilian courts.
- Establishing mental health testing for soldiers being redeployed to combat zones.

There's a more complete list of fifty top accomplishments that you can see in the Appendix.

On January 8, 2015, after news of my decision not to run for re-election in 2016 broke on the network news and in the major print media, I received telephone calls from President Barack Obama, President Bill Clinton, Vice President Joe Biden, Secretary of State John Kerry, former Secretary of State Hillary Clinton, Robert Redford, and many other colleagues, friends, and family.

I had announced my decision in a unique fashion: a sit-down "interview" with my nineteen-year-old grandson, Zach. The interview idea was mine. The idea to have Zach ask the questions came from my son, Doug, and was heartily approved by Zach's mom, my daughter, Nicole. I didn't want to do the usual hectic press conference because I had a few important points to make. Those were:

1. I am not leaving the Senate because of all the partisan fighting there.
2. I am not leaving the Senate because of my age.
3. I am not retiring from working on the issues I love.
4. I intend to grow my PAC for a Change in order to help others win elections.
5. I intend to work to elect a Democratic president who will make history in 2016.

We taped the interview at our home in California on a Monday three days before it was released. It was nostalgic because my four-time-winning campaign manager Rose Kapolczynski had organized its rollout. Rose is an extraordinary strategist and showed a male-dominated field that yes, a woman can win a statewide race in a state that, if it were a country, would be the eighth largest in the world.

The reaction to the announcement was overwhelmingly rewarding. A few thought the interview was "soupy." One right-winger called it "weird." That's fine with me.

The only truly vicious response was from southern California Congressman Darrell Issa, whose numerous shady dealings in the private sector have never inhibited him from wild attacks against me. Even when I announced my retirement from the Senate, he could find no gracious utterance.

"It's always been a vacant office," was his only comment.

Huh?

Well...I wrote at the beginning of this memoir that I never elicit a neutral response. I've always done it my way. I've always had this emotional fire, this art-of-tough way of operating. I've always believed if you are pleasing everyone, then you're probably not doing a heck of a lot. And doing nothing for me is not an option. Not until I am horizontal.

As we approach the end of this memoir, moreover, I want to say again that my story is not unique. "The art of tough" is an approach to all the challenges of my life, but using techniques that can apply to everyone. Whether you're in politics like me, or trying to be a great parent while holding down a job, running a small business, building or changing a career under difficult circumstances, out of work, or just between things—the principles are the same.

So this book is *about* me but *for* you. I've had the good fortune to learn a lot that I think can work for you, too. It's an approach to the problems and challenges we all face based on our own strong set of values and our own sense of purpose. That's the key. The art of tough must be accompanied by something unique...*you*. You need to be authentic and stay authentic, or being tough doesn't work. It will only be a technique, not a way of life.

And I hope I've sparked your interest in getting more involved politically, now that you understand how one person *can* make a difference.

One of my close friends who knew I was writing this memoir told me that she felt there was nothing about her life that was worth a memoir or even an article. I was incredulous. This was a woman who was born into an ethnic family who held their children close. She rebelled as a teenager and became quite independent. She blazed the trail for women in business. She led a number of philanthropic causes and quietly befriended many in need. She found the love of her life in her fifties. She battled bouts of cancer with an attitude that made her a life force for me and many others. I told her, "Nothing for a memoir? I say there's enough there for a movie."

I wish more people understood that they have a unique story to tell about their lives. Each of us has so much to tell. My daughter, Nicole, wrote, produced, and directed a documentary film called *How I Got Over*. It's about fifteen formerly homeless and addicted women who tell their life stories in a way that not only frees them from the grief but also inspires others.

Now I'm closing the door on my life as an elected official. I have a wide-open door for the next chapter. I'm excited about the future and I know whatever form it takes I will continue to stand up, speak up, and perhaps even make more history. Who knows? There is so much out there. The problems I care about will always need attention, many advocates, and dedicated people working to solve them.

But I bet I'll still have to be tough.

Here's a little lyric with no melody on this subject, the last for this memoir.

The Senate is the place where I've always made my case
For families, for the planet and the human race.
More than twenty years in a job I love
Thanks to California and the Lord above.

Although I won't be working from my Senate space
And I won't be running in that next tough race
As long as there are issues, challenges and strife
I will never retire 'cause that's the meaning of my life.

Acknowledgments

My deepest thanks to my dynamic agent, Kimberley Cameron, for encouraging me and leading me in just the right direction in every way including introducing me to Alan Rinzler, whose skill set included teaching me to weave my stories together.

Kimberley also made sure I met my editor, Mauro DiPreta from Hachette Books, who has been a tough, talented, and wonderful teacher.

His team has been a pleasure to work with, including Ashley Yancey, Betsy Hulsebosch, and Michelle Aielli.

Also thanks to David Brody, who cheered me on and made sure I told the toughest stories in the most direct ways, and to Kevin Keegan, who brought to life the senators who held "my" seat since California became a state.

My deepest thanks to every one of my staff members throughout the years. From my first election to my last re-election—a period of forty years—these top staffers have worked their hearts out for our state and our nation.

Listed here are those top staffers who started me off when I got elected to the Marin County Board of Supervisors in 1976, those who helped me when I won election to the House of Representatives in 1982, those top staffers who started me off in my first Senate office, and those top staffers who served on my Senate team in my last term. I include those on the Environment and Public Works Committee and on my campaign team. All of these are shining stars:

Jason Albritton, Tom Bohigian, Kelly Boyer, Sam Chapman, Zachary Coile, Grant Cope, Jackie DeNevers, Andrew Dohrmann, Joaquin Esquivel, Kate Gilman, Jana Haehl, Dan Hammer, Shannon Hart, Alicia Henry,

Maggie Henderson, Ted Illston, Tony Intintoli, Claudette Josephson, Matt Kagan, Nicole Kaneko, Rose Kapolczynski, Mary Kerr, Drew Littman, Gloria Littman, Jim Margolis, Yvette Martinez, Kaye Meier, Mark Mellman, Sean Moore, David Napoliello, Gina Pennestri, Bettina Poirier, Karen Olick, Paul Ordal, Wyman Riley, Beatriz Rogalski, Tyler Rushforth, Laura Schiller, Elaine Shamir, Stacey Smith, Liz Tankersley, Peter True, Eric Vizcaino, Michael Weiss, and Urcel Williams.

Appendix

Top Fifty Legislative Accomplishments

1. **Led passage of the Moving Ahead for Progress in the 21st Century Act,** which modernized federal highway, highway safety, and transit programs to make them more efficient and help address the infrastructure crisis facing our nation by reauthorizing and funding federal surface transportation programs for two years (fiscal years 2013 and 2014). MAP-21 transferred a small loan program into a dynamic program that is funding huge job-intensive infrastructure projects all across the nation. Signed into law on July 6, 2012.

2. **Protected more than 1 million acres of federal public land in California as wilderness.** The Omnibus Public Lands Package, which became law in 2009, included three bills I wrote to protect 57,000 acres in Big Sur and the Los Padres Forest plus 273,000 other acres of California coast as wilderness.

3. **Passed the first-ever specific authorization for after-school programs.** In 2001, the bipartisan bill was signed into law by President George W. Bush in 2002. After-school programs are now being funded at $1.15 billion, allowing them to serve 1.6 million children.

4. **Chaired House-Senate conference and led the effort to pass the Water Resources Reform and Development Act of 2014,** which invests in

water infrastructure that protects communities from flooding, maintains navigation routes for commerce and the movement of goods, restores ecosystems, and provides a boost to the economy by creating jobs.

5. **Wrote two laws to enhance economic and security cooperation with Israel.** In 2012, I worked with Republican Senator Johnny Isakson to write the United States–Israel Enhanced Security Cooperation Act, which extended loan guarantees to Israel, increased the U.S. military stockpile in Israel, and encouraged NATO–Israel cooperation. In 2014, I worked with Republican Senator Roy Blunt to write the U.S.–Israel Strategic Partnership Act of 2014—further strengthening economic and security cooperation between the two countries.

6. **Introduced bipartisan legislation to prevent abusive treatment of victims of sexual assault in the military.** In November 2013, Republican Senator Lindsay Graham joined me to amend Article 32 of the Uniform Code of Military Justice (UCMJ) to help prevent abusive treatment of sexual assault victims in a pretrial setting. The legislation gained broad support from military law experts and victims' advocacy groups, and was signed into law as part of the National Defense Authorization Act for 2014.

7. **Led the effort to stop unethical human pesticide testing.** In 2005, the Senate adopted my amendment to the Interior appropriations bill prohibiting human pesticide testing until rulemaking was completed establishing standards consistent with National Academy of Sciences recommendations and the Nuremberg Code.

8. **Helped establish a combat care center in San Diego to treat wounded service members.** I filed an amendment to provide funding for a Comprehensive Combat Casualty Care Center (C5) at the San Diego Naval Hospital. As a result, the Department of Defense approved funding for the project.

9. **Wrote the law to keep felons out of the military.** The fiscal year 2013 Defense Authorization Act included my bill to prohibit any individual who is convicted of a felony sexual assault from being issued

a waiver to join the military. According to an Army report, soldiers who received conduct waivers were more likely to commit a felony sexual assault while on active duty than soldiers who entered the military without waivers.

10. **Passed a bill to help eliminate lead in drinking water.** Joined Senator James Inhofe along with nine additional bipartisan co-sponsors to strengthen standards to protect people from toxic lead in drinking water by uniformly reducing the allowable lead content in drinking water pipes, pipe fittings, and plumbing fixtures to nearly zero.

11. **Wrote amendments on toy safety to protect children.** The first required the same "choking hazard" warnings printed on toy packaging to be displayed prominently on online retail websites or catalogues. The second required manufacturers of durable infant or toddler products to provide consumers with postage-paid registration forms so consumers could be better informed if the product they bought was recalled.

12. **Prevented DMVs from disclosing personal information that could be used to stalk or harm drivers.** I wrote a bipartisan amendment with Republican Senator John Warner to prohibit any state motor vehicle department from disclosing certain personal information. The amendment passed the Senate and was signed into law as part of the 1994 crime bill and was later upheld by the Supreme Court.

13. **Created the Senate Climate Action Task Force.** I led the formation of a large group of senators dedicated to taking action to reduce dangerous carbon pollution and address climate change. On March 10, 2014, the Senate Climate Action Task Force had more than thirty senators speak on the Senate floor throughout the night to focus attention on the serious impacts to the country that are occurring because of climate change.

14. **Created the first-ever Defense Task Force on Mental Health to address post-traumatic Stress and other wartime psychological health issues.** I amended the fiscal year 2006 Defense Authorization bill to create the Defense Task Force on Mental Health, which held

public meetings in California and submitted a long-term plan to help the Department of Defense improve the efficacy of mental health services in the armed forces. A Center of Excellence for Psychological Health and Traumatic Brain Injury was subsequently opened at the Naval Medical Center in Bethesda, Maryland.

15. **Extended essential foster care services to young people between eighteen and twenty-one.** My bill to extend essential foster care services to young people between the ages of eighteen and twenty-one was incorporated into the Fostering Connections to Success and Increasing Adoptions Act, which became law in 2008. This law helps those young people who want to stay in their foster care homes after the age of eighteen to do so, as many have a hard time being on their own as teenagers. Many were becoming homeless.

16. **Spurred new rules to protect airline passengers' rights.** Several provisions from my Passenger Bill of Rights legislation were enacted into law as part of the FAA Modernization and Reform Act of 2012 that ensured that passengers experiencing excessive tarmac delays would have access to food and water, working restrooms, comfortable cabin temperatures, and medical treatment. Airlines are also required to give passengers the option to deplane after three hours on domestic flights and four hours on international flights.

17. **Brokered agreement to restore the Gulf Coast after the Deepwater Horizon oil spill.** As chair of the Environmental and Public Works Committee, I negotiated a compromise bill that was co-sponsored by nine of the ten members of the Gulf Coast delegation. The Resources and Ecosystems Sustainability, Tourist Opportunities, and Revived Economies of the Gulf Coast Act of 2011 (RESTORE Act) established a Gulf Coast Restoration Trust Fund and dedicated 80 percent of all civil penalties paid by responsible parties in connection with the Deepwater Horizon oil spill for projects and activities to restore the long-term health of the coastal ecosystems and local economies in the Gulf Coast Region. It was enacted as part of MAP-21 (HR 4348) on July 6, 2012.

18. **Wrote the measure ending taxpayer bailouts of Wall Street.** In 2010, the Senate, on a ninety-six-to-one vote, passed my amendment ending taxpayer bailouts by ensuring that Wall Street firms—not taxpayers—pay all the costs of liquidating a failing financial firm. The measure required that any expenses associated with liquidating a failing financial firm be paid for by the sale of the firm's assets or an assessment on the financial industry. The measure was included as part of the Wall Street reform law signed by President Obama.

19. **Fought to pass the Violence Against Women Act.** As a member of the House of Representatives, I teamed up with Senator Joe Biden to introduce the original Violence Against Women Act (VAWA). This legislation, which became law in 1994, has raised awareness about violence against women, increased the number of shelters for abused women, and trained judges, police, and prosecutors on how to deal with violent crimes against women.

20. **Wrote an amendment to increase AIDS funding by $30 million.** In 2000, I passed a bipartisan amendment with Republican Senator Gordon Smith to the Foreign Operations Appropriations bill that increased international AIDS funding by $30 million to $255 million, and tuberculosis funding by $10 million to $66 million. The amendment passed by voice vote and was signed into law in November 2000.

21. **Wrote the Dolphin-Safe Tuna Label law.** As a member of the House of Representatives in 1990, my law required that companies that sell dolphin-safe tuna be able to prove that the fish was not caught with methods harmful to dolphins. The Senate version was sponsored by Senator Joe Biden. In July 2012, I worked with the Obama administration to comply with a World Trade Organization (WTO) ruling regarding the U.S. dolphin-safe tuna label.

22. **Passed a bill to name the Environmental Protection Agency headquarters in honor of President Bill Clinton.** My Federal Buildings Designation Act of 2012 (S. 3304) redesignated the Environmental Protection Agency Headquarters at 1200 Pennsylvania Avenue N.W.

in Washington, D.C., as the "William Jefferson Clinton Federal Building," and redesignated the federal building and United States courthouse located at 200 East Wall Street in Midland, Texas, as the "George H. W. Bush and George W. Bush United States Courthouse" and "George Mahon Federal Building."

23. **Created a provision for the conversion of the San Francisco's Presidio military base into a national park.** Representative Nancy Pelosi wrote the House version of the bill. The bill became law after I led the Senate fight to defeat an attempt to sell the Presidio, which would have led to the loss of this historic military site.

24. **Defeated an effort to overturn EPA's endangerment finding on carbon pollution.** I led the opposition on the Senate floor to a Congressional Review Act resolution of disapproval (S.J. Res. 26) that would overturn EPA's scientific finding that greenhouse gases endanger public health and welfare. The motion to proceed to consideration of the measure was rejected on June 10, 2010, by a vote of 47 to 53.

25. **Honored Malala Yousafzai by expanding scholarships for women in Pakistan.** I wrote language to honor Pakistani schoolgirl and advocate Malala Yousafzai. The final fiscal year 2015 Omnibus Appropriations bill included my legislation expanding university scholarship opportunities for disadvantaged women in Pakistan. As a result, USAID committed to provide 50 percent of future scholarships to Pakistani women.

26. **Helped secure millions for military burn trauma research.** Millions of dollars were needed to support multicenter clinical burn treatment trials that advance the treatment of service members who suffer burns during military service. I received an award from the American Burn Association in 2010 for this work.

27. **Spearheaded legislation to protect Peace Corps volunteers.** In September 2011, the Senate passed the Kate Puzey Peace Corps Volunteer Protection Act, authored by Senator Isakson and me, to honor the slain Peace Corps worker in Benin, West Africa, by providing better

security and protection measures for Peace Corps volunteers. It was signed into law by President Obama on November 21, 2011.

28. **Wrote a provision that prioritized cleanup of brownfield sites affecting children and vulnerable populations.** My brownfields cleanup bill that gives priority in cleanup to sites affecting children and other vulnerable populations was signed into law in January 2002.

29. **Established the Manzanar National Historic Site commemorating the infamous relocation camp.** I wrote the Senate version of Representative Robert Matsui's bill to acquire land to honor Japanese Americans who were unjustly interned during World War II.

30. **Wrote a bill to permit the use of highway funds to retrofit bridges.** My 1994 law ensured the use of funds under the highway bridge replacement and rehabilitation program for seismic retrofit, so bridges could withstand earthquakes.

31. **Established the first-ever subcommittee focused on global women's issues.** In 2009, I worked with Chairman John Kerry on the Senate Foreign Relations Committee to create the first-ever subcommittee focused on global women's issues. As chairman of the subcommittee, I've held numerous policy hearings and taken legislative action to address challenges facing women across the globe—from Afghanistan to the Democratic Republic of the Congo to Egypt to Syria.

32. **Wrote an amendment requiring the president to determine whether POWs who died in captivity were eligible for the Purple Heart.** The fiscal year 2007 Defense Authorization bill included an amendment by Republican Senator Olympia Snowe and me requiring the president to submit a determination as to whether all prisoners of war who died in captivity should be eligible for the Purple Heart. On October 6, 2008, the Department of Defense announced that U.S. soldiers who died in prisoner of war camps as long ago as World War II could receive Purple Heart medals once reserved for troops killed or wounded in combat, which could allow an estimated 17,000 POWs who died in captivity to receive the honor.

33. **Expanded research activities of the National Heart, Lung, and Blood Institute with regard to cardiovascular diseases in women.** I worked with Representative Maxine Waters to pass the Women's Cardiovascular Diseases Research and Prevention Act, which expanded research and authorized appropriations of the National Heart, Lung, and Blood Institute with regard to cardiovascular diseases in women.

34. **Created a provision requiring new standards for public protection from arsenic.** My 2001 amendment established a standard level of safety for arsenic that took into account infants, children, pregnant women, the elderly, and those with a history of serious illness. The amendment also lifted the suspension on the effective date for the community right-to-know mailers letting people know how much arsenic is in their water. The amendment passed the Senate ninety-seven to one, and was signed into law as part of the VA/HUD Appropriations bill in November 2001.

35. **Wrote an amendment to the Safe Drinking Water Act protecting children, pregnant women, and seniors.** My 1996 amendment sets standards to protect vulnerable populations, including children, infants, and the elderly. It passed the Senate by voice vote.

36. **Created recognition for Japanese American World War II heroes.** I wrote the law awarding the Congressional Gold Medal to the Army's 100th Infantry Battalion, the 442nd Regimental Combat Team, and the Military Intelligence Service in recognition of their dedicated service during World War II. After working to secure the co-sponsorship of two-thirds of the Senate, my bill passed the Senate unanimously and became law in 2010.

37. **Worked to secure assistance after California earthquakes.** I advocated for federal disaster assistance for California following the Loma Prieta, Northridge, and Napa earthquakes, all of which received a Major Disaster Declaration, which freed up federal funding and helped communities get back on their feet.

38. **Wrote a law to allow research into organ donations from HIV-positive donors to HIV-positive recipients.** In 2013, Congress passed and the president signed into law the bipartisan Boxer–Coburn HOPE Act, which

ends the federal ban on research into organ donations from HIV-positive donors to HIV-positive recipients and opens a pathway to the eventual transplantation of these organs and could provide life-saving assistance to HIV-positive patients who are at risk of liver and kidney failure.

39. **Created a provision to combat child trafficking.** The Violence Against Women Reauthorization Act (VAWA)—which was passed by Congress in February 2013 and signed into law by President Obama in March 2013—included a provision based on my Child Protection Compact Act (CPCA), a bipartisan bill that would give the State Department additional tools to combat child trafficking, exploitation, and enslavement across the globe.

40. **Wrote a provision to improve mental health screening for military members prior to deployment.** Senator Lieberman and I amended the fiscal year 2007 Defense Authorization bill to require new guidelines to prevent the deployment of military service members with serious mental health problems.

41. **Exposed Pentagon waste.** As a member of the House of Representatives in the 1980s, I revealed spare-part overcharges by Pentagon contractors—such as the infamous $7,600 coffeepot—that led to several procurement reforms that saved taxpayers millions of dollars.

42. **Secured funding for college entrance and financial aid counseling for low-income and first-generation students.** I wrote an amendment that increased funding for the Department of Education's Upward Bound program that provides tutoring, mentoring, and counseling on college entrance and financial aid applications for low-income and first-generation college bound students.

43. **Increased Pell Grant awards to community college students.** My 2007 Pell Grant Equity Act was included in the College Cost Reduction Act. This bill eliminated the "tuition sensitivity" clause in the Pell Grant system that had unfairly prevented students who attended community colleges and lower-tuition institutions from receiving the maximum Pell Grant.

44. **Worked to protect doctors, nurses, and patients from acquiring life threatening diseases from accidental needle sticks.** My Health Care Worker Needlestick Prevention Act was in large measure enacted in late 2000 as part of the Needle Stick Safety and Prevention Act. It requires hospitals, doctors' offices, and other healthcare providers to use drug delivery methods least likely to cause accidental needle sticks.

45. **Worked with the California poultry industry to stop deceptive advertising of previously frozen poultry.** In a victory against false advertising, I worked to ensure that previously frozen poultry couldn't be sold with a label marking it as fresh.

46. **Wrote an amendment protecting military children from pesticides.** My 2000 amendment prevented the Department of Defense from using pesticides that contain known or probable carcinogens in areas used by children, including parks, playgrounds, recreation centers, day care centers, and base housing.

47. **Provided assistance to salmon fishermen.** I introduced legislation in 2006 to provide financial relief to salmon fishermen, tribes, and related industries affected by the Klamath River salmon collapse and to support recovery efforts for wild salmon populations in the Klamath River. Assistance totaling $47.2 million was distributed to fishermen and other affected groups.

48. **Led the fight to secure passage of the Water Resources Development Act of 2007.** As chair of the Environment and Public Works Committee, I worked with ranking Republican Jim Inhofe of Oklahoma to craft a comprehensive water resources bill. This law authorized $1.3 billion for fifty-four flood control, ecosystem restoration, and navigation projects in California. In my first year as chairman, I successfully fought to pass the act and override a veto by President George W. Bush, and the bill was enacted on November 9, 2007.

49. **Wrote a law to establish Pinnacles National Park.** On January 10, 2013, President Obama signed my bill to elevate the Pinnacles National Monument to a national park. Pinnacles National Park was

the fifty-ninth national park created by Congress and the first since 2004. Elevating this site to a national park has since drawn more national recognition and an additional 90,000 visitors over the previous year to this spectacular piece of California's natural and cultural heritage.

50. **Championed expansion of marine sanctuaries.** In June 2011, the Senate Commerce Committee approved my Gulf of Farallones and Cordell Bank National Marine Sanctuaries Boundary Modification and Protection Act. The bill would protect the entire coastline of Sonoma County and as far north as Point Arena in Mendocino County. On December 20, 2012, the Obama administration announced that it would begin working to expand the Gulf of Farallones and Cordell Bank National Marine Sanctuaries administratively.

A Brief History of My U.S. Senate Seat

The title of this section isn't entirely accurate. The California United States Senate seat that I have held since 1993 is not really "my" Senate seat. If it's going to be named after anybody, it should probably be William McKendree Gwin, the first senator to hold it. But I've had this seat for four terms, nearly twenty-four years as I write, and I've grown fond of it. It's comfortable and familiar to me, like a family heirloom. So I'm taking liberties here and calling it "my" seat.

Since there are two Senate seats for each state, our leaders wanted to make sure that when a state became part of our nation, as California did in 1850, each senator had different term lengths. So after the two were chosen they picked straws for the six-year seat or the two-year seat and Gwin got the six-year term. All the fifteen senators to follow him are listed in his seat. In the other seat, John Charles Fremont was chosen and served briefly. Dianne Feinstein currently occupies the "Fremont" seat.

Hanging in my office are the photos of all my predecessors. As I gaze at them from time to time, particularly when things are tough, I know that they too faced the same kind of difficult issues that I have. Well, not exactly. Until the Seventeenth Amendment was ratified in 1913, two years after my mother's birth, senators were not directly elected by the voters. So before that time, senators were only responsible to the politicians in their state. A terrible situation for democracy, but easier for half the senators who occupied "my" seat, since far fewer people were holding them accountable.

What follows, in any case, is a brief description of the men who held the seat before the good people of California gave me this incredible opportunity. It is just a little bit of history that perhaps will interest you enough to learn much more about each of my predecessors, because each is interesting and provocative in his own way. What becomes clear even in this tiny history lesson is that events shape our careers, a point I have tried to make in this memoir.

SENATOR #1: William McKendree Gwin, Democrat, 1850–1861 (with a pause in 1856 due to a fight over his reappointment)

Senator Gwin was very involved in California's drive for statehood. William was a southerner and a slave owner from the Deep South, having already represented a Mississippi district in the House of Representatives. He knew he could never win a Senate seat from the south because other politicians had it locked up, with more influence than he did with the southern power brokers. Remember, there wasn't a chance to go out to the people, like I did. You needed connections—big connections—to win the appointment from the state legislature.

Standing on the steps of the Willard Hotel near the White House on March 5, 1849, therefore, William Gwin turned to his friend, Senator Stephen Douglas of Illinois, and declared he was headed for California. Douglas was stunned, but he expressed his wish that Gwin would succeed in his quest to become a United States senator from that state that was yet to be admitted to the Union.

So Gwin, with the support of his wife, Mary, traveled to San Francisco in 1849. He had to take a steamship to Panama, then a boat up a river, through a jungle, and transfer by mule to a boat in Panama City and then north to San Francisco. The trip was so difficult that he left on March 5 and didn't get to the San Francisco Bay until June 4. And I complain about the airline commute!

Gwin didn't waste time. He brought with him a copy of the Iowa state constitution, became a delegate to the California state convention, and played a huge role in crafting the state's constitution, which prohibited slavery.

Gwin was a slave owner himself, having spent most of his life in the south. But he knew he had to get this slot as a senator and that was an imperative. California would not be admitted to the Union as a slave state.

Gwin went back to D.C. and had the satisfaction of being a senator-elect, but he couldn't serve until California was admitted to the Union. That debate over California's admission to the Union was the last debate for Daniel Webster, Henry Clay, and John C. Calhoun. It was a *very* convoluted and difficult one. Had it not been for the sudden death of President Zachary Taylor in 1850, some historians feel it would have taken California much longer to become part of the United States. They believe that the opposition in Congress to California's admission dissipated due to shock over the president's death. Consequently, the "great compromise" of 1850 allowed California into the Union as a free state.

Senator Gwin became known as a tireless advocate for California. He introduced many bills, always explaining how the "unprecedented nature of life" in California required attention. Some things never change.

He was known for construction of lighthouses along the Pacific coast and for expanding the federal judiciary. He worked to set up schools and universities and a code to regulate the working of the mines. He established a branch of the U.S. Mint in San Francisco, a building I saved after the treasury closed it down early in my Senate term. I guess Gwin would have been happy at that.

He worked to construct Mare Island Naval Shipyard, which was part of my House district in the eighties before it closed as a base. He also worked to give California more than one million acres of public lands. One of my proudest accomplishments is gaining wilderness designation for more than one million acres of public land in California, the highest level of protection.

Gwin left the Senate before the Civil War and despite his amazing work for California, he supported slavery and the Confederacy. His son even fought for the south. This taints his tenure, but I am glad that much later in life he said: "The institution of slavery would be a curse to the white inhabitants where it prevailed."

That's the story of the first senator to hold "my seat," a man from the south who was so instrumental in California becoming a part of America.

SENATOR #2: James McDougall, Democrat, 1861–1867

General James McDougall, who had served one term in the U.S. House of Representatives, was declared the U.S. senator after twenty-two "ballotings" by California's legislature. It was a very controversial election.

In 1861, the *New York Times* described the reasons the paper had supported McDougall: "He is sound on the Pacific Railroad, he was confirmed in the Episcopal church...and no doubt has learned the habits of self-denial since." That was alluding to McDougall's well-known fondness for imbibing "a great deal of whiskey." But the most important issue, as the *Times* explained it, was that McDougall was "openly and earnestly a Union man." So the second senator was fiercely opposed to secession and had strong support from President Lincoln. And that was the clear reason he won over the legislature.

The war gave impetus to the construction of the Transcontinental Railroad with California's congressional delegation uniting to push for it with a sense of urgency. California elected officials wisely asked, "Psychologically how are the Far West states to be stabilized in relation to the Union if they remain disconnected from the east for decades to come?" President Lincoln agreed, and he became intimately involved. The Pacific Railway Act of 1862 authorized and financed the construction of a transcontinental railroad and a second Pacific Railway Act of 1864 increased the land grant and financial incentives. In that time frame, President Lincoln also acted to protect Yosemite.

It turns out that Senator McDougall, while giving his vote for these important projects, didn't have a major influence over those momentous events, because his skills as a legislator continued to be diminished by alcoholism. The addiction must have been a terrible one, because it is reported that he didn't even visit California once during his six-year term.

SENATOR #3: Cornelius Cole, Republican, 1867–1873

As a member of the House, Senator Cole was one of the delegates who gathered at Gettysburg to dedicate a burying ground for the soldiers who had given their lives in the Civil War. Hundreds of thousands had died. This is what Cole wrote about President Lincoln:

> I sat only a few feet from Mr. Abraham Lincoln and had a rare opportunity to study him. He appeared rather depressed and only rarely did his face brighten... When he rose to speak, he began in a firm clear voice: "Four score and seven years ago, our fathers brought forth upon this continent a new nation, conceived in liberty and dedicated to the proposition that all men are created equal."

Cole was so moved by that speech and that issue. Senator Cole cast a vote for the Thirteenth Amendment, abolishing slavery. "I never felt so much excitement over any measure before," he said. Indeed.

Many years later, when he was nearing a hundred years of age, he was invited to the House to address that body and he said:

"Our destiny no one can forecast. Our hopes are wide awake. From a few weak colonists we have become what we are today, and I think we ought all to remember above all things, the wonderful character of those who created the Republic and government in America."

Cole lived to be 102. While he was in the Senate, he was a leader in negotiations to acquire the land known as "Russian America" that today is Alaska. He was also active in gaining grants for our harbors and forest preservation and for greater efficiency of the postal service on the Pacific Coast.

SENATOR #4: Aaron Sargent, Republican, 1873–1879

While I relish my connection to Senator Cole, who voted to abolish slavery, I'm also proud that Senator Sargent, encouraged by his wife, Ellen, proposed to the Senate the language that was eventually adopted as the Nineteenth Amendment…women's suffrage. Women wouldn't get the right to vote until 1920, but the Sargents were definitely part of the movement.

Mrs. Sargent was president of the California Woman Suffrage Association and became treasurer of the national organization.

In addition to his progressive politics on women, Senator Sargent was very involved in the transportation system in southern California. He knew how important it was to give farmers the ability to ship their products. Los Angeles could not be isolated and he worked to ensure that. His impetus was that it was a two-day steamboat trip from San Francisco. He probably would like Governor Brown's bullet train.

SENATOR #5: James Farley, Democrat, 1879–1885

California had a couple of major milestones in 1879 when James Farley took office. One was that agriculture replaced mining as a big factor in the state's economy.

Farley, an attorney, was acknowledged as a leader in the Democratic Party in California. He served in the State Senate from 1869 to 1876. Clearly he was very interested in state affairs and perhaps not that interested in national affairs.

I say that because according to the website Govtrack.us, Senator Farley missed 785 votes out of 1,818 roll call votes. Or maybe it was because he wasn't well: he died less than a year after he left the Senate.

SENATOR #6: Leland Stanford, Republican, 1885–1893

Senator Stanford was the former governor of California, founder of Stanford University, and one of California's "big four" businessmen, who would earn millions from the fruits of the railroad business. Leland Stanford was the seventh-richest man in the nation, the year he was appointed to the Senate.

Stanford was said to be reluctant about seeking the Senate seat, but his wife, Jane, encouraged him to accept the nomination and enter the race, which still took place inside the California legislature.

Stanford was very talented and respected, but he had been a chief executive and therefore was frustrated by, in his own words, the "deliberative processes of the Senate," a feeling shared by most governors then and since. He complained that his constituents were "working him to death sending him 100 letters a day and expecting personal responses to each." California had more than one million residents at that time, and they were making themselves heard.

Believe it or not, Senator Stanford maintained two other jobs while he was a senator. He managed the university he founded and was also president of the Southern Pacific Railroad Company. Maybe that's the reason he only addressed the Senate fewer than two dozen times in his eight years there.

Senator Stanford dedicated his time as a senator to several issues including interstate commerce, currency, and public education. In an amazing situation, he rallied support against the Interstate Commerce Act and said it was about regulating railroads. Whoa! He owned a railroad, but that was no impediment then. He turned out to be on the losing side of that issue.

Stanford put forward a "cooperation bill" that he really cared about. It was about the need to have more cooperation between workers and business owners. He envisioned that workers would work better in a cooperative relationship. To me it sounds like giving workers ownership in part of the business they work for.

He failed to get that legislation passed too.

Stanford was very progressive on worker policy and public education. He supported a bill called the Blair Education Bill, which would have set up a federal grant to help the states educate their children. He said, "The national government could have no more important objective than improving the intelligence of the nation's citizens."

Education was Stanford's great passion, but despite his best efforts the Blair Act never became law.

Although Senator Stanford, a man of many careers and a major contributor to the state of California in the nineteenth century, did not deliver legislative accomplishments while in the Senate, he did receive this high compliment from one of his colleagues, Senator William M. Stewart of Nevada, who said:

"Every suggestion Stanford made, every speech he ever delivered and every bill he introduced had for its object the good of all the people."

To me, that is a very high compliment.

Leland Stanford was the only senator in my seat to die while still serving the people of California.

SENATOR #7: George Perkins, Republican, 1893–1915

Senator Perkins was a former governor of California and was appointed to Leland Stanford's seat after Stanford's death. He was the last senator to serve in this seat before the Seventeenth Amendment was ratified, ensuring that United States senators would from then on be elected by popular vote.

Significant changes occurred in California and nationwide during his service. The first World Series was held in 1903, the Pacific Fleet was established, the first Model T rolled off Henry Ford's assembly line, and the movie industry was established in Los Angeles.

Perkins served during the 1906 earthquake, which was so horrific for San Francisco. More than three thousand people died and most of the city was leveled. He also worked with his colleagues on the investigation of the loss of the SS *Titanic* in 1912.

The very big issue that the senator embraced was the Raker Act. It passed in 1913 and is still an issue in San Francisco today. Perkins was a leader in the passage of this act, which declared that: "If the source of water is on public land, no private profit could be derived from the development."

The senator was chairman of four Senate committees during his tenure, a situation not permitted today. He chaired Fisheries, Civil Service and Retrenchment Committee, the Naval Affairs Committee, and the Railroads Committee. Today, you can only be chairman of one committee. (I actually chaired two committees, the only one in my time in the Senate to do so. In addition to the Environment and Public Works Committee, I was the head of the Ethics Committee.)

Senator Perkins was really the first senator to begin to deal with the issue of water. He was involved in the beginning of California's complicated water delivery system, which one expert called "a reorganization of nature."

SENATOR #8: James Phelan, Democrat, 1915–1921

James Phelan was the first U.S. senator in my seat to be elected by the people, not appointed by the powers that be.

To give you the sense of his politics, when he was still the mayor of San Francisco, he faced off about water against the president of the Sierra Club, the great John Muir. The issue was whether a dam should be built 170 miles east of San Francisco. It was in Yosemite National Park. Phelan proposed this Hetch Hetchy Valley reservoir as a new supply. Debate was drawn out over a decade. Phelan believed that the needs of San Franciscans should take "precedence over the recreation of a few."

Phelan won and the environmentalists lost when President Woodrow Wilson signed the legislation right before Phelan came to the Senate. The debate over Hetch Hetchy was very difficult. This issue is still alive today as part of the battle between development and preservation.

World War I had broken out by the time Phelan was elected to the Senate. In 1917, seven months after President Wilson asked Congress to declare war against Germany, Senator Phelan delivered a speech that called attention to California's contribution to the war effort, including the invention of the caterpillar tractor in Stockton, California, which allowed tanks on the front lines that "broke the Hindenburg line."

"The smokestacks are something of which we should be proud and are a new glory to California," he said. "The wreaths which issue from their tops crown enterprise and labor. There can be no defilement of our California sky by smoke which brings prosperity and attendant happiness to our people and greatly serves our country in arms."

Well, Senator Phelan was not a visionary in one regard. It would take years to clean up the air pollution that was harming California until the Clean Air Act was passed in the 1970s. Phelan's support of economic growth regardless of its consequences would be tempered over time.

Phelan's view of the war can be summed up in his words: "It has been said that it is cruel to take life, but to take away the joy of life is a crueler thing to do, because a man without hope in poverty and suffering brokenly lives on."

SENATOR #9: Samuel Shortridge, Republican, 1921–1933

Samuel Shortridge took his seat in the Senate as the Jazz Age and roaring twenties took off.

In California, the movies were captivating the nation, attendance doubled, and the American culture was changed forever. The industrial infrastructure of southern California was being fueled by oil. Pumps and derricks were everywhere. California's population was headed toward five million.

Samuel Shortridge supported the National Origins Act of 1924, which limited immigration with quotas that tied immigration to American ancestry. Shortridge supported this kind of exclusion, which was very hurtful to any immigrants from Asia, especially the Japanese.

Then the stock market crashed on October 24, 1929, and the Great Depression began. Unemployment in San Francisco and Los Angeles was estimated to have reached 30 percent by late 1932. Department stores reported a 38 percent decline in sales. Dorothea Lange's famous 1936 photograph of what she called a "hungry and desperate mother" taken in San Luis Obispo County, California, encapsulates the times.

Clearly the people of California wanted change, so in the 1932 Republican primary Shortridge was defeated, and in the general election the seat went to a Democrat.

SENATOR #10: William McAdoo, Democrat, 1933–1938

William McAdoo was elected to the Senate in the year construction began on the Golden Gate Bridge.

McAdoo was fortunate to be running at a time when FDR crushed his opponent, Herbert Hoover. Democrats still do better in Senate elections today when they run the same year as the presidential election.

McAdoo had many ties to Hollywood, having served as general counsel to United Artists; he was also the son-in-law of President Woodrow Wilson. He supported the programs of the New Deal, which transformed the nation by undertaking a massive rebuilding of roads, schools, dams, post offices, and other infrastructure.

Senator McAdoo quit his seat early because he saw he was about to lose the primary to Sheridan Downey; Downey supported the first old age pension proposal and people wanted that kind of champion for them in the Senate. McAdoo opposed the bill that carried this idea: the Townsend Plan.

SENATOR #11: Thomas Storke, Democrat, 1938–1939

Senator Storke, having been appointed to fill out McAdoo's term, was only in the Senate for two months, so there is not much to say here. He was perhaps the most accomplished senator in the outside world. He won a Pulitzer Prize in journalism, helped establish the Santa Barbara Municipal Airport, and led the effort to upgrade Santa Barbara State College to a University of California campus.

His departure coincided with the rise of Hitler in Germany.

SENATOR #12: Sheridan Downey, Democrat, 1939–1950

In 1939, the year Senator Downey was elected, whatever good feelings citizens had from the amazing growth of California came tumbling down when the Japanese attacked Pearl Harbor and our installations there.

Senator Downey supported the declaration of war against Japan and knew his constituents in California were gravely concerned that an attack could come to their state. "If the empire of Japan can reach the islands... what's to stop them from striking a coastal state?" he said.

The panic set in further when a Japanese submarine actually surfaced in a Santa Barbara channel and fired shells at oil storage tanks. The physical damage was minor but the psychological blow was heavy.

In 1941, Senator Downey was named chairman of a special committee on old age pensions. He had worked on this issue for years and had run on the issue.

Downey was very progressive in his first term and called for a special committee to investigate discrimination against African Americans in the military. He also fought for increased veterans' benefits.

His politics veered right after his re-election in 1944, and before facing a difficult Democratic primary, he retired.

He was being challenged by Congresswoman Helen Gahagan Douglas.

SENATOR #13: *Richard Nixon, Republican, 1950–1953*

Before Ronald Reagan and Arnold Schwarzenegger, California had a Senate candidate who had performed as an actress—Helen Gahagan Douglas, the wife of actor Melvyn Douglas and the first Democratic woman to be elected to the Congress. She represented California's fourteenth district and served three terms from 1944 to 1950. Her issues were women's rights, civil liberties, and world disarmament. She became a major figure in Richard Nixon's ascent to the United States Senate.

In the late forties, Nixon was also in the House of Representatives and gained notoriety for going against communists. Nixon had his opening to run for the Senate when Sheridan Downey lost the support of the liberal elements of the Democratic Party. Helen Gahagan Douglas ran against Nixon, whose campaign focused on the implication that she was a communist. She in turn gave him the long-lasting title of "Tricky Dick."

It's been reported that John F. Kennedy quietly donated money to Nixon's campaign, though I can't say why.

Nixon didn't write anything in his memoirs about his time in the Senate.

He had his eye on the vice presidential nomination and clearly used his Senate seat as a stepping stone.

There were many issues at that time: the Korean War, the intensification of the Cold War; the Civil Rights movement was starting. But Nixon had his eyes turned elsewhere.

Eisenhower picked Nixon as his running mate because, according to Alice Longworth, Teddy Roosevelt's daughter, he wanted "someone on the ticket who could reassure party regulars, particularly conservatives."

SENATOR #14: Thomas Kuchel, Republican, 1953–1969

When Nixon left to become vice president, California Governor Earl Warren chose Thomas Kuchel to fill the vacancy. He was subsequently elected twice and served as minority whip. He was a very moderate Republican. I would say a very liberal Republican, since when he died in 1994, the *Los Angeles Times* called him "the last of the state's GOP progressives."

Kuchel was a strong supporter of Medicare. He managed the Civil Rights Act of 1964 and 1965 on the floor of the senate. Those two laws were the gems of the Civil Rights movement.

He had a huge falling-out with his party because of the party's failure to disown the John Birch Society. The John Birch Society termed him a communist sympathizer.

He prepared a carefully researched speech taking on the society. The far right of the Republican Party never forgave him. Their response turned him against his own party. He withheld support from many Republican leaders, deeming them "too far to the right," and lost the Republican primary to conservative Max Rafferty in 1968.

SENATOR #15: Alan Cranston, Democrat, 1969–1992

Senator Cranston took the oath of office when the state's population expanded to 20 million. It would be nearly 30 million when he retired in 1992 and I won the seat.

His first decade was eventful, encompassing the Vietnam War and Watergate. Cranston developed a reputation for being able to round up votes. According to the *New York Times,* he was "tireless in pushing for an end to the Vietnam War."

Cranston was a graduate of Stanford and very proud of California start-up companies like Apple and Intel. He supported computer research and development. As the seventies wound down, he led the Senate on arms control, and became a leader of the peace movement in California and the nation. He formed the California Democratic Council in the state, which became a very effective liberal grassroots organization.

Alan's work on arms control generated support all over the country, and he tried to run for president in 1984. While he won a few straw polls, he failed to generate momentum and dropped out.

He did all he could to help after the 1989 Loma Prieta earthquake. In the early 1990s his reputation took a hit due to an ethics investigation into the savings and loan scandal. He was also diagnosed with prostate cancer.

When he announced he wasn't running for re-election to the Senate, I jumped into the race.

And that's the story so far from "my" Senate seat.

Lyrics and Poems

I wrote one of my soupier songs about Tip O'Neill, to the tune of "On the Sunny Side of the Street":

Vote your brains and vote your heart
Be a Democrat and feel good
Find yourself some style
On the TIP side of the aisle

Now just avoid the right
The Falwells, Helms, and Reagans
Tip will make you smile
On the donkey side of the aisle

Its fairness jobs and peace
They're the framework of our party
Even walk a mile
To the TIP side of the aisle.

Words to the tune of "Ballin' the Jack" to express my frustration with President Reagan's arms buildup:

First you put a missile here and there
Then pretty soon there are missiles everywhere
It's all okay 'til they start to blow
And then we turn around and look around
And what do you know

All the trees and buildings
The people too
All the dogs and cats just to name a few
The things we love they are no more
And that's what we call nuclear war

It's strange to sing about a thing like war
But talking does no good to Ron, we've tried before
We've shown him the graphs but he takes no heed
So what's the point building bombs that we don't need

Stop all the testing, ask your congressman
To cut off the funding get a real test ban

Then join with colleagues one by one
And lead our children into the sun.

One thing that helped me recover from the attempt to impeach President Clinton, at least temporarily, was to write a song that celebrated all the good things about the Clinton–Gore years (lyrics to the tune of "The Way We Were"):

Memories
Of the days of Bill and Al
We have happy White House memories
Of the way we were

Oh the victories
Like the deficit we slew
And the children getting health care
They're insured, that's new

We put cops on streets where there were killers
We put teachers right in every class
We passed bills by one vote,
They were thrillers
Like clean air
Child care

Yes we've got memories
Big surplus memories
Those balanced budget memories of
The way we were.

My way to deal with awful things I haven't been able to prevent was, as always, to write a song. This one has the title "The Supreme Disappointment" and is to the tune of "My Favorite Things."

Scalia and Rehnquist and Sandra and Tony
How could you find our election laws phony?
Don't you think every vote counts in the land?
Why didn't one of you just take a stand?

Where's the statute?
Where's the refute?
Where's the precedent?
I'm not on the court but I think it's a tort
It's not what our founders meant!

About the Bush–Gore contested 2000 election to the tune of "It Was Just One of Those Things":

It was just one of those nights
We needed a fantasy flight
At nine we were tops
At ten we were flops
Just one of those nights.

It was just one of these nights,
Just one of those terrible nights
At twelve we had won,
At one we were done
Just one of those nights

CNN was wrong, ABC was wrong
But it's clear that Fox was the worst
Channel two was wrong
Channel nine was wrong
How could Bush, who lost, wind up first?
It was just one of those nights

Those nights that bring heat and not light
What a good fight
But it was just one of those nights!

To the melody of "Don't Cry For Me, Argentina," I wrote this during the
Iraq War:

Don't cry for us, Condoleezza
You are the one who told us of tubes aluminum
Of weapons there were none
Your truth was half baked with yellow fake cake

Colin Powell, call some fouls, Condoleezza
But no, not you
You gave us nothing
That was true.

Here's a non-musical little rhyme I wrote about being mistaken for Nancy
Pelosi:

I don't look like Nancy
She doesn't look like me
But Californians mix us up
Explain how can that be?
We've pondered this for years
We've held some seminars
We think it's 'cause we're in the face
Of right-wing demagogues
From Limbaugh to Hannity
From Savage to Coulter
We view their attacks
As a huge badge of honor.

After the 2004 Ohio voting fiasco to the tune of "Smiles":

There are lines
That make me happy
Like baseball lines
That lead from base to base

There are lines
That also make me grumpy
Like these lines
Right here upon my face

But the lines that make me sad and worried
Are the ones that foil democracy
'Cause those lines
Prevent our folks from voting
And without votes we can't be free.

Harry Reid often tells me I'm the sister he never had. And, Harry, you are the brother I never had. I wrote a song about him, to the tune of "Sunny."

Harry . . . thank you for the strength you give to us
Harry . . . thank you for the way you make them cuss
So you're not a TV star
We just take you as you are
Harry blue and true
No one like you

Harry . . . working from the day until the night
Harry . . . never turns away when there's a fight
We're so glad you changed the rules
Good thing there are no Senate duels

Harry blue and true
No one like you.

I wrote words about how good it would be if more women were in politics, to the tune of "If I Ruled the World":

When girls rule the world
Major problems will be
Solved every way
We'd use friendship and some
Guilt every day
Hear us say
If girls ruled the world.

There would be fairness in slices of pie
If your shoe heels are low or they're high
When the time ever comes
That girls rule the world.

Bibliography

U.S. Senate Seat History, California

Agel, Jerome B., editor. *We, the People: Great Documents of The American Nation.* New York: Barnes and Noble, Inc., 1997.

Binder, David. "Thomas H. Kuchel Dies at 84; Ex-Republican Whip in Senate." *The New York Times*, November 24, 1994.

Biographical Directory of the United States Congress, http://bioguide.congress.gov Center for Legislative Archives, The. http://www.archives.gov/legislative/features/17th-amendment/

Cherny, Robert, Gretchen Lemke-Santangelo, and Richard Griswold del Castillo. *Competing Visions: A History of California.* Boston: Houghton Mifflin Company, 2005.

Dinkelspiel, Frances. *Towers of Gold.* New York: St. Martin's Press, 2008.

"Ellen Clark Sargent," http://en.wikipedia.org/wiki/Ellen_Clark_Sargent

"Gen. James McDougall Declared United States Senator," *New York Times*, March 23, 1861.

Gould, Lewis L. *The Most Exclusive Club.* New York: Basic Books, 2005.

"Helen Gahagan Douglas," http://en.wikipedia.org/wiki/Helen_Gahagan_Douglas

Hosefros, Paul. "Alan Cranston, Former U.S. Senator, Is Dead at 86." *New York Times*, January 1, 2001.

Hundley, Norris, Jr. *The Great Thirst.* Berkeley: University of California Press, 2001.

"James Farley," https://www.govtrack.us/congress/members/james_farley/403982

Kazin, Michael, editor. *The Concise Princeton Encyclopedia of American Political History.* Princeton, N.J.: Princeton University Press, 2011.

Nixon, Richard. *RN: The Memoirs of Richard Nixon*, New York: Simon and Schuster, 1978.

Phelan, James D. "On the United States and the War Situation." Address by Honorable James D. Phelan, United States Senator, November 26, 1917.

Phillips, Catherine Coffin. *Cornelius Cole: California Pioneer and United States Senator*. San Francisco: John Henry Nash, 1929.

Reich, Kenneth. "Ex-Sen. Kuchel Dies; Last of State's GOP Progressives." *Los Angeles Times*, November 23, 1994.

"Sheridan Downey," http://en.wikipedia.org/wiki/Sheridan_Downey

Starr, Kevin. *California: A History*. New York: Modern Library, 2005.

Thomas, Lately. *Between Two Empires: The Life Story of California's First Senator*. Boston: Houghton Mifflin Company, 1969.

Thomson, David. *The Big Screen: The Story of the Movies*. New York: Farrar, Straus and Giroux, 2012.

Tutorow, Norman. *Leland Stanford: Man of Many Careers*. Menlo Park, Calif.: Pacific Coast Publishers, 1971.

"William Gibbs McAdoo," http://www.knoxfocus.com/2013/01/william-gibbs-mcadoo/

Reading Group Guide

The Art of Tough

1. The "art of tough" has nine rules:
   1. Never compromise about doing the right thing.
   2. Don't be afraid to step up.
   3. Beware of anger.
   4. Forgive.
   5. Fight against racism.
   6. Be strong on the issues you care about, even if it means sometimes being wrong.
   7. Sing.
   8. Go for your dreams.
   9. Never settle for less than love.

   Which of them do you use in your life? Which do you hope to learn to use more? Are there any elements of your own toughness not included in Senator Boxer's rules?

2. Which politicians most clearly embody the art of tough to you? What is the difference between those who pursue the art of tough and those who are merely aggressive and loud?

3. Why do you think the all-male judiciary committee was so uncomfortable with the Anita Hill/Clarence Thomas hearing? How might the environment have been different if there had been women on that committee?

4. Senator Boxer credits Professor Anita Hill for cultivating the political environment that led to the "Year of the Woman" in the 1992 election. Why did it require her tumultuous hearing to finally lead America to a more representative Congress?

5. Do you think Senator Boxer was right to keep quiet about the way she was treated by Senator John McCain after she testified before his committee? Did she betray the art of tough?

6. Why did Senator Boxer, when Hillary Clinton and Barack Obama were running against each other for President, choose to stay neutral? Have you ever been put in a position—at work or at home—where you felt you couldn't take sides in a conflict?

7. Senator Boxer cast some lonely votes on gay marriage, "Don't ask, don't tell," and the Iraq War. How is thinking independently an aspect of the art of tough? What challenges did Senator Boxer face in voting against the consensus?

8. Senator Boxer shows how far apart the political parties have moved, noting how, during the 1990s, the House of Representatives evolved "from a functional legislative pillar of democracy [in]to a polarized fist-fight" (Chapter 5). Assuming you agree, what are the issues that you find most clearly illustrate the growing divide between Democrats and Republicans?

9. Are women are still discriminated against in politics? Can you give some examples? Are women still discriminated against in other professions? In what ways can one use the art of tough to fight discrimination?

10. In *The Art of Tough*, Senator Boxer laments so many Americans' indifference to politics and reluctance to vote, revealing that Democrats tend

to do better in presidential election years because constituents turn out in far greater numbers. Do you believe the blame for so many people's disengagement from the political process rests with the politicians or the constituents themselves?

11. Senator Boxer was in the nation's capital when the 9/11 terrorist attacks occurred and describes seeing "smoke billowing out of the Pentagon" (Chapter 7). Do you remember where you were when you first learned of the attacks? Did they change your view, as they did Senator Boxer's, on the proper balance between security and liberty?

12. Senator Boxer served in elected life for forty years and was in the middle of many historic movements and events, including the Vietnam War, the women's liberation movement of the 1960s and '70s, the AIDS crisis, the environmental movement, 9/11, and the Iraq War. Which of these had the greatest effect on the course of the nation, and why? Are there other significant movements or events from the past forty years not listed here?